Geovisualization: Current Trends, Challenges, and Applications

Geovisualization: Current Trends, Challenges, and Applications

Guest Editors

Vassilios Krassanakis
Andriani Skopeliti
Merve Keskin
Paweł Cybulski

Basel • Beijing • Wuhan • Barcelona • Belgrade • Novi Sad • Cluj • Manchester

Guest Editors

Vassilios Krassanakis
Department of Surveying and Geoinformatics Engineering
University of West Attica
Egaleo
Greece

Andriani Skopeliti
School of Rural, Surveying and Geoinformatics Engineering
National Technical University of Athens
Zographos
Greece

Merve Keskin
Department of Geoinformatics and Cartography
University of Salzburg
Salzburg
Austria

Paweł Cybulski
Department of Cartography and Geomatics
Adam Mickiewicz University
Poznań
Poland

Editorial Office
MDPI AG
Grosspeteranlage 5
4052 Basel, Switzerland

This is a reprint of the Special Issue, published open access by the journal *Geographies* (ISSN 2673-7086), freely accessible at: https://www.mdpi.com/journal/geographies/special_issues/Geovisualization_Current_Trends.

For citation purposes, cite each article independently as indicated on the article page online and as indicated below:

Lastname, A.A.; Lastname, B.B. Article Title. *Journal Name* **Year**, *Volume Number*, Page Range.

ISBN 978-3-7258-4231-5 (Hbk)
ISBN 978-3-7258-4232-2 (PDF)
https://doi.org/10.3390/books978-3-7258-4232-2

© 2025 by the authors. Articles in this book are Open Access and distributed under the Creative Commons Attribution (CC BY) license. The book as a whole is distributed by MDPI under the terms and conditions of the Creative Commons Attribution-NonCommercial-NoDerivs (CC BY-NC-ND) license (https://creativecommons.org/licenses/by-nc-nd/4.0/).

Contents

About the Editors vii

Vassilios Krassanakis, Andriani Skopeliti, Merve Keskin and Paweł Cybulski
Geovisualization: Current Trends, Challenges, and Applications
Reprinted from: *Geographies* **2023**, *3*, 801–805, https://doi.org/10.3390/geographies3040043 . . . 1

Steffen Goebbels and Regina Pohle-Fröhlich
Automatic Unfolding of CityGML Buildings to Paper Models
Reprinted from: *Geographies* **2021**, *1*, 333–345, https://doi.org/10.3390/geographies1030018 . . . 6

Leda Stamou
Cartography and Art: A Comparative Study Based on Color
Reprinted from: *Geographies* **2022**, *2*, 87–110, https://doi.org/10.3390/geographies2010007 . . . 19

Polixeni Iliopoulou and Elissavet Feloni
Spatial Modelling and Geovisualization of House Prices in the Greater Athens Region, Greece
Reprinted from: *Geographies* **2022**, *2*, 111–131, https://doi.org/10.3390/geographies2010008 . . . 43

Su Zhang, Christopher D. Lippitt, Susan M. Bogus, Tammira D. Taylor and Renee Haley
Mapping Construction Costs at the National Level
Reprinted from: *Geographies* **2022**, *2*, 132–144, https://doi.org/10.3390/geographies2010009 . . . 64

Mingke Li, Heather McGrath and Emmanuel Stefanakis
Geovisualization of Hydrological Flow in Hexagonal Grid Systems
Reprinted from: *Geographies* **2022**, *2*, 227–244, https://doi.org/10.3390/geographies2020016 . . . 77

Kenji Wada, Günter Wallner and Steven Vos
Studying the Utilization of a Map-Based Visualization with Vitality Datasets by Domain Experts
Reprinted from: *Geographies* **2022**, *2*, 379–396, https://doi.org/10.3390/geographies2030024 . . . 95

Natalia Blana, Ioannis Kavadas and Lysandros Tsoulos
A Constraint-Based Generalization Model Incorporating a Quality Control Mechanism
Reprinted from: *Geographies* **2023**, *3*, 321–343, https://doi.org/10.3390/geographies3020017 . . . 113

Georgios Lampropoulos, George Panagiotopoulos, Christina Giannakoula and Alexandros Kokkalas
Geovisualization of Historical Geospatial Data: A Web Mapping Application for the 19th-Century Kaupert's Maps of Attica
Reprinted from: *Geographies* **2023**, *3*, 398–415, https://doi.org/10.3390/geographies3020021 . . . 136

About the Editors

Vassilios Krassanakis

Vassilios Krassanakis, Diploma of Rural and Surveying Engineering, National Technical University of Athens (NTUA), Doctor of Engineering NTUA, is an Associate Professor at the Department of Surveying and Geoinformatics Engineering, School of Engineering, University of West Attica, who specialized in Cartography and Visual Perception of Maps. At the undergraduate and postgraduate level, he teaches courses mainly in the areas of cartography, visual perception of maps, web mapping, and programming in geoinformatics. He has also taught as a Visiting Professor, Invited Speaker, and Instructor, at the National and Kapodistrian University of Athens, the Harokopio University, and the School of Topography of the Hellenic Military Geographical Service, as well as at the Institute of Education and Training of Members of the Technical Chamber of Greece. Previously, he has worked as a Postdoctoral Researcher the Université de Nantes and the NTUA, as a Visiting Researcher at the Ghent University, as an External Research Collaborator at the National Observatory of Athens and the Hellenic Centre for Marine, and as a Technical Researcher at the NTUA. He is a member of the Editorial Board of the *Journal of Eye Movement Research* and Guest Editor of the Special Issues "Geovisualization: Current Trends, Challenges, and Applications" (in *"Geographies"*), "Geographic Information Systems and Cartography for a Sustainable World" (in *"ISPRS International Journal of Geo-Information"*), and "Latest Research on Eye Tracking Applications" (in *"Applied Sciences"*). He has participated in several research projects funded by European, French, and Greek grants. He has authored numerous scientific publications, including journal papers, conference proceedings, book chapters, and an academic book. His current research activities are mainly focus on the areas of map and landscape perception, eye movement analysis and gaze behavior modeling, geovisualization and spatial data infrastructures (SDIs).

Andriani Skopeliti

Andriani Skopeliti [Dipl. Ing. Surveyor Engineer NTUA (1994) and PhD NTUA (2001)] is an Assistant Professor at the School of Rural, Surveying and Geoinformatics Engineering in the National Technical University of Athens in Greece. She specializes in analytical processing and the visualization of geospatial data. She teaches courses in the areas of cartography, geographic information science, and web mapping at both undergraduate and postgraduate levels. She has authored numerous research papers and book chapters. Her overall work has received extensive recognition, accumulating more than 780 citations. She is also a Reviewer and Guest Editor for scientific journals. She has participated in many research projects as a Scientific Manager and Researcher with international, European, and Greek funding. She is a member of the board of directors of the Hellenic Cartographic Society. Her main research interests focus on web cartography, cartographic generalization, VGI use in mapping, and VGI quality.

Merve Keskin

Merve Keskin is a Postdoctoral Research Associate in the Department of Geoinformatics (Z_GIS) at the University of Salzburg (PLUS), Austria. She is a geomatics engineer and cartographer, holding doctoral degrees from Ghent University and Istanbul Technical University, obtained through a joint PhD program. She currently serves as a vice-chair of the International Cartographic Association Commission on User Experience. Her expertise includes spatial cognition and behavior, the integration of HCI/UX/UI principles in map use and design, and mixed-methods multimodal user experiments (eye tracking, EEG, EDA). She supervises undergraduate and graduate students in these areas and strives to integrate new technologies and methods from various disciplines (psychology, computer science, urban planning) into geoinformatics through innovation and open science. She is the author of more than 35 peer-reviewed publications (see ORCID and Google Scholar).

Paweł Cybulski

Dr. Paweł Cybulski is a Cartography Researcher specializing in spatio-temporal visualization, animated maps, and user cognition. He earned his PhD in Geographical Sciences (Cartography) in 2017, following degrees in Geoinformation as well as Geodesy and Cartography. His research focuses on the effectiveness of animated cartographic techniques, change blindness, and preattentive processing, often employing eye-tracking to evaluate user experience and spatial cognition. Dr. Cybulski has led and co-investigated several international and national research projects, including a National Science Centre Poland grant on the perception of dynamic point symbols. He is the author or co-author of over 40 scientific publications and several monographs, including Multimedia Cartography, published by MDPI. He has served as a Guest Editor for Special Issues in the *ISPRS International Journal of Geo-Information*, and as an Editor for *Scientific Reports*. His work integrates experimental methodologies with applied cartography, contributing to a deeper understanding of how visual variables influence perception and map usability, particularly on digital and mobile platforms. Dr. Cybulski is affiliated with the Department of Cartography and Geomatics at Adam Mickiewicz University in Poznań, Poland.

Editorial

Geovisualization: Current Trends, Challenges, and Applications

Vassilios Krassanakis [1,*], Andriani Skopeliti [2], Merve Keskin [3] and Paweł Cybulski [4]

[1] Department of Surveying and Geoinformatics Engineering, School of Engineering, University of West Attica, Egaleo Park Campus, 12243 Egaleo, Greece
[2] Cartography Laboratory, School of Rural, Surveying and Geoinformatics Engineering, National Technical University of Athens, 15780 Athens, Greece; askop@survey.ntua.gr
[3] Geo-Social Analytics Laboratory, Department of Geoinformatics (Z_GIS), Paris Lodron University of Salzburg (PLUS), 5020 Salzburg, Austria; merve.keskin@plus.ac.at
[4] Department of Cartography and Geomatics, Faculty of Geographical and Geological Sciences, Adam Mickiewicz University, 61-712 Poznań, Poland; p.cybulski@amu.edu.pl
* Correspondence: krasvas@uniwa.gr

1. Introduction

Geovisualization (or *Geographic Visualization*) represents an interdisciplinary scientific field spanning cartography, geographic information science (GIScience) and technology, computer science and human–computer interaction (HCI), psychology, and cognitive science. All of these diverse specialisms have fostered the development of the robust methodological frameworks implemented in this field over the years. Geovisualization utilizes several spatial data representation techniques, including qualitative and/or quantitative attribute representation, which can be associated with a specific timestamp or considered in terms of periodic changes. In any case, geovisualization products permit users to visually explore the existing or potential relationships (i.e., spatial interactions), patterns, and/or trends connected to geographic entities and phenomena. Archetypal geovisualization digital products involve different types of maps, including static, animated, multimedia, and/or interactive spatial configurations, working either in local environments (as standalone applications) or across the Internet. Equally, these products can translate into virtual or augmented reality environments.

The implementation of geovisualization methods and techniques is vital to educational and professional research that aims to study geographical spaces. Hence, geovisualization is integral to spatial analysis and planning, hydrology, as well as history and archaeology. At present, the vast number of geospatial data collected by terrestrial, aerial, and satellite sensors is the principal challenge to tackle. Geovisualization products are the "vehicles" that support the communication between designers and users. However, the effectiveness of these spatial representations is inextricably linked with the principles followed during the cartographic design process.

This Special Issue (SI) collected eight different contributions to the geovisualization domain. In Section 2, the published papers are briefly introduced. In this section, the major points and outcomes of each contribution are highlighted and discussed. Finally, Section 3 reflects on the SI based on the contributions provided, as well as the existing challenges and opportunities in geovisualization. A complete list of the published papers is reported at the end of the editorial.

2. An Overview of the Published Papers

Goebbels and Pohle-Fröhlich's article (contribution 1) delves into an examination of paper models as a cost-effective and user-friendly tool for urban planning, offering an alternative to virtual 3D visualization and traditional architectural models. The study introduces an innovative algorithm tailored to automatically unfolding CityGML models into precise, scaled paper model kits, facilitating straightforward assembly using a single sheet of paper. The focus of the algorithm is generating CityGML building parts that unfold without overlap, as accomplished by establishing a graph based on the vertices and edges of the polygons within the CityGML building, subsequently creating a dual graph representing the ground, wall, and roof polygons. Prospective developments include the application of inpainting algorithms for vegetation removal, the simplification of CityGML models for their ease of assembly, and exploration of the potential of streamlining the production process using 2D laser cutting to enhance the texture patterns. The primary drawback associated with paper models is the manual effort required for assembly, despite each model taking less than five minutes. Although 3D printing is time-consuming, paper models require manual tasks that use smaller areas and simple geometries, as constrained by paper size and the space for 3D printing and building.

Furthermore, Leda Stamou's article (contribution 2) discusses the relationship between colors in maps and colors in artistic movements in order to investigate whether color can be used to identify artistic trends and their corresponding time periods. The study addresses the artistic period from the end of the Middle Ages to the 21st century that took place in Western Europe, including in Italy, incorporating both descriptive and quantitative color comparisons. Initially, color is examined according to properties such as hue, brightness, and saturation. Additionally, map and painting colors are plotted on the color wheel in order to visualize the range and location of color sequences. Despite the subjective selection method for the maps and paintings included, the reasonable assertion that the results may not be universally applicable, and the fact that colors differ over time, the research findings are interesting and significant enough to support its conclusions. The study verifies that in almost all of the comparisons made, the color sequences of the paintings and selected maps reside in the same part of the color wheel, across the same range. The author also points out that the color similarity is supported both for the colors used and for the color character resulting from saturation and brightness. In summary, the selected paintings and maps examined support the correlation between the use of color in paintings and maps, without implying intentionality.

Next, Iliopoulou and Feloni (contribution 3) utilized geovisualization techniques in order to visualize and interpret spatial analysis results for houses on the market. The authors considered both the structural and locational characteristics of houses in the Greater Athens Region, Greece. The geovisualization process was founded on the implementation of kriging interpolation techniques. Equally, these geovisualization techniques supported the depiction of both Moran's and Getis–Ord Gi* coefficients, which were calculated to examine the existing spatial autocorrelation, as well as to identify existing hot and cold spots, that is, clusters, of houses with similar characteristics, correspondingly. A Geographically Weighted Regression (GWR) model was developed to predict house prices based on their characteristics. The model was employed to calculate a regression equation for each house under study. Spatial variation in both the size and age coefficients was also depicted using typical geovisualization techniques. Hence, the mapping process supported the visual exploration and interpretation of both positive and negative coefficient allocation within the study area.

The piece authored by Zhang et al. (contribution 4) investigated the cartographic visualization of construction cost indexes (CCIs) at the national level, recognizing the limitations of the current tabular formats for 649 cities in the conterminous United States. The data utilized for the CCIs spanned from 2004 to 2015 and was sourced from RSMeans. Construction cost maps at the national level were generated using the NN (Nearest Neighbor), CNN (Condensed Nearest Neighbor), and IDW (inverse distance weighting) methods. These maps offered a complete picture of the construction costs, aiding construction practitioners, real estate developers, and the general public in identifying regional patterns and hotspots. The article also discusses the accessibility of these national construction cost maps via WebGIS technologies, which offer interactive and dynamic visualization to a broad audience. They concluded that potential future research directions include the broader applicability of interpolation methods in geovisualization, and suggested extending this approach to mapping other construction-related costs at a similar scale.

Moreover, the article by Li et al. (contribution 5) elaborates on the use of a hexagonal grid for hydrological flow calculation and geovizualization. Indeed, flow calculation is highly pertinent in supporting hydrological analysis, as applies to flow accumulation, watershed delineation, stream networks, and so on. While hexagonal grids have been lauded over rectangular grids, calculation methods have not adapted to accommodate this. In this workflow, the water flow direction was computed using five methods based on slope aspect calculation in the ISEA3H DGGS: the Maximum Adjacent Gradient (MAG), Maximum Downward Gradient (MDG), Multiple Downhill Neighbors (MDN), Finite-Difference Algorithm (FDA), and Best-Fit Plane (BFP) methods. Both visually and quantitatively, this study investigated the flow accumulation and hydrological indices, proving that the results vary among the different approaches, and that ultimately the impact of these variations propagates to hydrological products. As the outcome of the study, the D6 algorithm is endorsed for its ability to eliminate close loops after pit-filling processes. According to the authors, this research can be used to supplement future flood inundation modeling or susceptibility modeling in a pure hexagonal DGGS environment.

In addition, the mixed-methods study conducted by Wada et al. (contribution 6) explores the efficacy of map-based visualizations containing vitality data in supporting visual analysis processes in government, business, and research. Accordingly, it confirms that map-based data visualization is an visual analysis effective tool for domain experts in the context of vitality due to its coherent data presentation, the ease of spatial analysis, and its interactivity. The expert consensus deems geovisualization suitable for both quick novice insights and the deeper analysis conducted by intermediate or advanced users. However, it remains challenging to thematically tailor geovisualization to real-world domain expert projects and their in-depth and specific analysis requirements. To enhance its adaptability to diverse use cases, this study suggests aggregating datasets by theme and incorporating interactive features into map-based data visualizations.

Blana et al.'s (contribution 7) extended study of their own previous work (Blana and Tsoulos, 2022) presents a constraint-based generalization model that uses constraints to control the detail granularity while implementing a quality control mechanism to produce high-quality topographic maps at any scale; this comprises a structured framework and a thorough method for generalizing linear and area features. The authors take a standardizing approach to the semantic generalization process together, with applying a new quality control mechanism to evaluate the shape of the features. Their model identifies and resolves legibility violations based on quantitative criteria, and simplifies the resolution of geometric conflicts using density reduction techniques and quantitative legibility thresholds. It is also compliant with the ISO 19157 standard [1] on quality and map specifications and compatible with a wide range of GIS environments. The authors advocate for the inclusion of a quality policy and a quality management system (QMS) throughout the map production process, which necessitates evaluating the integrity of the input data and the output product to ensure the quality outcomes of the entire process.

Lampropoulos et al. (contribution 8) presented a new web mapping application for historical cartographic data representation. In particular, the platform provides access to high-resolution map images and geospatial data related to Kaupert's Maps of Attica from the 19th century, which supports the process of overlaying these maps onto modern cartographic backgrounds. Consequently, the application also includes querying, filtering, and measurement tools to aid user in navigating and interrogating the data provided. The application's implementation is based on modern geospatial frameworks (for both the client and server side), which streamline the interactive exploration of the ancient topography of Attica. The platform showcases a working example of how modern geovisualization techniques and digital technologies offer a modern approach to the digital humanities and cultural heritage.

3. Concluding Remarks

This SI collates eight contributions illustrating varied forms of geovisualization (i.e., building models, cartography and art, spatial modeling, constructions, hydrology, decision-making processes, cartographic generalization, and cartographic heritage), highlighting the existing trends and challenges in this scientific field. This variety proves that geovisualization is an active field significantly supporting geospatial modeling in the modern day. As indicated by prior studies (e.g., [2–6]), geovisualization meets a number of germane challenges, such as effectiveness and efficiency analysis [7] based on behavioral research methods and/or artificial intelligence (AI) techniques [8,9], as well as adaptation to modern virtual environments [10]. Undoubtedly, in the era of big data and AI, geovisualization will be crucial in conveying meaningful information to map users.

Conflicts of Interest: The authors declare no conflict of interest.

List of Contributions

The SI contains seven research articles and one technical note (contribution 4):

1. Goebbels, S.; Pohle-Fröhlich, R. Automatic Unfolding of CityGML Buildings to Paper Models. *Geographies* **2021**, *1*, 333–345. https://doi.org/10.3390/geographies1030018.
2. Stamou, L. Cartography and Art: A Comparative Study Based on Color. *Geographies* **2022**, *2*, 87–110. https://doi.org/10.3390/geographies2010007.
3. Iliopoulou, P.; Feloni, E. Spatial Modelling and Geovisualization of House Prices in the Greater Athens Region, Greece. *Geographies* **2022**, *2*, 111–131. https://doi.org/10.3390/geographies2010008.
4. Zhang, S.; Lippitt, C.; Bogus, S.; Taylor, T.; Haley, R. Mapping Construction Costs at the National Level. *Geographies* **2022**, *2*, 132–144. https://doi.org/10.3390/geographies2010009.
5. Li, M.; McGrath, H.; Stefanakis, E. Geovisualization of Hydrological Flow in Hexagonal Grid Systems. *Geographies* **2022**, *2*, 227–244. https://doi.org/10.3390/geographies2020016.
6. Wada, K.; Wallner, G.; Vos, S. Studying the Utilization of a Map-Based Visualization with Vitality Datasets by Domain Experts. *Geographies* **2022**, *2*, 379–396. https://doi.org/10.3390/geographies2030024.
7. Blana, N.; Kavadas, I.; Tsoulos, L. A Constraint-Based Generalization Model Incorporating a Quality Control Mechanism. *Geographies* **2023**, *3*, 321–343. https://doi.org/10.3390/geographies3020017.
8. Lampropoulos, G.; Panagiotopoulos, G.; Giannakoula, C.; Kokkalas, A. Geovisualization of Historical Geospatial Data: A Web Mapping Application for the 19th-Century Kaupert's Maps of Attica. *Geographies* **2023**, *3*, 398–415. https://doi.org/10.3390/geographies3020021.

References

1. ISO 19157; Geographic Information—Data Quality. International Organization for Standardization: Geneva, Switzerland, 2013.
2. Slocum, A.T.; Blok, C.; Jiang, B.; Koussoulakou, A.; Montello, R.D.; Fuhrmann, S.; Nicholas, R.H. Cognitive and Usability Issues in Geovisualization. *Cartogr. Geogr. Inf. Sci.* **2001**, *28*, 61–75. [CrossRef]
3. MacEachren, A.M.; Kraak, M.-J. Research Challenges in Geovisualization. *Cartogr. Geogr. Inf. Sci.* **2001**, *28*, 3–12. [CrossRef]
4. Kraak, M.-J. Geovisualization illustrated. *ISPRS J. Photogramm. Remote Sens.* **2003**, *57*, 390–399. [CrossRef]
5. Jiang, B.; Li, Z. Geovisualization: Design, Enhanced Visual Tools and Applications. *Cartogr. J.* **2005**, *42*, 3–4. [CrossRef]
6. Çöltekin, A.; Bleisch, S.; Andrienko, G.; Dykes, J. Persistent challenges in geovisualization—A community perspective. *Int. J. Cartogr.* **2017**, *3*, 115–139. [CrossRef]
7. Fuhrmann, S.; Ahonen-Rainio, P.; Edsall, R.M.; Fabrikant, S.I.; Koua, E.L.; Tobón, C.; Ware, C.; Wilson, S. Chapter 28—Making Useful and Useable Geovisualization: Design and Evaluation Issues. In *Exploring Geovisualization*; Dykes, J., MacEachren, A.M., Kraak, M.-J., Eds.; International Cartographic Association: Bern, Switzerland, 2005; pp. 551–566. ISBN 978-0-08-044531-1.
8. Chen, M.; Claramunt, C.; Çöltekin, A.; Liu, X.; Peng, P.; Robinson, A.C.; Wang, D.; Strobl, J.; Wilson, J.P.; Batty, M.; et al. Artificial intelligence and visual analytics in geographical space and cyberspace: Research opportunities and challenges. *Earth-Sci. Rev.* **2023**, *241*, 104438. [CrossRef]

9. Robinson, A.C.; Çöltekin, A.; Griffin, A.L.; Ledermann, F. Cartography in GeoAI: Emerging Themes and Research Challenges. In Proceedings of the 6th ACM SIGSPATIAL International Workshop on AI for Geographic Knowledge Discovery, Los Angeles, CA, USA, 6 October 2023; Association for Computing Machinery: New York, NY, USA, 2023; pp. 1–2.
10. Hruby, F.; Ressl, R.; de la Borbolla del Valle, G. Geovisualization with immersive virtual environments in theory and practice. *Int. J. Digit. Earth* **2019**, *12*, 123–136. [CrossRef]

Disclaimer/Publisher's Note: The statements, opinions and data contained in all publications are solely those of the individual author(s) and contributor(s) and not of MDPI and/or the editor(s). MDPI and/or the editor(s) disclaim responsibility for any injury to people or property resulting from any ideas, methods, instructions or products referred to in the content.

Article

Automatic Unfolding of CityGML Buildings to Paper Models

Steffen Goebbels * and Regina Pohle-Fröhlich

iPattern Institute, Niederrhein University of Applied Sciences, Reinarzstr. 49, 47805 Krefeld, Germany; regina.pohle@hsnr.de
* Correspondence: steffen.goebbels@hsnr.de

Abstract: 3D city models are mainly viewed on computer screens, but many municipalities also use 3D printing to make urban planning tangible. Since 3D color printing is still comparatively expensive and the colors often fade over time, many of these models are monochrome. Here, color textured paper models offer an inexpensive and under-appreciated alternative. In this paper, a greedy algorithm adapted to CityGML building models is presented, which creates print templates for such paper models. These 2D layouts consist of cut edges and fold edges that bound polygons of a building. The polygons can be textured or left blank depending on the existence of CityGML textures. Glue tabs are attached to cut edges. In addition to the haptic 3D visualization, the quality of the 3D models can sometimes be better assessed on the basis of the print templates than from a perspective projection. The unfolding procedure was applied to parts of the freely available CityGML model of Berlin as well as to parts of models of the cities of Dortmund and Krefeld.

Keywords: 3D city models; CityGML; unfolding

1. Introduction

Virtual 3D city models are used for simulation purposes (e.g., solar potential analyzes, flood maps, heat requirement mapping) as well as for vivid visualization of urban planning, e.g., see [1]. They are also a data source for Building Information Modeling (BIM), see [2]. Over the past decade, CityGML (see [3]) and more recently CityJSON (https://cityjson.org/specs/ (accessed on 23 November 2021)), have become the standards for representing 3D city information.

Most CityGML models are currently specified in a level of detail that provides somewhat simplified roof facets and walls but lack detailed facade information. In the CityGML level of detail 1 (LoD 1), the building footprint is extruded to obtain a 3D object with a flat roof. The CityGML level of detail 2 (LoD 2) allows for arbitrary planar roof facets. The representation of facades with windows and doors requires a higher level of detail, which is usually not available. The simple LoD 2 structure with few surfaces, which must also be planar, is ideal as a basis for paper models, cf. [4]. If color printing is used, this is even more true for those models that have been textured with oblique aerial images, see Figure 1.

Figure 1. Detail of a textured CityGML model of Krefeld.

Physical building models are important for participatory planning because they reduce the level of abstraction, see, e.g., [5]. These models are a tool for exploration and communication, and they can show the interplay between structures and their surrounding environment, see [6]. The role of haptic visualization of geospatial data is described in [7]. Handmade physical architectural models (made of cardboard, plaster, or wood in the past, cf. [8]) are quite expensive but now the presence of virtual 3D models allows for (semi-) automated production. Laser cutting is used to cut (also colored) pieces that have to be assembled manually. One can distinguish between subtractive (CNC milling) and additive techniques (3D printing) as well as forming techniques (deep drawing) to automatically create physical models, cf. [9]. With the advance of cheap 3D printers, various 3D printing techniques like stereolithography, powder printing, and Fused Filament Fabrication (FFF) have been applied to create architectural models in recent years, cf. [10]. Powder printing is capable of reproducing multi-colored surfaces, and many FFF printers allow for a few differently colored filaments within one print process. For example, the city of Essen used color 3D powder printing to reproduce the entire city center, see Figure 2.

Figure 2. Upper left image: 3D-printed city model of Essen, created by "Amt für Geoinformation, Vermessung und Kataster der Stadt Essen"; other images: Manually colored 3D print of buildings in Krefeld.

However, 3D printing is a slow process, and compared to FFF printing with few colors, color powder 3D printing requires expensive materials and hardware. As the Essen model shows, the colors can fade away over time. In an experiment, we converted CityGML to the STL format, manually increased the level of detail, printed monochrome with a cheap FFF printer, and then manually painted facades. Although the results are promising (Figure 2), the manual effort is tremendous. Textured paper models also show realistic facades but can be assembled without the need of manual coloring in a fraction of 3D print time if there are not too many facets.

Paper models are created from printed 2D layouts by cutting along certain edges and by folding. The transformation of a 3D model to a 2D layout is called unfolding (cf. Section 2.1 for a formal definition). A general heuristic unfolding algorithm based on computing a minimum spanning tree is described in [11].

For CAD programs such as Blender (https://docs.blender.org/manual/en/latest/addons/import_export/paper_model.html (accessed on 23 November 2021)), there exist plug-ins that can be used to convert 3D models into print templates for paper models, cf. [12]. However, currently available free tools do not support an easy conversion of textured CityGML and CityJSON objects into textured CAD models. In contrast to general optimization approaches as described in [13,14], the typical geometry of the building models allows a specific greedy procedure for unfolding the models into 2D structures that results in small 2D layout sizes, see Figure 3.

Until now, it has been an open question if every convex polyhedron can be cut along some of its edges (cut edges) to allow a non-overlapping unfolding onto a 2D plane ([15] pp. 73–75). There exist special polyhedra with convex faces that do not have a non-overlapping unfolding [16]. Many building models do not even consist of only convex polygons. For example, a dormer might be placed over an opening in a roof facet. Then walls and roof of the dormer do not fit into the space of the opening such that no non-overlapping unfolding exists. For practical purposes, this is not a problem as we can generate multiple 2D layout images for a given building if necessary. The next section describes our unfolding approach. It has been implemented for CityGML data only, since CityJSON and CityGML can be easily converted into each other with freely available tools, github.com/citygml4j/citygml-tools (accessed on 23 November 2021). The paper concludes with a discussion of the results.

Figure 3. Print templates of CityGML buildings with automatically added glue tabs.

2. Materials and Methods

2.1. The Greedy Algorithm

In CityGML, buildings can be divided into building parts that can share opposite walls. Usually, only large buildings are split up into parts. Since 2D layouts of such buildings may not fit on a single page, the proposed algorithm computes a separate unfolding for each building part.

Let V be the set of vertices and E be the set of undirected edges of all polygons of a CityGML building part or building. The graph (V, E) describes the outer hull of the (watertight) object, it has exactly one connected component. Its dual graph (V_d, E_d) has a vertex set V_d that consists of the CityGML polygons (the faces of graph (V, E) are now the vertices), and has a set of edges (1),

$$E_d := \{\{p_1, p_2\} : p_1 \neq p_2 \in V_d \text{ have at least one common edge in } E\}. \quad (1)$$

The vertex set V_d is the disjoint union of a set $V_{d,G}$ of ground plane polygons, a set $V_{d,W}$ of wall polygons, and a set $V_{d,R}$ of roof polygons. We assume that adjacent polygons lie in different planes. Otherwise, they must be merged before applying this algorithm. An unfolding of the CityGML object is a spanning tree of (V_d, E_d). If and only if this tree has an edge between p_1 and p_2, then the two polygons have at least one common fold edge in E. Then all common edges of p_1 and p_2 are fold edges and lie on a straight line. Edges in E that are no fold edges are cut edges.

Instead of a spanning tree, our greedy algorithm computes a spanning forest of non-overlapping unfoldings, see Algorithm 1. Unlike the algorithm in [11] that computes a minimal spanning tree of (V_d, E_d) first and then cuts it into a forest to fulfill the nonoverlap condition, now the tree is successively constructed by adding new polygons until it can no longer grow due to overlaps. Then a new tree is started.

Polygons are allowed to have openings (interior polygons) in CityGML. Such openings are usually too small to accommodate another polygon along with a neighbor or a glue tab. Therefore, polygons that are adjacent to edges of an inner polygon are not treated within the same tree as in which the inner polygon is considered.

Algorithm 1 Greedy Unfolding

componentNo = 0
while unprocessed polygons exist **do**
    componentNo:=componentNo+1
    Initialize new output image
    if componentNo = 1 **then**
        Find a largest ground plane face p_G
        Find a wall polygon p adjacent to longest edge of p_G
        Draw p as the first polygon to the output image
        while attachable wall polygons exist **do**
            ▷ An attachable wall polygon is so far not drawn, with an edge adjacent to a drawn wall
            ▷ polygon, such that it can be attached in 2D without overlaps
            Draw this polygon attached to the adjacent edge
    else
        Find a polygon p with largest area size
        Draw p as the first polygon to the output image
    added := 1
    while added **do**
        added=0;
        for all remaining polygons p in descending area size **do**
            Edges $e \in E$ of p are determined which are also edges of a polygon q already drawn in the current output image
            for each such edge e in descending order (2) **do**
                if p can be attached at e without overlaps **then**
                    Draw polygon p into the output image
                    added = 1

CityGML building models have ground plane polygons $p_G \in V_{d,G}$. All wall polygons $p_W \in V_{d,W}$, which have vertices with a (largest) ground plane face p_G in common, i.e., $\{p_G, p_W\} \in E_d$, can be linked to form an initial tree that is a sub-graph of (V_d, E_d). Two-wall polygons $p_{W,1}$ and $p_{W,2}$ can be connected with an edge if and only if they share a common vertex $v \in V$ with p_G, i.e., v is a vertex of all three polygons. The greedy algorithm (Algorithm 1) starts with a wall polygon adjacent to a longest edge of p_G, and then iteratively adds more wall polygons until all adjacent polygons are added to the tree or until overlaps occur, see Figure 4. By definition, an unfolding is a spanning tree of the dual graph. It is not guaranteed that cutting along the cut edges and folding along fold edges will result in a planar layout in which polygons do not overlap. This has to be checked additionally (see below).

Figure 4. The initial layout consists of wall faces that are adjacent to a ground plane polygon.

Iteratively, further polygons $p \in V_d$ are added to the initial tree. For this purpose, the remaining polygons are sorted and processed in descending order by area size. For each of these polygons p, those of its edges $e \in E$ are determined, which are also edges of a polygon q already added as a vertex in the tree. These edges e are sorted in descending order by a combination of edge length l, type of the matching polygon q, and number of common edges between the two polygons p and q. Edges e with wall and ground plane polygons $q \in V_{d,W} \cup V_{d,G}$ have a higher priority $t = 10$ than with roof polygons $q \in V_{d,R}$ where $t = 1$. Thus, roof planes are attached to wall polygons whenever possible. This leads to a compact print size and, if possible, avoids chains of roof polygons on the paper. If the two polygons p and q share more than one edge e, then they are weighted with a low priority $m = 0.01$ because it might be difficult to later add other polygons between the different shared edges. Otherwise, m is set to one. The overall priority is:

$$l \times t \times m. \tag{2}$$

During the iterative tree assembly, a 2D representation of the unfolding is maintained. The vertices of each considered polygon are projected into the two-dimensional space by computing coordinates with respect to two orthogonal vectors that span the plane of the polygon. In the 2D space, affine transformations are then applied to connect projected polygons along fold edges.

In the described sequence of selected edges e of p, the algorithm tries to extend the tree by connecting p if possible. To this end, checks have to be performed to identify overlaps. Thus, intersection points between 2D edges of p and all other 2D edges so far belonging to polygons of the tree are computed (with the exception of the potential fold edge e used for the connection). In addition, (partially) overlapping edges on a same straight line with the projection of e have to be considered. If there exists an intersection point, the polygon p cannot be connected in this way, and its next selected edge is examined instead.

With this procedure, an attempt is made to connect each remaining polygon with those already present in the tree, see Figure 3. If it succeeds for at least one polygon, the procedure is repeated, as there are now new polygons to connect to.

For most buildings, a single tree and thus a non-overlapping unfolding can be constructed. However, if polygons remain, the largest remaining one is selected, and then the procedure is repeated with this new seed to generate a forest. This happens especially when a polygon has an opening since then the edges of the opening are not considered in the unfolding process, see Figure 5.

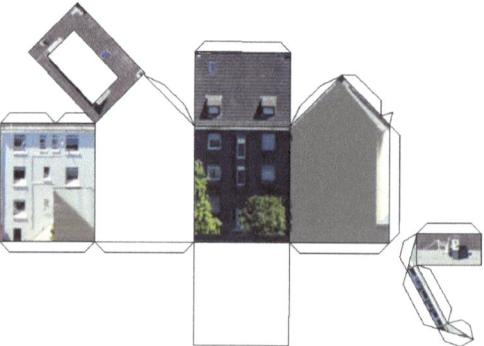

Figure 5. Dormers lead to openings.

Figure 6. A cupola from the Berlin model forms one connected component belonging to an opening of a roof.

Figure 7. Examples from the Berlin city model.

Figure 8. Unfolding examples without and with glue tabs.

Each tree of the forest is used to draw a separate image of the corresponding part of the unfolded model, see Figure 6. Textures are added to polygons in CityGML via the appearance model. They are positioned with an UV mapping using 2D coordinates for each polygon vertex. For simplicity however, we assume that texture coordinates are limited to the interval $[0,1] \times [0,1]$ such that no repetitive patterns occur. Such patterns should not occur in automatically textured models from oblique aerial images. Instead of the UV mapping, an affine transform based on three iteratively selected polygon points and their corresponding texture coordinates is applied. After choosing a first point with a smallest *x*-coordinate, the other points are chosen such that the minimum distance from the previously selected points is maximal. The drawn 2D polygon is filled with the transformed texture image.

Pairs of cut edges separated by unfolding require a glue tab. This must be placed on one of the two corresponding 2D edges in a layout image. To do this, different sizes and shapes of glue tabs are tried iteratively and each is checked for intersections with polygon edges as well as with edges of other glue tabs in the output image. If an intersection occurs, the next smaller size is selected. Building edges shorter than one meter are not given a glue tab.

To print with exact scaling, the typesetting system LaTeX can be used. LaTeX allows to scale included images exactly by specifying the unit *truecm*. If the page size is exceeded, the 2D layout has to be divided into smaller pieces. This is done by cutting a bounding rectangle into pieces. For optimal positioning of the pieces on the paper, a 2D bin packing problem can be solved, see [11].

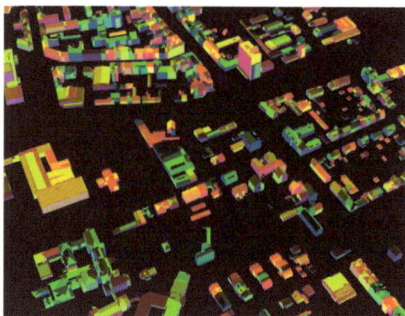

Figure 9. Visibility mask for identifying occluded regions.

2.2. Data Preparation

We tested the algorithm with single buildings from the textured Berlin LoD 2 CityGML data and a textured LoD 2 city model of Dortmund. These buildings were chosen because of their texture quality. To show that performance is no issue, we also applied the algorithm to all 6485 building parts of two square kilometers of LoD 2 buildings within the interval [330,000; 5,688,000] × [331,000; 5,690,000] of UTM coordinates in zone 32U. This is the area around our institute in Krefeld. The Berlin model is freely available (Berlin Partner für Wirtschaft und Technologie GmbH, https://www.businesslocationcenter.de/downloadportal/ (accessed on 23 November 2021)). Disadvantages of this model are the low resolution of the textures and the fact that the footprint areas are often divided into several ground plane polygons. This can lead to multiple layout images, even if the building can be represented by one. Therefore, we computed are own textured models based on oblique aerial images obtained with IGI UrbanMapper digital aerial survey cameras. The cities of Dortmund and Krefeld supported us not only with these images, but also with meta data indicating camera positions and camera parameters. With these parameters, we applied a perspective transform to match an image area with a CityGML polygon of an LoD 2 city model that was derived with the algorithm in [17] from cadastral footprints and airborne laser scanning point clouds that are available from the state cadastral office of the German state, North Rhine-Westphalia (https://www.bezreg-koeln.nrw.de/brk_internet/geobasis/hoehenmodelle/3d-messdaten/index.html (accessed on 23 November 2021)). The perspective transform was applied before storing the texture images. That allowed us to correctly replace the UV mapping by an affine transform when drawing 2D layouts. The obtained textures had a resolution of more than 100 pixels per square meter. Besides projecting images to model faces, we also identified occluded areas that were then not textured. This is in contrast to the Berlin model, in which all walls are textured, such that occluded segments show perspective distortions, see Figure 7.

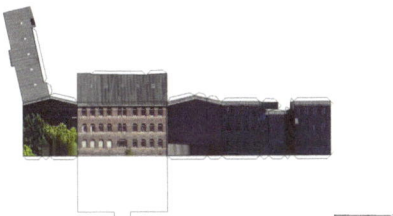

Figure 10. The algorithm divided the layout into three connected components.

Leaving occluded wall and roof segments blank reduces printing costs and actually looks better. This also reveals texture errors, as they can be distinguished from occlusion artifacts. In Figures 5–8, occluded areas of partially hidden walls are gray while fully occluded walls are white. To determine occluded areas, we drew the CityGML model with camera parameters of an oblique aerial image by using a Z-buffer. Each facet was assigned a unique color as ID, see Figure 9. Within a drawn polygon, only areas with its corresponding color were visible.

2.3. Histogram Matching

The brightness of texture images in all three city models varies greatly depending on the orientation of polygons towards the sun, see Figure 10. We experimented with histogram matching to adjust the brightness. Pixels outside the polygon, pixels of occluded areas, and green pixels indicating vegetation were masked out. Then we processed wall and roof textures separately. For both sets of images, we determined a reference image each. This is the brightest image with more than half the maximum number of non-masked-out pixels in the set under consideration. Then all other images of the set were adjusted to the reference image, see Figures 11–13.

The histogram function:

$$h_c : \{0, \ldots, 255\} \to \mathbb{N}_0 := \{0, 1, 2, \ldots\} \tag{3}$$

counts the occurrence of byte values in an image channel c. When (3) is interpreted as a density function, the corresponding distribution function is $H_c : \{0, \ldots, 255\} \to [0, 1]$ defined by:

$$H_c(k) := \frac{\sum_{0 \leq j \leq k} h_c(j)}{\sum_{0 \leq j \leq 255} h_c(j)}. \tag{4}$$

Let $H_{\text{ref},c}$ be the distribution Function (4) of channel c of the reference image, and let $H_{A,c}$ be the corresponding distribution function of an image A to be adjusted. Then the classical histogram matching replaces byte values k of channel c of A with $k' := \min\{j \in \{0, \ldots, 255\} : H_{\text{ref},c}(j) \geq H_{A,c}(k)\}$.

We applied an independent histogram matching of RGB channels as well as of HSV channels and also a matching of only the Y channel of the YCbCr color schema, see Figure 13.

However, the histogram-based approach did not work sufficiently. Buildings often looked too different on different sides, with rear facades having a dissimilar color to the corresponding front facade. The different color distribution in connection with independent matching of the RGB channels led to noisy hue values. Much better results were obtained by applying histogram matching to the original aerial images before the generation of the CityGML textures (which unfortunately is not possible when only the final textured models are available, as in the Berlin city model). These much larger images cover up to a thousand buildings. Typically, aerial images are taken with four cameras mounted on an aircraft. During a flight, these cameras look roughly in the directions of north, south, east, and west. We worked with images taken around noon, so the images from the camera facing north were brightest. Using these images as a reference, the other images could be adjusted quite well if adjusted and reference images showed the same area (and therefore had similar color distribution), see Figure 14.

Figure 11. Histogram matching of all RGB channels applied to the first unfolding in Figure 3.

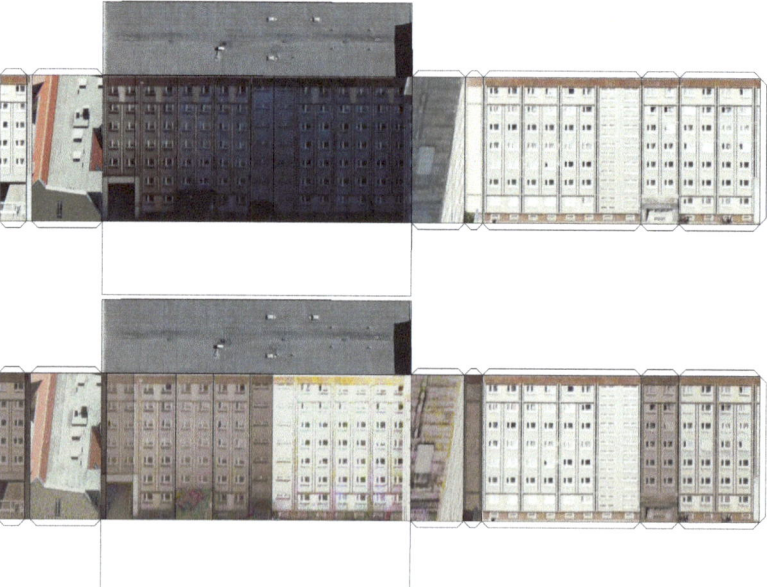

Figure 12. The comparison of original textures (upper image) and textures adjusted with RGB histogram matching (lower image) shows the limitations of the method. The prerequisite that adjacent polygons do not lie in the same plane is not given with this building of the Berlin model.

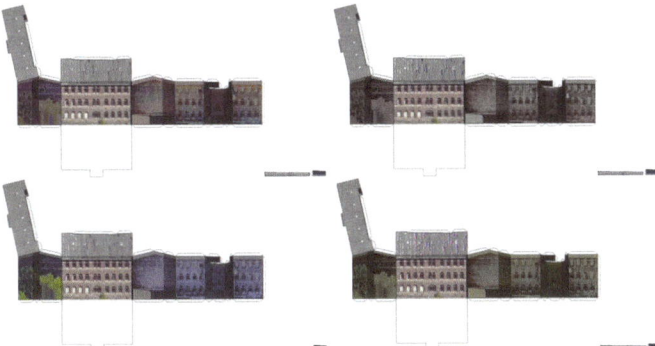

Figure 13. Histogram matching applied to Figure 10, from top left to bottom right: Independent matching of all RGB channels, independent matching of all HSV channels, matching of Y channel in the YUV schema, independent matching of all YUV channels.

Figure 14. Adjustment of aerial images, (**left**) detail of the original image, taken in the south direction (showing dark facades in Figures 10 and 13), (**right**) adjusted image.

2.4. Implementation

With the Xcode IDE on a MacBook Pro computer with i5 processor, the algorithm was implemented in C++ based on the OpenCV library (https://opencv.org (accessed on 23 November 2021)) that is used for image transformation. All tests were performed on the MacBook with 16 GB memory that was sufficient to handle textures and oblique aerial images.

3. Results and Discussion

Due to the greedy approach, the unfolding results were available immediately. Most buildings consist of a few wall and roof facets. Then it is easy to fold the 2D layout back into a physical 3D model as shown in Figure 15. Figure 16 summarizes some numbers for two square kilometer tiles around our institute. The fist tile (blue plots) consists of 2502 building parts and the second consists of 3443 building parts (red plots). The 0.75-quartile of connected layout components in both tiles was one. More precisely, 85% and 79% of all building parts could be unfolded to only one connected component. The 0.95-quantile of connected components was two and three, respectively. A few of these components were needed because of interior polygons (openings). The maximum number of openings per building was eight, but the 0.95-quantile was only zero and one, respectively. The numbers demonstrate that the chosen greedy approach is sufficient.

A higher number of connected components were often associated with buildings that had many small facets, see Figure 17. Such buildings were also difficult to assemble, and the level of detail should be reduced prior to unfolding. A simple but effective technique is to remove openings and any polygons that are inside openings. Another technique reduces the set of building corners to dominant corners, see [18].

Figure 15. Assembled paper models.

The prerequisite that adjacent polygons do not lie in the same plane was sometimes violated. This could lead to cut edges that should be fold edges. Merging faces prior unfolding also requires merging textures. To avoid this effort, the algorithm simply does not draw glue tabs along these cut edges. This is done by temporarily coloring non-textured facets and adding glue tabs only after all polygons are drawn. Then a check is performed to see if the glue tab vertices are already colored. If so, the tab is omitted.

We only checked for occlusion by buildings. Unfortunately, many facades were covered by vegetation. This was indicated by green areas. However, this type of occlusion occurred on some walls to an extent that did not allow inpainting.

The slope angles of some roof surfaces were inaccurate in the CityGML models. In addition, bay windows and balconies were not represented in the simple models. Both problems led to perspective distortions in the textures, which were clearly visible, cf. Figure 18.

Table 1 summarizes our experiences with paper models compared to 3D printing. The main disadvantage of paper models is the manual work required to assemble the printed kits. However, it took less than five minutes to cut out and glue together each of the models shown in Figure 15. Preparation for a 3D print (cleaning, handling of materials, supervising the print, removing support structures, etc.) also takes some time. Nevertheless, unlike color 3D printing, manual interaction limits the paper kit approach to smaller areas like single streets and to simple geometries, i.e., buildings should not consist of too many facets. Facets should not be too small. The size of models is bounded by the paper size and by the build space of a 3D printer, respectively. For both techniques, it is therefore often necessary to (automatically) cut the models into smaller pieces.

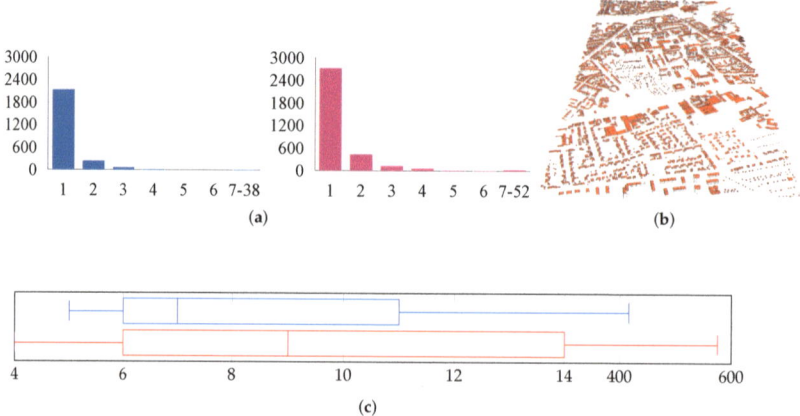

Figure 16. Blue bars: Square kilometer with southwest corner (330,000; 5,687,000) in zone 32U UTM coordinates, red bars: Square kilometer with southwest corner (330,000; 5,688,000). (**a**) *x*-axis: Number of connected components, *y*-axis: Building parts with this number of connected components; (**b**) models of the two square kilometer test region; and (**c**) polygons per building part.

Figure 17. A fragmented flat roof leads to multiple connected components, three are shown here.

Figure 18. The left roof surface in the first, the right roof surface in the last image, and two roof polygons in the second image do not perfectly match the texture. The balconies in the last image originate from two aerial images taken from different angles to avoid occluded areas.

Table 1. Comparison between paper models and 3D print models, colors from dark red to dark green indicate a scale from bad to good.

	Paper Model	Color Powder 3D Print	FFF with Multiple Filaments Colors
time needed for model creation	light green	red	red
manual interaction	pink	light green	white
costs of materials and equipment	dark green	red	white
stability of models	dark green	dark green	dark green
quality of color	dark green	dark green	white
number of colors	dark green	dark green	red
durability of structure	pink	light green	dark green
durability of colors	pink	dark green	dark green
precision of scale	dark green	dark green	dark green
applicability for simple geometries	dark green	dark green	dark green
applicability for complex geometries	pink	dark green	dark green
scalability of models	pink	dark green	dark green

4. Conclusions and Future Work

Paper models can potentially be used for urban planning and are a comparatively easy-to-create and cost-effective alternative to virtual 3D visualization as well as manually-created or 3D-printed architectural models.

We presented a greedy algorithm for automatically unfolding CityGML models into paper model kits with exact scaling, so that in most cases only a single piece of paper needs to be cut out, folded, and glued together. However, even without assembling the models, the kits are an alternative to virtual 3D rendering because unfolding to 2D is helpful for finding model and texture errors. The fold edges indicate how the 2D facets fit together in 3D. The 2D rendering shows hidden walls and internal structures that are not readily apparent when viewing virtual city representations. Thus, textures of walls between buildings can be checked. Building models in LoD 2 should consist only of the outer shell such that interior walls indicate errors. At the moment, this 2D representation is also complimentary to some city model viewers (like the "azul" (https://github.com/tudelft3d/azul (accessed on 23 November 2021)) viewer) that are not capable of displaying textures from files. In addition, the current CityJSON plugin for QGIS does not support the appearance module needed to handle textures, see [19].

Our future work will be to apply algorithms for inpainting to occluded image areas so that vegetation is removed from the facade images. It would also be useful to simplify given CityGML models so that cutting and gluing together becomes easier. It should also be investigated how the production process can be simplified by 2D laser cutting. Laser cutting would not only eliminate the need to cut out the layouts, but could also prepare the folding edges by weakening the material. In addition, raised texture patterns would be possible, which could be obtained from the textures.

Author Contributions: Section Histogram Matching: R.P.-F., other sections: S.G.; writing—review and editing, S.G. All authors have read and agreed to the published version of the manuscript.

Funding: This research received no external funding.

Institutional Review Board Statement: Not applicable

Informed Consent Statement: Not applicable

Acknowledgments: The authors are grateful to Udo Hannok from the cadastral office of the City of Krefeld for providing the oblique aerial images. The authors are also grateful for valuable comments by the anonymous reviewers as well as by our colleague, Christoph Dalitz.

Conflicts of Interest: The authors declare no conflict of interest.

References

1. Biljecki, F.; Stoter, J.; Ledoux, H.; Zlatanova, S.; Çöltekin, A. Applications of 3D City Models: State of the Art Review. *ISPRS Int. J. Geo-Inf.* **2015**, *4*, 2842–2889. [CrossRef]
2. Kolbe, T.; Donaubauer, A. *Semantic 3D City Modeling and BIM*; Urban Informatics. The Urban Book Series; Shi, W., Goodchild, M., Batty, M., Kwan, M., Zhang, A., Eds.; Springer: Singapore, 2016; pp. 609–636.
3. Gröger, G.; Kolbe, T.H.; Nagel, C.; Häfele, K.H. *OpenGIS City Geography Markup Language (CityGML) Encoding Standard. Version 2.0.0*; Open Geospatial Consortium: Arlington, VA, USA, 2012.
4. Schmidt, P.; Stattmann, N. *Unfolded*; Birkhäuser: Basel, Switzerland, 2012.
5. Al-Kodmany, K. Visualization tools and methods for participatory planning and design. *J. Urban Technol.* **2001**, *8*, 1–37. [CrossRef]
6. Hull, C.; Willett, W. Building with Data: Architectural Models as Inspiration for Data Physicalization. In Proceedings of the 2017 CHI Conference on Human Factors in Computing Systems, Denver, CO, USA, 6–11 May 2017; Association for Computing Machinery: New York, NY, USA, 2017; pp. 1217–1264.
7. Griffin, A.L. Feeling It Out: The Use of Haptic Visualization for Exploratory Geographic Analysis. *Cartogr. Perspect.* **2001**, *39*, 12–29. [CrossRef]
8. Schilling, A. *Architektur und Modellbau: Konzepte-Methoden-Materialien*; Birkhäuser: Basel, Switzerland, 2018.
9. Pottmann, H.; Asperl, A.; Hofer, M.; Kilian, A. Die Erstellung von Modellen im Kontext der Architektur. In *Architekturgeometrie*; Springer: Vienna, Austria, 2010; pp. 423–453.
10. Bañón, C.; Raspall, F. *3D Printing Architecture: Workflows, Applications, and Trends*; Springer: Berlin, Germany, 2021.
11. Straub, R.; Prautzsch, H. Creating Optimized Cut-Out Sheets for Paper Models from Meshes. *KarlsRuhe Rep. Inform.* **2011**, *36*, 1–15.
12. Cankova, K.; Dovramadjiev, T.; Jecheva, G.V. Methodology for creating 3D paper unfolded models with complex geometry using open-source software and resources with free personal and commercial license. *Annu. J. Tech. Univ. Varna Bulg.* **2018**, *2*, 39–46.
13. Haenselmann, T.; Effelsberg, W. Optimal strategies for creating paper models from 3D objects. *Multimed. Syst.* **2012**, *18*, 519–532. [CrossRef]
14. Korpitsch, T.; Takahashi, S.; Gröller, E.; Wu, H.Y. Simulated Annealing to Unfold 3D Meshes and Assign Glue Tabs. *J. WSCG* **2020**, *28*, 47–56. [CrossRef]
15. Croft, H.; Falconer, K.; Guy, R. *Unsolved Problems in Geometry*; Springer: Berlin/Heidelberg, Germany, 1991.
16. Bern, M.; Demaine, E.; Eppstein, D.; Kuo, E.; Mantler, A.; Snoeyink, J. Unfoldable polyhedra with convex faces. *Comput. Geom.* **2003**, *24*, 51–62. [CrossRef]
17. Goebbels, S.; Pohle-Fröhlich, R. Roof reconstruction from airborne laser scanning data based on image processing methods. *ISPRS Ann. Photogramm. Remote Sens. Spatial Inf. Sci.* **2016**, *3*, 407–414. [CrossRef]
18. Goebbels, S. Convergence rates for Fourier partial sums of polygons and periodic splines. *J. Fourier Anal. Appl.* **2019**, *25*, 1902–1920. [CrossRef]
19. Vitalis, S.; Arroyo Ohori, K.; Stoter, J. CityJSON in QGIS: Development of an open-source plugin. *Trans. GIS* **2020**, *24*, 1147–1164. [CrossRef] [PubMed]

Article

Cartography and Art: A Comparative Study Based on Color

Leda Stamou

Cartography Laboratory, School of Rural, Surveying and Geoinformatics Engineering, National Technical University of Athens, 9 Iroon Polytechniou, 15780 Zografou, Greece; lestamou@central.ntua.gr

Abstract: Color occupies a prominent place in the bibliography of cartography, as it is an important element in the formation of cartographic symbolization. Apart from the technical issues of its application to maps, color theory is one of the elements that connect maps with art. In this paper various cartographic trends and their origins are examined and correlated with the artistic periods in which they were developed in order to investigate and document the extent to which maps follow the artistic movements and, particularly in the art of painting, concerning the form and the content of the maps and whether color can be used as an identification element of the art trend and the corresponding period. The research spans from the end of the Middle Ages to the 21st century and is referred spatially in Western Europe, including Italy. The comparison of colors is made in both descriptive and quantitative terms through the commentary of hue, brightness, and saturation, as well as through plotting them in the color wheel, a process that allows an overview of the range and location of color sequences. Concluding, the paintings and maps that were selected and examined in detail support the effect of painting on maps, without implying that it is intentional.

Keywords: color; color theory; color schemes analysis; visual variables; cartographic symbolization

1. Introduction

In the evolution of cartography, remarkable relations between cartography and art appear, not only during those periods when maps were created by highly skilled engravers and artists, but also later. Even during the mature period of cartography since the last decades of the 20th century, the map composition is widely related to the appearance of the map, both in terms of the symbols used, the layout, and the overall visual impression. Despite the fact that, nowadays, cartography has been completely dominated by science and technology, without the artistic skills required as in earlier periods of the history of cartography, during the phase of cartographic composition, the cartographer is called upon to be imaginative and creative in order to support the "good map design". It is quite clear that the theory of cartography, along with the cartographic tradition and practice, allow the cartographer much less freedom than art allows to the artist, provided that cartographic design challenges the cartographer to find effective solutions to graphic design issues. The issue of the relationship between cartography and art is one of the issues that concern the cartographic community. The ICA "Art and Cartography Commission" has a significant role in promoting creative research and scholarly publications on art and cartography in all of its aspects, for both the academic audience and the general public.

Cartography has benefited greatly from science, as far as the cognitive areas of cartographic representation, communication, color vision theories, optics, color theory, visual perception, and psychology are concerned. Art has also. Many artistic movements, such as Impressionism, Neo-Impressionism, Pointillism, Fauvism, and Modernism, were based on the scientific knowledge that emerged from the theory of color, the trichromatic theory, and the opponent process theory. It should also be noted that contemporary art shares additional characteristics with science: modern artists, having rejected aesthetics as the defining feature of their work, have based art on a practice that can be imaginative, creative, provocative, and exploratory [1].

In addition, part of exploring the relationship between cartography and art focuses on the use of color [2,3]. Paintings can be a source of inspiration for cartographers when it comes to choosing and using color. Color, due to its inherent characteristics is perhaps the most complex and multifaceted element of the cartographic design. Painters have highlighted color and form as the two dominant elements of their work, as evidenced by the study of art history [4]. In particular, color has been a central element in various artistic movements [4] and, in fact, is often enough to determine the artistic period of a painting and often the painter.

Another notable issue that frequently arises in the cartographic bibliography is the fact that maps inspire and stimulate the interest of artists, being the subject or medium for artistic creations. Great Dutch painters such as Vermeer, Pieter de Hooch, and many others have portrayed maps in their paintings during the exploration period, emphasizing this way the important role played by this medium, as it portrayed the new territories. Johannes Vermeer in particular, portrayed maps in ten of his paintings [5]. For example, the map made by Balthasar Florisz van Berckenrode and published by Willem Jansz Blaeu in 1621, is portrayed in the "Officer and laughing girl" (Figure 1, adapted from [6], Attribution: Johannes Vermeer, Public domain, via Wikimedia Commons) and also in the "Woman in blue, reading a letter" [5].

Figure 1. Johannes Vermeer: Officer and the laughing girl.

The Surrealists published their world map in 1929, which they intentionally distorted by formulating a political message against Imperialism and the conventional ethnocentric representation of the world [7,8]. It was published in a special issue of the Belgian magazine Variétés on "Le Surréalisme en 1929" in June 1929. Respectively, Situationists drew the map "The Naked City", which shows how this group of artists and activists perceived the neighborhoods as they wandered around the city, with the aim of providing alternative ways of urban space, and the crossing of psychogeographical boundaries [9,10]. Jasper Johns (b. 1930), has created paintings and collages portraying the map of the USA using bright colors and vivid touches of abstract expressionism [11]. So maps are often a source of inspiration for many artists. Joyce Kosloff and Mona Hatoum utilize maps to format their iconic artistic works [12,13]. From the anthropomorphic maps of Bunting and Münster [14,15] in the 16th century to "Carto-morphic" people in the 21st century: Matthew Cusick's collages of cartographic people and landscapes in the "Map Works" collection [16] are part of the cartography and art dialogue. This dialogue transcends the boundaries of the visual arts and in several cases infiltrates in literature, a fact indicative of the power of the map. The case of Rebecca Solnit and her book "Unfathomable City: A New Orleans Atlas" is typical. There, she uses a performance map of the concentration of lead in the soil, superimposing texts with political lies from 1699 that influenced the social and racial development of the city [9,17].

One could claim that the common elements of art and cartography are representation and symbolization. In art, the representation comes to light via the expressive means of the artist, while in cartography via the skills and knowledge of the cartographer, that is, the method of symbolization, the symbols themselves, and the structure of the map. The aggregation of the individual symbols of a map constitutes the result of its objective, which is usually the geographical reality. As an inevitable stage of cartographic composition, symbolization could be defined as the graphical encoding of information, or, in particular, the use of visual variables to represent data aggregates resulting from categorization, simplification, and amplification [18].

A map is a graphic representation of geographical reality, which is implemented through cartographic symbolization. Unlike the image characterized by the property of similarity, the map emerges as a result of an abstract process: the entities to be represented are selected and symbols with conventional relation to the signifier are used. Arthur Robinson emphasizes cartographic representation as: "The principal task of cartography is to communicate environmental information ... The task of the map designer is to enhance the map user's ability to retrieve information" [19] (p. 17). The symbols are determined by cartographic rules and design constraints. In the course of information from the geographical reality to the user through the map, the role of the cartographer is crucial as he/she implements the cartographic abstraction that concerns both the selection of the information to be displayed and the selection and configuration of the symbolization. The cartographic rendering of spatial information is a process of transformation from its physical form to a form of non-literal symbolization contained in the map. The visual perception, the mental processing, and then the recognition and/or interpretation of these symbols by the user of the map are critical components in achieving the goal of its creation, i.e., in the transmission of the geographical information. If cognitive and geometric accuracy are taken for granted, based on our knowledge of the world and the available technological means, the main task of the map composition is the selection of appropriate symbols and their organization in a functional communication dipole between the cartographer and the map user, using the symbol as a carrier.

Color and its application to the individual cartographic elements is a critical factor, not only because it is one of the elements of symbols formation, but also because it establishes harmony, balance, contrast, visual hierarchy, and image-background organization. In the image formed by the map, what will pop-up, what will recede, what will be clear, and what will be blurred, bright or dark, what will be different or similar, depends mainly on the color [20]. From an artistic point of view, color is a powerful means of artistic expression and activates the feelings of the observer. It is remarkable that three of Bertin's visual variables are related to color: hue, brightness, and saturation [21]. Indicatory of its distinguished role in cartographic design, cartographic symbolization, and cartographic communication is the fact that every single cartographic textbook written by prominent cartographers and scholars, devotes a special section to color description, analysis, and perception, as well as color models and color spaces [19,22–24].

Socio-political changes and technological progress have had a catalytic effect on both the acquisition of knowledge about the geographical area and the means of cartographic expression. This study is an attempt to investigate and document the influence of art—and particularly the art of painting—on the form and the content of the maps, with emphasis to the use and the role of color. The comparison is based on the change of the subject, as well as the means of expression in paintings and maps, over time. The form of maps, paintings, and other graphic works is also the subject of commentary, as well as the infiltration of the dominant artistic point of view in cartographic design. To some extent, this approach is based on historical, artistic, and cartographic elements. The aim of this study is to investigate whether and to what extent maps are influenced by the prevailing artistic trend of the time and whether this can be exploited today.

Based on the way color is used in various artistic movements, the aesthetic and artistic relationship between paintings and maps is sought, that is, whether and to what extent the paintings infiltrate the works of cartographers and, in some cases, vice versa. Thus, an attempt is made to examine and/or correlate the parallel evolution of the artistic and cartographic periods. For this reason, maps are examined based on the artistic period. For this research, maps and paintings related to space and time are sought. The choice of maps examined in this study does not constitute historical documentation, but are considered as an anthology of those that signal the change in the format and content of the maps, in the context of the history of cartography.

2. Methodology

Before describing the methodology, a reference to the selection of maps and paintings is necessary. The reasonable question raised is "which maps compare with which paintings". Based on the history of cartography, cartographic schools in Europe were used as the fundamental criterion. Maps of well-known Italian, Spanish, Portuguese, German, Dutch, French, and English cartographers defined the framework as well as the timeline. For the selected cartographic periods, from the medieval European world maps ("mappae mundi") to the Italian and Portuguese portolans, the world maps and atlases of the Age of Exploration to the maps produced by scientific and technical developments, even up to the online map services, the corresponding artistic period was examined, with respect to their general characteristics and the use of color. Thus, the history of cartography is linked to the history of art and this resulted in a visual examination and comparison between maps and paintings of the same period. As the original works (maps and paintings) are not accessible, the study is based on the search for the corresponding digital images and the selection was made through/from official national digital libraries, museum websites, and collectors' websites. For each map examined, paintings from the same period are selected and common formatting elements are sought. The colors, the structure, and the margin of the map try to find their counterparts in the paintings.

The methodology followed in this research has two phases: the qualitative approach and the quantitative one. During the qualitative phase, the comparison of the colors is initially descriptive, i.e., their visual characteristics are examined based on the visual variables related to color: hue, brightness (value), and saturation (chroma) [25]. It is examined which hues have been used, which part of the color wheel they cover, and what is the variation of brightness and saturation. At the same time, the role of color as a means of expression, as well as the way it is used to distinguish spatial information, is identified, as described in the next sections. Thus, the qualitative phase concludes to a verbal description of the colors used. In order to visualize the results of the verbal description and comparison, as well as to highlight the affinities of the colors, a quantitative phase has been adopted to support and document the results with metrics concerning color coordinates, as described below.

The quantification phase is then implemented, using a combination of ColorSchemer Studio 2 and Adobe Photoshop software (depending on the quality of the image), so that color schemes of maps and paintings are created and plotted in the color wheel as shown in Figure 2, which is a typical example of color analysis. In this case, the selected colors correspond to the colors of line and area symbols of an examined map. In ColorSchemer Studio 2, the colors can be selected from the image, either automatically or manually, to form the image's color scheme, which is portrayed as a set of color patches. The selected colors are then automatically transferred to the color wheel using their RGB primaries (identified by the software) and they are examined on a case-by-case basis for their perceptual attributes (hue, brightness, saturation), as well as the affinities of the colors. This transfer can also be made by manually deriving colors from an image through a different application (e.g., Adobe Photoshop). The color schemes can then be exported to standalone image files of color patches or can be combined with the source image for presentation purposes (see to the right of Figures 4, 5, and 10). Additionally, the color schemes can be exported to various formats (e.g., html, css, etc.) for any further use. Thus, lists of coordinates, either in RGB or HEX, can be used for numerical presentation, as shown in Table 1. It is noted that the color "coding" in Figure 2 and Table 1 are used here for reference purposes.

Figure 2. Color analysis, typical example.

Table 1. Color coordinates, typical example.

Color	HEX	RGB
C1	#AADAFF	170,218,255
C2	#89BCF3	137,188,243
C3	#FFFFFF	255,255,255
C4	#EDEBE8	237,235,232
C5	#D7DADD	215,218,221
C6	#FDF4E2	253,244,226
C7	#C3ECB2	195,236,178
C8	#F9EDED	249,237,237
C9	#FFE99E	255,233,158
C10	#ECF7EA	236,247,234

In Figure 2, the color scheme of the image is shown on the color wheel, and thus, each color is visually arranged in relation to the set of colors displayed on the screen. This kind of visualization supports conclusions about the range of colors used, which area of the color wheel they occupy and their brightness (or saturation, depending on the choice). Especially for the brightness (or saturation), it is visualized and assessed by the distance of the color from the center of the color wheel (Figure 2), while numerically it is expressed through the corresponding HSB (Hue-Saturation-Brightness) built-in tool.

Due to the use of digital images, the issue of color accuracy in relation to the original work (map or painting) is raised. This is uncontrollable in quantitative terms. For this reason, the research is made using more than one source, in order to cross-reference the data, and it is preferred that the selection be made from official organizations and institutes that demonstrate the required dependability. This is one of the reasons why the numerical description of the colors is not emphasized, but to a considerable extent the main weight is given to the verbal and visual (via the color wheel) description. Nevertheless, the numerical results (color coordinates) could be further used, for example, as a base in cartographic compositions and symbols creation. Any color profiles attached to digital images are retained during processing.

Due to possible Creative Commons restrictions, most of the images used are not included in this article, but the relevant source links are provided. More than 100 maps and paintings were compared and analyzed as part of an extended research [20], for the period from the end of the Middle Ages to the beginning of the 21st century, in Western Europe. It is pointed out that many more had been visually examined prior to the final selection. This paper presents a limited number of them, that is indicative and on the same time representative for each period. Results and discussion are presented in the following paragraphs.

3. Analysis and Results

3.1. Gothic Period

During the Middle Ages (from the 5th to the 15th century A.C.), maps, known as mappae mundi, reflect the influence of the Church: the cartographic representation is allegorical, as is the pictorial representation in images and murals. Typical examples are the map of Ebstorf (Germany, c. 1234) and the map of Hereford (United Kingdom, c. 1285). They are oriented with the East at the top, and Jerusalem is located in the center. The perception and description of the world revolves around the teachings of religion and this is also expressed cartographically. Maps of this era are characterized as "pictorial" [9], but it is easy to recognize the influence of early narrative painting. This artistic term describes an art form that "tells a story" and as general as it sounds, it is literal. It can describe a moment, an event, or a series of events. In early narrative painting the perspective, the actual sizes, and the relative positions are not as important as the transmission of information in the form of narrative. Typical examples of such paintings exist from the beginning of the history of painting until today, not only with the works of the so-called Naive painters, but also with works of historical and mythological content during the Renaissance, Baroque, etc. Note that one of the modern trends in cartography is the creation of storytelling maps utilizing software applications. This way of depicting landscapes, people, and events has left many samples in cartography and especially in the Middle Ages. The "mappae mundi" are a typical example, but the influence of this particular perception and performance of the space, gave important samples in other categories of maps, such as the portolans. This category of maps was created at the end of the 13th century, initially in Italy, and more specifically in Genoa and Venice (followed by Spain and Portugal), and formed the basis of the maps of the time of the discoveries (15th century). Portolans portray the shoreline and compass directions, typical names associated with the coast, ports and capes, while the interior of the coast is either left empty or decorated with symbols of power and compass roses that are depicted in characteristic positions. Toponyms along the coastal points of interest are written on the inner side and with a direction perpendicular to the coastline.

The oldest surviving portolan specimen is the Carte Pisane (c. 1292) and is attributed either to an unknown cartographer or to the Italian cartographer Pietro Vesconte (1310–1330). Contemporary of the Italian School of cartography is the School of Majorca, staffed by prominent Jewish cartographers, cosmographers, and instrument makers, as well as some Christian collaborators, which flourished from the 13th to the 15th century until the Spanish Holy Examination. This school also includes those who were active in Catalonia.

Vesconte's portolans are characterized not only by the religious themes in the marginal illuminations, but also by the influence of painters, such as Giotto di Bondone (1267–1337). Both the structure and the colors used in his portolans look like those used in Giotto's paintings. Inspecting one of his maps made in Venice at 1318 [26], (p. 21), the resemblance to Giotto's paintings is very impressive: the map is located in the center and the corner illuminations depict religious themes (i.e., the Annunciation of Virgin Mary), facing the map, exactly like the way peripherals are looking at the central person in the paintings of religious content. The forms on the map and in the painting are similar, since the era is characterized by a specific style based on the use of specific dyeing materials and dyeing methods for the depiction of leather, fabrics, and folds of clothing. The colors have a great resemblance: gold background, beige, green, red-tile, and blue, most of them located in the area of warm colors. Green (light and dark), tile, ocher, and gold are used not only in the decorative elements of the map, but also on the map itself. This particular cartographer maintains the same structure in his works, with the presence of persons or symbols of religious authority. The golden background, which is the backdrop to the religious scenes acting as a curtain separating the physical from the spiritual world, is also found in the maps of Vesconte, as well as in the paintings of the time (e.g., Giotto di Bondone: "The Madonna Di Ognissanti", c. 1310 [27], Duccio di Buoninsegna: "The Calling of the Apostles Peter and Andrew", c. 1308–1311 [28], and many others).

3.2. Cartography in the Renaissance or the Renaissance of Cartography?

The nautical atlas of Battista Agnese (compiled in 1544) [29] is compared to Titian's "Bacchus and Ariadne" (1523) [30] and the results are portrayed in Figure 3. Both color schemes are located to the same partition of the color wheel, most of them covering the sector from red to yellow.

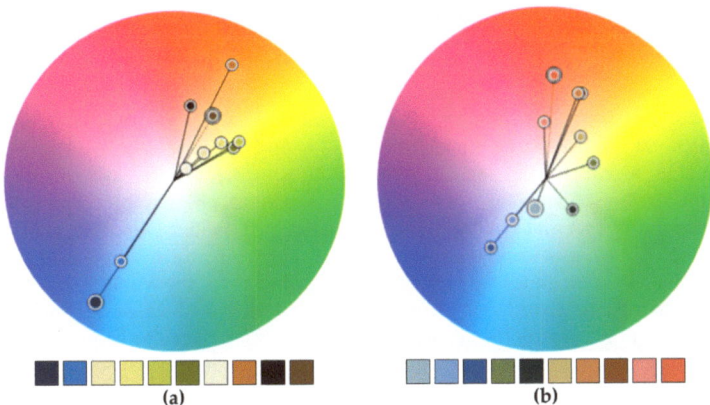

Figure 3. Color analysis and comparison: (a) Battista Agnese nautical atlas (b) Titian painting.

Angelo Freducci's portolans are characterized by vivid colors: blue, green, red, ocher, green-gray, the design of colorful compass roses, and the use of different ways of coloring the islands. On his map of the Caribbean for example (c. 1550) [31], the small islands are filled with solid colors, the middle ones have a colored border that follows the interior of the coastline and fill background with the same color in a lighter tone, while on the large islands the coastline is reinforced with a colored border to the interior of the island. The color impression produced by this map is very close to that of the painting by Domenico Beccafumi "The Holy Family with Angels", c. 1545/1550 [32]. In both cases, the color is used to highlight the important: the islands and the cruising directions in the case of the map and the central face in the painting, while the remaining elements or faces are lost in the neutral background. The visual characteristics in most of his maps are similar and it is notable that some of them carry a very strong pictorial character, especially in terms of cities and mountains symbolization. The mountains are represented by triangular shapes and, in color, by the imitation of chiaroscuro, with the light tones to the east where the light source is placed and the dark tones to the west. Blue is used for rivers, green for lowlands, beige and brown for cities, and almost orange for mountains. Remarkable color similarity is noted between this map and the painting "The Miraculous Draft of Fishes" (1545) by the Venetian painter Jacopo Bassano [33]. From the comparison of the color analysis, it is obvious that the color sequences are placed in the same part of the color wheel, in the area of the warm ones, with small differences in saturation.

Worth mentioning is the Vatican "Maps Gallery" (Galleria delle carte geografiche, 1580–1585) a gallery decorated with 40 maps-murals that cover a length of 120 m. Impressive topographic details, perspective, plasticity, and rich colors have been used to tell stories related to the places: battles, naval battles, cities, and symbols of power. The application of light shading and color gradation for the representation of the relief of the land and the waves of the sea is remarkable, as well as the use of a realistic dark blue for the depiction of the sea. Colors and symbols are in harmony with Michelangelo's paintings that adorn the Capela Sistina to which the gallery leads. The inherent characteristics—harmony, colors, and plasticity of forms—of the mature Italian Renaissance period are predominant, but these maps are a unique case. It will take a long time for the technical means of creating maps to evolve, in order to continue this way of cartographic rendering. However, it should be noted that for the relief rendering, two different modes have been used, depending on the scale. On the larger scales maps, the tonal gradation has been used for the representation of the 3D relief, just like in the works of the representational painting. The impression of the relief, just like the plasticity of the figures, is achieved by the combination of tonal gradations, so that the one closest to the observer (higher altitudes) is lighter and the farthest (lower altitudes) more dark. On the smallest scales maps, the method of representation uses the expressive means of narrative painting. The land relief is represented in front view and the tonal gradations are used in relation to a light source: the light tones are located on the side from which the mountain masses are illuminated. Swiss relief rendering maps approach this style.

The first map printed by copper plate engraving, the map of the Mediterranean (Figure 4, adapted from [34]) by the Italian cartographer and engraver Paolo Forlani, was published in 1569. A portolan, but without following the previous structure and content of the maps of this category where color is used to represent political or geographical divisions and the corresponding pictorial symbols that prevailed in the previous two centuries have been eliminated. The countries and the continents are depicted by the inscription of their name, with color along the inner side of the coastline of some of them and by coloring their interior with a lighter color tone. The sea background is covered by sparse tiny black dots, but the coastline towards the sea is highlighted in blue. Its color sequence is in complete correlation with that of Paolo Veronese's painting (Figure 5, adapted from [35], Attribution: Paolo Veronese, Public domain, via Wikimedia Commons) as shown in Figure 6. Slightly warm colors of medium and low saturation: green, beige, ocher, orange, and blue. The differences in saturation, although relatively small, are expected due to the technical means of creating the two images, copperplate and oil painting, respectively, but also to the different aesthetic requirements of their shaping.

Figure 4. Paolo Forlani's portolan of the Mediterranean Sea and its color scheme.

Figure 5. Paolo Veronese: "Jesus among the doctors at the Temple" and its color scheme.

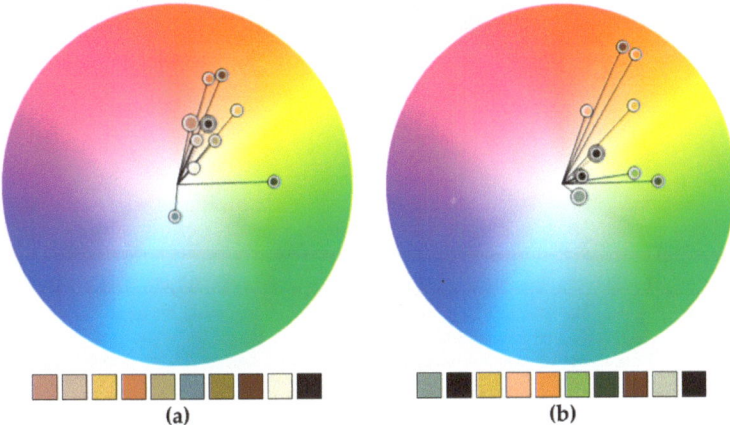

Figure 6. Color analysis and comparison: (**a**) Paolo Forlani's portolan (**b**) Paolo Veronese's painting.

Despite the gradual changes in maps in the late 16th century, the portolan atlases continued to emphasize the interest in depicting the world as new landscapes were discovered. Thus, the work of the Portuguese Fernão Vaz Dourado is very popular. Both Atlas [36] and Atlas with Portolans of the Old and New Worlds [37] (1568–1580) reflect a period when map features had to be visually impressive, on the one hand, and useful in navigation, on the other. These atlases are attributed to Dourado, based on their illustration and design style. Apart from the descriptive richness of these maps and the semiology of the design, the vivid colors of the illustration and many intricate design details give them great visual power (Figure 7). The colors of the symbols of power, blue, red, and gold, bring dominance to the foreground. Crowns, fleurs de lys, flags, and coats of arms pop up in the foreground of the image, forcing the conquered geographical area—both on land and at sea to retreat as a vassal in the background. The influence of Renaissance painting is clear: the color combinations (green, red, blue, gold, and earth tones) give naturalness to the objects, but also intensity and reason for existence in the decorative elements, which support the whole. The maps are based on color, just like many paintings of the Italian Renaissance and Mannerism. Examining the color scheme adopted by El Greco in his work "Christ healing the blind" (1570) [38] and comparing it with the corresponding map, it becomes obvious that both cover the area from the end of the warm to the cold blue through the green, have medium and low saturation values, and have a wide common section (Figure 8).

Figure 7. Fernão Vaz Dourado: The Atlas of Naval Maps of the Old and New Worlds.

The Guillaume Le Testu World Atlas ("Cosmographie Universelle selon les Navigateurs") [39] published in 1555, is another excellent specimen of 16th-century manuscripts and a typical example of the Dieppe School of cartography. It includes nautical charts that follow the style and content of the portolans as it had been established since the 14th century, but has been created with a strong painting visual character. This atlas, in addition to maps of individual areas, also includes six (6) depictions of the Earth, called "Projections". In all maps, the land part is covered by a green color that has a "tonal" gradation from inland to shores, while the small islands are colored red and some larger ones with ultramarine blue (lapis lazuli). Mountains are also designed in green, while rivers and lakes in gray. The sea is covered with low saturated light blue and brown wavy patterns, except for the Red Sea which is depicted in the "Sixth Projection" map and is drawn with a red line. Ships and sea creatures or monsters sail in the oceans, and symbols of royal power and sovereignty are visible on all maps of this atlas. The background of the sky in medium blue harmonizes with the corresponding green background of the land, with lighter clouds and winds painted as male faces. The toponyms are written in bold font in red and gray. The color schemes that have been adopted are mostly cool (Figure 9) and harmonious in terms of the value of the colors. The high saturation is used to emphasize the symbols of power, which mark the domination of the lands. The atlas' color scheme is integrated in the context of the appearance of the Italian Renaissance's paintings.

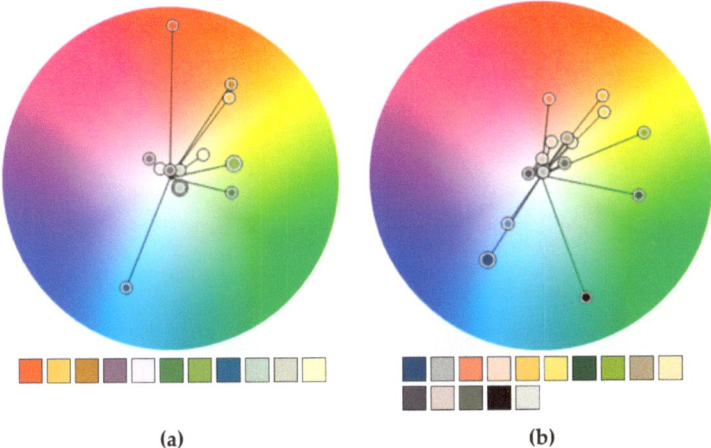

Figure 8. Color analysis and comparison: (**a**) Fernão Vaz Dourado maps (**b**) El Greco painting.

Figure 9. Guillaume Le Testu World Atlas color analysis.

The last quarter of the 16th century is marked by the Flemish cartographers Gerardus Mercator and his almost contemporary Abraham Ortelius. Mercator maps were sought not only for their content, but also for the italics fonts used to indicate toponyms. The Mercator Atlas [40] (Figure 10) published as a whole in 1595, is a combination of three sections published in 1585, 1589, and 1595, respectively. Mercator's maps signal significant changes: emphasis is placed on the geographical space and the use of pictorial elements is limited to the use of frontal aspects for the rendering of the mountains (with brown color and light shading that gives them a highly dramatic character), forests (green), and castles/cities (red). The settlements are symbolized with a small circular symbol and are accompanied by the inscription of their name. The colors chosen in this atlas (orange, beige, green, and yellow) have a strong visual affinity with the colors chosen by Pieter Bruegel the Elder [41]. These are low and medium saturated colors, which are placed in almost one third of the color wheel (Figure 11), on the warm side, except for the blue-gray which marks the sea beyond the coastline, which is placed in the cool side.

Figure 10. Gerardus Mercator Atlas and its color scheme.

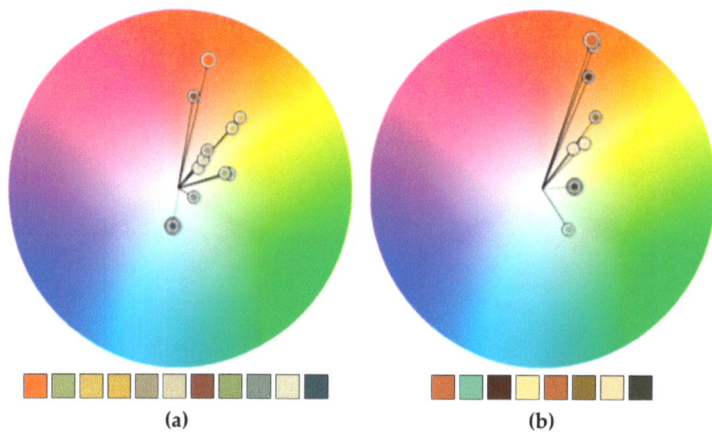

Figure 11. Color analysis and comparison: (a) Mercator atlas (b) Pieter Bruegel the Elder painting.

3.3. The Era of Baroque

In the golden age of the Dutch discoveries, the need to demonstrate the power, sovereignty, and grandeur brought about by land conquests determined the character of maps: magnificent compositions with complex visual character and rich marginal decoration. As in many paintings, the elements surrounding the central theme are not related to it, but are spectacular and they often have a strong allegorical character. Observing the overall appearance and structure of maps of that period, one can see the complexity of its composition. Geographic information is complemented by elements of astronomy, history, and mythology. The density of the image refers to complicated compositions, characteristic of the painting movements of the late 16th and early 17th century, the transition from the Renaissance to Mannerism and Baroque. The controversy of "form" over "color" continued with the controversy of the beauty of forms over "naturalism". The Flemish painter Peter Paul Rubens, despite being in Rome, which was the center of developments in painting and discussions around it, maintained the tradition of Flemish painters who focused on the realistic rendering of visible reality, but also on the emphasis on detail. In his works, the elements of the painting composition are crowded around a central object; there is a wealth of light, a variety of textures and great vibrancy that contribute to the emergence of the subject, which is often allegorical. His artistic style belongs to the Baroque period and is characterized mainly by large, impressive compositions that tend to grandeur.

The aim of the Baroque style is to impress through intricate designs and luxurious decorative elements that shape and dramatic and theatrical style add imposingness to the work. These features are also found on Willem Janszoon Blaeu's map, as well as on other maps of Flemish, Dutch, and German cartographers of that period (e.g., Willem & Johannes Blaeu, Jodocus Hondius, Henricus Hondius, Mattias & Johann Bussemachaer, Joan Blaeu etc). Color not only has a decorative role, but is used to distinguish states or continents or individual elements (compass roses, etc.). As in the Baroque artistic style, the striking effects played an important role and intricate decorations defined the painting itself, the same way with the maps of the Baroque era, the constant addition of decorative elements made the maps intricate and striking, emphasizing the fringe elements. This fact adds to the maps the prestige and the glamour of the murals (religious paintings) with which churches and monasteries are decorated. The striking details of the physiographic elements and the intricate fonts are added to the intense painting decoration of the margin of the map, give an exuberant character, and are in line with the characteristics of this artistic movement that was definitively formed until the first half of the 17th century. The overall visual impression of these maps is characterized by color harmony between the main theme and the peripheral decoration. Vibrant or hazy colors of medium or high saturation, add intensity, luxury, and visual power. These are the characteristics of Baroque colors and are recognized not only in the masterpieces of painting, but also in the maps of the same era. From the study of maps and paintings of the Baroque period, the results of the color comparison are presented selectively in Figure 12 for one map made by Blaeu [42] and one of Rubens' painting [43]. The similarity of the colors is confirmed, both for the hues and the saturation range. Of course, due to the different technical means, the highest saturation values in the painting are expected.

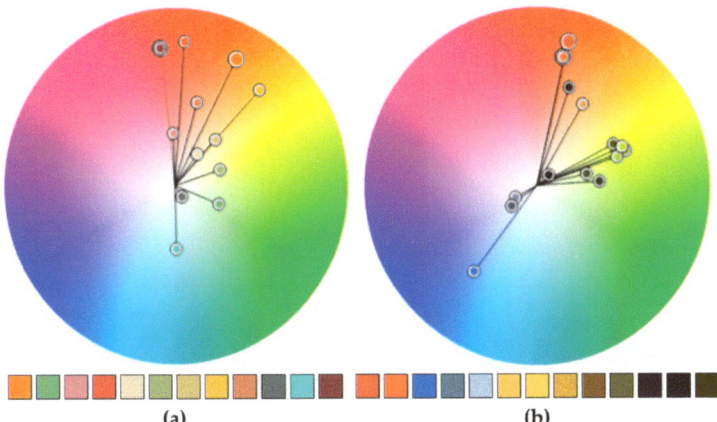

Figure 12. Color analysis and comparison: (a) Blaeu map (b) Rubens painting.

3.4. The Trends during the 18th Century

As part of the transition from Baroque to Romanticism, the marginal decorative elements are gradually eliminated from the maps, or limited to the cartouche. Their form gradually changes, overcoming the intensity and complexity of the Baroque and going to the grace and kindness of Rococo, as reflected in the paintings of the early 18th century in France, but also in Italy, England, Germany, and Austria. The paintings try to capture the pleasant everyday scenes, with idyllic landscapes and people from the aristocracy in various occupations, going beyond the strict limits imposed by the church. The colors are soft and transparent with pastel tones, without deep shadows. They try to give the works a graceful, light tone and elegance. The decoration acquires a character of subtlety that expresses the taste of the French aristocracy and chivalrous grace [4]. Leading painters are Jean Antoine Watteau, Jean Honoré Fragonard, François Boucher, Giovanni Battista Tiepolo, and William Hogarth. Scientific developments, such as astronomical discoveries and the measurement of longitude, reinforce the autonomous identity of the map and weaken the need for decoration. An excellent example is the world map of Guillaume De L'Isle maybe the most important French cartographer of the time. Based on the-then-recent astronomical observations, not only did he contribute to the recalculation of latitude and longitude, but he incorporated this information into his maps, thus changing the accuracy of the maps. The change that is taking place in the appearance of maps in Northern Europe is great for the conditions of the time. Even the maps of Dutch cartographers with the heavy heritage of intense decoration, have replaced, in whole or in part, the decorative themes with cartographic inserts, visibly lightening the image and removing the dramatic and imposing elements. The emphasis is on the depiction of the geographical space, as, in the subjects of the paintings, the emphasis is on calm and carefree scenes, without action, without intensity. Colors are used without the chromatic visual strength of colors used in the 17th century; they are duller, lighter, as in the works of Antoine Watteau. A selective example of the similarity of the colors between maps and paintings during the Rococo period, is presented in Figure 13 about the comparison of the 1721 map by John Senex [44] and the painting of Antoine Watteau "Pilgrimage to Cythera" (1717–1719) [45]. The colors belong to the same area of the color wheel, so they have a common range of mainly cool shades and even with similar values of brightness and saturation.

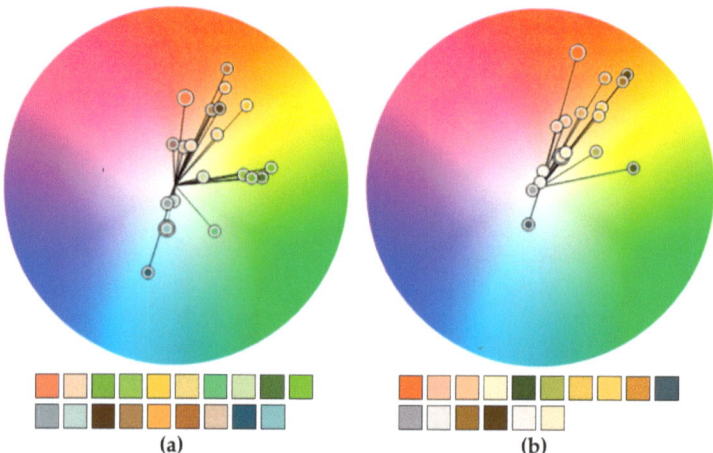

Figure 13. Color analysis and comparison: (a) John Senex map (b) Antoine Watteau painting.

Neoclassicism succeeded Rococo, a style that embodied grace, asymmetry, and enhanced appearance with the use of elegant and delicate decorative elements. It was developed in Europe in the second half of the 18th century and relied on symmetry and harmony, virtues of ancient Greek and Roman art, bringing them back to the Renaissance. The works of the artists should be imbued with the "gentle simplicity and calm grandeur" of the works of classical antiquity. Neoclassicism opposes the exaggerated character and complex expression of Baroque, as well as the lightness and division of the Rococo form. Neoclassicism painting is characterized by the idealization of forms, clarity, and emphasis on outlines, the superiority of design over color, the accuracy and limited use of detail, and the avoidance of depth rendering. The forms become strictly descriptive and, due to the clarity of the outlines, they emerge from the painting like sculptures. The shadows and fluctuations of the lighting—a strong element of Baroque painting—are constantly softening and in some cases completely disappearing. The viewer is obliged to focus his attention on the first level of the work and usually on the center, where the most important part of the composition is located. The rigor of Neoclassicism pervades the 1784 map of the Homann Heirs publishing house [46]. The map is located in the center of the observer's attention. There is no margin decoration; there is information in the form of text and tables instead. The colors, yellow, orange, green, and red, are also found in the work of Benjamin West "The Death of General Wolfe" (1770) [47].

3.5. The First Half of the 19th Century

In the context of the industrial revolution in the 19th century, mass mechanical production dominated over hand-made creation and production. During this period, artistic creation shifted more and more to the capitalist bourgeoisie and national academies, with merchants and art critics gaining a strong foothold. Paris had become the artistic capital of Europe, with the French Academy and official painting exhibitions defining developments in art. It is in this context that the transition from Neoclassicism (which began in the second half of the 18th century) to Romanticism takes place. In the field of cartography, the 19th century is characterized as the "Age of cartography". Cartographic creation and production in the 19th century acquired characteristics of professional specialization and the gradual standardization of maps began internationally, mainly through the establishment of official state cartographic organizations and institutes. With the development of lithography and the implementation of color printing, it became feasible to reproduce a large number of copies, which was used extensively to disseminate the map for economic, military, and educational purposes. The methods of map production and reproduction inevitably affected its style. Uniform cartographic practices and topographic maps were gradually standardized. In art, during the first half of the 19th century, Romanticism prevailed. Its main feature is the emphasis on evoking strong emotion through art, as well as the greater freedom in form, compared to most classical concepts. In Romanticism, the dominant element is the emphasis on emotion, not so much against logic as against its one-sided domination. Emotion, imagination, and lyricism are opposed to logic and pettiness. The colors are rich, the outline is slimming, the composition is full of movement and energy and the touches are free. Intense and contrasting movements and dramatic shading are some of the main features of this art and are very reminiscent of Baroque art. Typical are the artistic work of: Goya (Spain), Turner (England), Géricault and Delacroix (France), and Friedrich (Germany). Romanticism opposes the effects of the Industrial Revolution which led to the decline of handicrafts and replaced handicrafts with machine production. At the same time, a new middle class was developed that lacked tradition. Landscape painting, in the context of Romanticism, is part of the artist's freedom to choose a subject. Turner is considered one of the greatest landscape painters of the 19th century; he was a member of the Romantic Movement and became known as "the painter of light". Gilbert's world map (1839) [48] shows the use of colors similar to Turner's works, but it is not possible to ignore the aspects of the terrain at the base of the map and not to relate them to the imposingness of the visual scene of Caspar David Friedrich's artistic work, especially the emblematic painting "Wanderer above the sea of fog" (1818) [49]. The same approach is observed in the world map of Alexander Keith Johnston (1854) [50] and in the impressive Natural Atlas of Johnston & Humboldt (1850) [51].

Romanticism was overthrown in France by Realism. In painting, Realism rejects the emotional tone of Romanticism and advocates the depiction of real scenes in a realistic way, without a mood of embellishment. The leading Gustave Courbet, Jean-François Millet, Honoré Daumier, and Jean-Baptiste-Camille Corot are important painters of this movement, which had an impact and influenced artists in other countries, such as Britain, Germany, and Russia. The hazy colors of the paintings of this period are characteristically found on the map of Europe, which was published in London on 1861 [52].

3.6. The Second Half of the 19th Century and the 20th Century

Synonymous with the 20th century, the philosophical and artistic movement of Modernism is characterized by the spirit of opposition and deconstruction of conventional ways of thinking, expression, and representation. Modernist movements overthrow what is considered outdated or inappropriate in the new environment of a fully industrialized world. In painting, Modernism undoubtedly began with Edward Manet, but its peak is evident from the beginning of the 20th century until 1930, while its existence continues until Postmodernism.

One of the main artistic movements that used color as the main expressive means of individual and artistic expression is Impressionism. For the Impressionists, the characteristic of the visual scene is the light, which determines the impression, totally and partially. The light creates areas that are recorded with specific local color characteristics, without keeping the form unchanged, that is, the shape of the object. On the contrary, the fragmentation of the structure in combination with the special character of the colors, with emphasis on the primary shades, but also a pastel overall impression, realized with small visible touches, are special features of this artistic movement, the main means of expression of which is color. Another feature, which is found in several works, but mainly in those of Renoir, is a diffuse haze that is mainly due to the lack of outline, but also to the tendency to implement in the work the way in which a visual scene is perceived by the human visual system: everything in the central field of view is clear (focused), while what is perceived by the peripheral vision is blurred. Emblematic figures of this movement, apart from August Renoir, are Claude Monet, Edgar Degas, Camille Pissarro, and many other painters associated with it, without being considered its exponents, as either they had more influences by other movements, or the main character of their work (their identity) is part of later artistic movements. In Edward Stanford's color map [53], the main visual characteristics of the colors brought to the painting by the Impressionist painters are present. Despite the differences in the coverage area, on the map the areas of colors are larger, while in the works of the Impressionists the colors occupy small fragmented areas, which makes color analysis difficult, a comparison can be made with Monet's work [54]. The color sequences of the map and the table are placed in close areas of the color wheel, they cover a similar area in it, that is, they are similar shades; they have low saturation and high brightness (Figure 14).

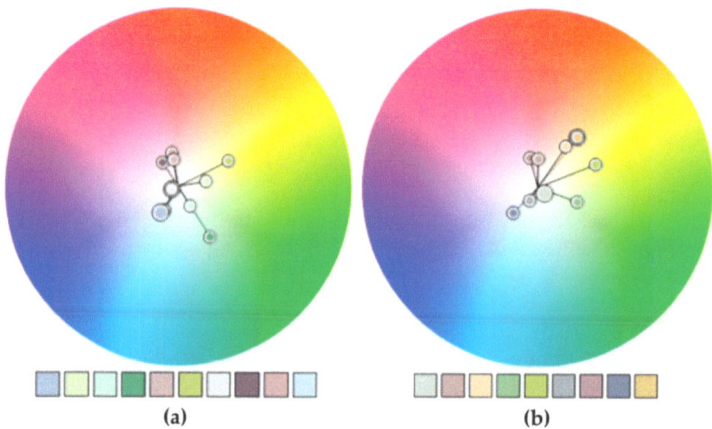

Figure 14. Color analysis and comparison: (a) Stanford map (b) Claude Monet painting.

The end of the 19th century finds artistic movements succeeding each other at a speed that would have been unthinkable a century or two ago. Impressionism handed over the baton to Post-Impressionism, which developed from 1886 to 1905 and that, in turn, to Fauvism. The Post-Impressionists reacted to the fragmentation of the theme structure used by the Impressionists and used color to reinforce form, with no interest in naturalness. With Cézanne at the forefront, the form began to approach its geometric simplicity, a path that would lead modern art to abstraction. Despite the lack of common beliefs, post-Impressionist painters, each with their own unique character, used color in a more flat way. The deep Baroque light and shades contrast passed into the color gradations of Impressionism and began to become flat in the Post-Impressionism, Fauvism, Symbolism, and Expressionism that would follow. Paul Cézanne used a lot of burnt orange, blue, and bluish green, medium and low saturation colors in general [55,56]. Vincent Van Gogh is famous for the sulfite yellows he combined with the blue and the characteristic brush strokes of the shading, widely used in engraving. Paul Gauguin is famous for the use of complementary colors. The Fauvists, led by Henri Matisse, brought the bold color combinations, but at the same time established modern art. In various editions of Johnston W&AK Atlas [57], the use of green and burnt orange at various brightness levels recalls Cézanne's color vocabulary. The colors of [55,57] are located mainly in the cool part of the color wheel, except for the orange, with low brightness colors and medium and low saturation (Figure 15).

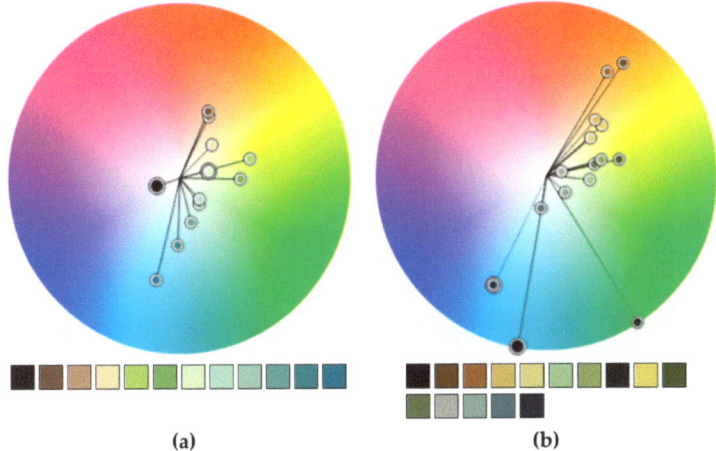

Figure 15. Color analysis and comparison: (a) W&AK Atlas (b) Cézanne painting.

The color map of 1897 [58] was published by the French publishing house Didot-Bottin during the Belle Époque, and is clearly part of the Art Nouveau with the characteristic curved decorative elements, inspired by plants and flowers, the flat colors that prevailed in commercial posters, and also in paintings (Toulouse Lautrec, Gustav Klimt, Alfonse Mucha etc.). In the map [58] and in the Alfonse Mucha poster [59], the colors occupy a very narrow area of the color wheel (Figure 16); they are earthy beige, hazy green, and brownish red. A similar comparison can be made between the Le Petit Journal map [60] and other Mucha posters.

In Expressionism the artist primarily expresses himself/herself and the visual medium for this is color, without form being so important, thus establishing the abstract art. Pioneer of abstract art Wassily Kandinsky studies, uses, and teaches color and transcends physical experience giving weight to its spiritual dimension. The point is that Fauvists and Expressionists have one thing in common: bold, strong, opaque color [61,62] and will influence not only paintings, but also graphic works in general. The map of climate zones [63] is in the spirit of Wassily Kandinsky's color choices. High saturation, high brightness for colors mainly warm, but also with the presence of some cool ones, all placed in the same part of the color wheel (Figure 17).

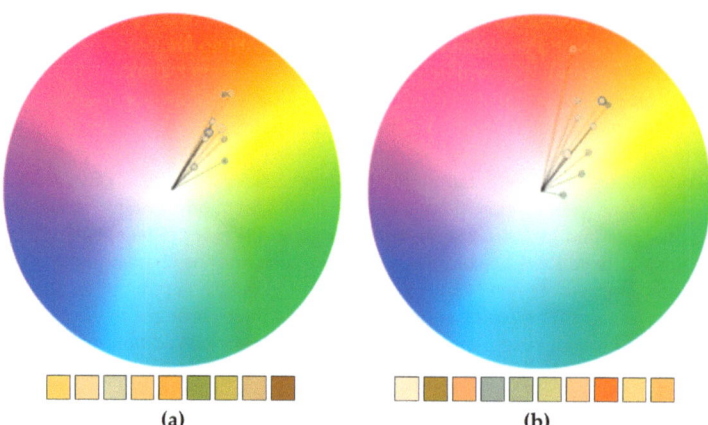

Figure 16. Color analysis and comparison: (**a**) Didot-Bottin color map (**b**) Mucha poster.

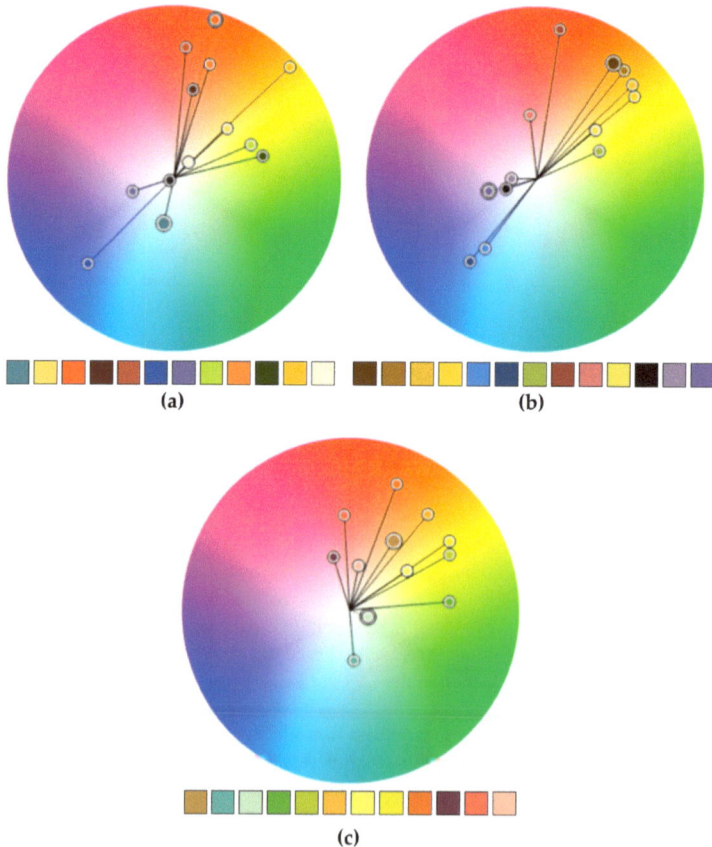

Figure 17. Color analysis and comparison: (**a**,**b**) Kandinsky paintings (**c**) Climate zones map.

The top moment (specimen) of Modernism in cartography is the map of Henry Beck, which is a landmark for the topological depiction of geographical information [64]. Chronologically it belongs to the era of Art Deco style with influences from the abstraction and geometry of Cubism, and the bold and vivid colors of phobia. Piet Mondrian had similar influences and since 1915 he has been experimenting with abstraction, which he conquers by maintaining only simple geometric shapes and vivid colors in his painting discourse, developing the non-representational form of Neo-Plasticism [65]. After World War II, topographic maps of official national cartographic agencies are produced in accordance with the specifications and instructions issued by NATO through STANAGs. World maps are usually issued for educational purposes and are contained in school atlases: political, geophysical, and thematic. However, the value of the influence of Modernism is not degraded as the colors are vivid and flat and the abstraction has been assimilated not only in the content, but also in the form of the maps [66,67].

3.7. Early 21st Century

At the end of the 20th century, cartography, or better cartographic creation and production, is described by the terms digital cartography or automated cartography, both indicative of the complete use of computer systems in the cartographic process. After all, technical means have always played a determining role in the implementation of the map. Equally sweeping is the use of computers, software, and multimedia in artistic creation. If photography, with its entry into museums and art galleries and its integration into the Fine Arts, began to undermine the foundations of painting as one of the most powerful and creative artistic means of expression, digital photography, the creation of images using computers, video art, and installations, are just some of the contemporary artistic activities, which a few decades ago it was unthinkable, if not rejected, to be considered art. In the field of cartography today, the use of maps and geospatial data is adopted by the average internet user. Online maps are published either by official National Cartographic Agencies (e.g., IGN-France), or by private companies (e.g., Google) and voluntary crowd sourcing data actions (e.g., Open Street Map) etc. The online map services are widely used for locating points of interest, navigation, planning, and monitoring of trips, real-time information (e.g., traffic load), training, etc., but also as a background for the creation of (new) maps. They provide global coverage and are used by people all over the world. These services have a huge impact on the millions of Internet users, giving them a (realistic) view of the world. Competition between providers results in a continuous improvement of these products, but the most important thing is that nowadays, more than any other time in the history of cartography, the map itself is used daily at the same time and for different uses by people around the world. Nowadays, in the age of digital communication, the map as a medium is becoming more widespread in society. Never before were maps directly accessible by the user, never before were maps an integrated part of everyday life, and this is a huge achievement. It is the most unified and integrated means for simultaneous representation of position and descriptive information in textual form. The enthusiasm that comes from the ubiquitous online map service should not be a narrow self-referential limit, but should be matured with choices, utilizing the principles and heritage of cartography [68].

4. Discussion

A map is not a typical commercial graphic product. It conveys information about the geographical area, which has measurable and qualitative value and the signature of the body (or the individual) of its creation. It has the status of a symbolic image of geographical reality and with paintings they have common elements: image, symbolization, representation. Of course, the map lacks the freedom to choose the subject and the form of the paintings, but, over time, it has followed or assimilated the choices in the use of color as it emerges from the prevailing artistic trend.

From the Gothic rhythm and the exclusive influence of the Church to the era of digital technology domination, the journey of color in painting clearly influenced the application of color on maps. In many cases the visual comparison results in strongly similar visual impressions in such an eloquent way that you may not need color analysis and comparison in quantitative terms. However, the similarities are documented by creating the corresponding color sequences and comparing them with quantitative terms captured in the color wheel [20].

The paintings and maps that were selected and examined in detail and their subset presented in this paper, support the impact of painting, without implying that this trend was intentional. Apart from the cases of collaboration of cartographers with painters, painting is part of the intellect of a place and an era and shapes the culture as well as the aesthetic approach—among other things—of graphic products. Through art, an attitude is developed, familiarity with color is achieved, and a number of images that serve as a source of inspiration can support the adoption of artistic expression or the creation of a style.

The apparent distancing of cartography from art over time may be related to scientific knowledge, measurements, and the evolution of technology that made it possible to create and produce maps without collaboration with artists (for the design and/or coloring). However, it is not overlooked that not only cartography, but also painting gradually assimilated scientific knowledge and incorporated it into the means of expression of artists. A prominent example is Georges Seraut, the founder of Neo-Impressionism, who applied the trichromatic theory of color vision to his personal painting style [69]. Is this personal style related to color photolithography and the use of CMYK separation screens at a specific angle for each color of the four color printing method [70]? In addition, the application of perspective in the works of the Renaissance and its rejection by the Cubists in the shaping of their work connect art with science.

The power of the map lies in the application of cartographic symbolization and, here, the relationship with the precepts of art is inseparable. The foundation of the application of a more objective symbolization, Bertin's main visual variables [21] and, in particular, the three of them related to color, come from the standardization of color in painting and have exactly the same use that they have in paintings: the shade has the character of qualitative distinction, while the brightness (value) and the saturation a quantitative one [71]. Undoubtedly, the standardization of maps from the end of the 19th century created the need to establish rules, not only in the form (layout) and content of maps, but also in the application of cartographic symbolization in a less subjective way. This does not mean that a situation was created from scratch. On the contrary, the cartographic evolvement was formed based on the cartographic tradition and the integration of scientific knowledge, technological means, and the precepts of art. The heritage of art in cartography is important. The use of hue for the nominal differentiation of spatial entities and the use of brightness and saturation for quantitative differentiation [71] constitute a vivid paradigm.

The depiction of volume and plasticity of the three-dimensional objects in the relief representation, mainly in combination with the light shading, unequivocally substantiates this view. Here is the absolute application of the pop-up (warm) colors for the larger and the withdrawn (cool) colors for the lower altitude values, which are closer and farther from the observer, respectively [72]. The implementation of plasticity, i.e., the impression of volume, is created with the bright colors placed in the protruding areas. This technique was widely applied in the rendering of the plasticity of objects in paintings and during the evolution of the expressive means it was combined with the use of light and shadow [73].

The examples given above are part of a broader research and confirm the common path followed regarding the use of color in the maps and paintings of the respective periods. As is presumed through the experimental procedure followed, the color path in the maps tracks the color path in the paintings. From the works of the Middle Ages to the 21st century, the differences in color, both for aesthetic and for technical or practical reasons, are obvious. From heavy or luxurious colors with or without light shading applied even in complex shapes and compositions [74], the transition to flat colors and almost complete subtraction has taken place, as applied to the land-sea separation in the world online maps [75].

Until the middle of the 19th century the artistic movements used to change at a relatively slow pace, as did the style of maps. The influence of painting was then clearer as there was, on the one hand, collaboration of map makers with painters, but also more time to assimilate artistic achievements or choices. The artistic movements from the middle of the 19th century were less and less lasting and there are cases of painters whose conquest of a style, a means of expression, was the trigger for the next experimentation, as if it was important for the personal artistic expression and recognition who will be the first to create a trend, who will be the first to conquer an achievement, a goal; to whom will the originality be credited? Certainly this has to do with the gradual weakening of collaborative movements and the prevalence of individualism and individual expression; the possible "anxiety" of acquiring a very personal and recognizable identity, an identity that differentiates the individual from others and makes him/her special. Individualism, the commercialization of art, the predominance of the intangible (in the form of digital) in all activities of modern culture, often leads to the questioning of traditional methods of artistic expression by characterizing them as conservative. Currently, this also governs commercial cartographic applications, as it becomes clear from the comparison of the most popular online maps [20,68]. The issues of commercialization, the commercial value, but also the authenticity of the works exhibited in the museums, concern the intellectuals in many ways.

It could be said that if today the map had to be part of the "philosophy" of an artistic movement or an art school, then it would be part of the Bauhaus School, which approaches design by combining functionality, simplicity, usability with an emphasis on color and the geometry of "form", and, most important, applying the precepts of art to utilitarian objects.

Paintings are a field of realization of the characteristics of color, a field of highlighting the relations of colors and the simultaneous contrast. Each of these can replace experimental research on how colors look next to each other and how color observations, affinities, and contrasts are perceived by the observer. Each of them can be a source of inspiration for creative cartographic composition, and if the institutionalization of specifications standardized the topographic maps, and in part the general-use maps, there remains room for creativity in the thematic maps, mainly in the digital environment of the internet, which today is the dominant platform for creating and disseminating maps.

5. Conclusions

This research was not based solely on the visual similarities between the paintings and the maps. Undoubtedly, the greatest power of color lies in the image. No word, no description of color can be as apt and accurate as the color itself. However, the analysis of the color sequences and their recording in the color wheel reinforces the initial subjective judgement, giving it an objective character, through the description in quantitative terms.

Despite, to a certain extent, the subjectivity in the selection and the reasonable assertion that may not be universally applicable, the findings are interesting and significant enough to form the basis for further research. It is noteworthy that in almost all of the comparisons made, the color sequences are placed in the same part of the color wheel and have almost the same range. Therefore, the color similarity between the paintings and the selected maps is supported both for the colors used and for the color character resulting from their saturation and brightness. It should also be noted that colors differ over time: the red, green, or blue of the Italian Renaissance has a different visual character than in Mannerism or in Modernism. El Greco's red is very different from Bruegel's red and foreign to Renoir, Chagall, or Mondrian's red. This variation of the color character is also recognized in the journey of color in the maps: the red used by Mercator is quite different of the one used by Dourado or Agnese. It should also be emphasized that the atlases which have been studied are characterized by a unified color approach, which gives aesthetic and artistic unity to the work.

It would be interesting if a similar research would be done outside of the Western European culture. For example, consider this relationship in Asian or Arab culture or, in a narrower context, in the 20th century, in artistic expression during the period of "actually existing socialism" in Eastern Europe. Japanese or Chinese culture, as well as the masterpieces of Arabic culture from the depths of time to the present day, are remarkable and have left an important imprint on both art and cartography. The examination, for example, of Japanese paintings, has significant differences from those of the Western world. Japanese culture has a long tradition, among other things, in painting and design, with a strong minimalist approach. A glance at Sakai Hoitsu "Iris" [76] and Van Gogh "Iris" paintings, as well as a Japanese world map, is enough to deeply think about it [77]. It would be extremely interesting to consider further research on other symbol variables, especially for visually impaired people, as, in this case, any tactual perception cannot rely on color.

In conclusion, it is estimated that the initial objectives of this research have been achieved, not only through the experimental approach and the documentation of the respective conclusions through the listed color analysis, but mainly through the knowledge acquired during the study and analysis of the artistic and cartographic periods. The study of paintings and the ability to identify the respective period or the corresponding artistic movement based on how the color was used is an important resource that can be widely used, both in map composition and the evaluation of the cartographic result. The widespread use of online maps services is a great opportunity, but also a responsibility for cartographers not only to take advantage of the technological aspects, but to also integrate in cartographic practice and teaching the application of the precepts of art. In this way, maps can become as fascinating today as they have been in the past, without losing their contemporary character and functionality.

Funding: This research received no external funding.

Institutional Review Board Statement: Not applicable.

Informed Consent Statement: Not applicable.

Data Availability Statement: Images of maps and paintings were obtained from the Internet. Source links are mentioned in the References.

Conflicts of Interest: The author declares no conflict of interest.

References

1. Cosgrove, D. Maps, Mapping, Modernity: Art and Cartography in the Twentieth Century. *Imago Mundi* **2005**, *57*, 34–35. [CrossRef]
2. Friedmannova, L. What Can We Learn from the Masters? Color Schemas on Paintings as the Source for Color Ranges Applicable in Cartography. In *Cartography and Art*; Springer: Berlin/Heidelberg, Germany, 2009; pp. 93–105. ISBN 978-3-540-68567-8.
3. Christophe, S. Making Legends by Means of Painters' Palettes. In *Cartography and Art*; Springer: Berlin/Heidelberg, Germany, 2009; pp. 81–92. ISBN 978-3-540-68567-8.
4. Gombrich, E.H. *The Story of Art*, 15th ed.; Prentice Hall: Hoboken, NJ, USA, 1989; ISBN 9789602501443. (in Greek)
5. Livieratos, E.; Koussoulakou, A. "Vermeer"'s maps: A new digital look in an old masters mirror. *e-Perimetron* **2006**, *1*, 138–154.
6. File: Johannes Vermeer-De Soldaat en het Lachende Meisje. Available online: https://commons.wikimedia.org/wiki/File:Johannes_Vermeer_-_De_Soldaat_en_het_Lachende_Meisje_-_Google_Art_Project.jpg (accessed on 20 January 2022).
7. Wood, D. Map Art. *Cartogr. Perspect.* **2006**, 5–14. [CrossRef]
8. Available online: https://monoskop.org/images/6/6c/Varietes_Le_Surrealisme_en_1929.pdf (accessed on 20 January 2022).
9. Ribeiro, D.M.; Caquard, S. Cartography and Art. In *The Geographic Information Science & Technology Body of Knowledge*, 1st ed.; Wilson, J.P., Ed.; Springer: Berlin/Heidelberg, Germany, 2018. [CrossRef]
10. Foster, H.; Krauss, R.; Bois, Y.-A.; Buchloh, B.H.D. *Art Since 1900*; Cambridge Scholars Publishing: Newcastle upon Tyne, UK, 2004; ISBN 978-960-458-047-7. (in Greek)
11. Johns, J. Map. 1961. Available online: https://www.moma.org/collection/works/79372?artist_id=2923&locale=en&page=1&sov_referrer=artist (accessed on 20 January 2022).
12. Kozloff, J. 2017; Girlhood. Available online: http://www.joycekozloff.net/2015-girlhood/23o4a342voaou12awrbjgn9vg0obh3 (accessed on 20 January 2022).
13. Available online: https://mapsartblog.files.wordpress.com/2013/06/dsc_0293.jpg (accessed on 20 January 2022).
14. Available online: https://www.raremaps.com/gallery/detail/73197/europe-in-the-shape-of-a-queen-europa-prima-pars-terrae-in-bunting (accessed on 20 January 2022).
15. Available online: https://www.raremaps.com/gallery/detail/79363/europe-as-a-queen-munster (accessed on 20 January 2022).
16. Available online: https://www.mattcusick.com/portfolio/map-works/view/4005121/1/4005149 (accessed on 20 January 2022).
17. CV-27—Cartography and Art. Available online: https://gistbok.ucgis.org/bok-topics/cartography-and-art#Historical (accessed on 20 January 2022).

18. Kent, A. Aesthetics: A lost cause in cartographic theory? *Cartogr. J.* **2005**, *42*, 182–188. [CrossRef]
19. Robinson, A.; Morrison, J.; Muehrcke, P.; Kimerling, A.J.; Guptill, S. *Elements of Cartography*, 6th ed.; John Wiley & Sons: New York, NY, USA, 1995; ISBN 0-471-55579-7.
20. Stamou, L. Maps and Art: Color as a Critical Parameter. Ph.D. Thesis, National Technical University of Athens, Athens, Greece, 19 October 2019. (in Greek).
21. Bertin, J. *Semiologie Graphique: Les Diagrammes, les Reseaux, les Cartes/par Jacques Bertin*; Gauthier-Villars: Paris, France, 1967.
22. Slocum, T.; McMaster, R.; Kessler, F.; Howard, H. *Thematic Cartography and Geographic Visualization*, 2nd ed.; Prentice Hall: Hoboken, NJ, USA, 2005; ISBN 13-978-0130351234.
23. Dent, B. *Cartography, Thematic Map Design*, 5th ed.; William C Brown Pub: Dubuque, IA, USA, 1999; ISBN 978-0697384959.
24. MacEachren, A. *How Maps Work*; The Guilford Press: New York, NY, USA, 1995; ISBN 1-57230-040-X.
25. Brewer, C. Color Use Guidelines for Mapping and Visualization. In *Modern Cartography. Volume Two: Visualization in Modern Cartography*; Elsevier: New York, NY, USA, 1994; pp. 123–147. ISBN 0-0-042415-5.
26. Schuler, C.J. *Mapping the World*; Editions Place des Victoires: Paris, France, 2010; ISBN 978-2-8099-0203-7.
27. Madonna di Ognissanti di Giotto. Available online: http://www.uffizi.org/it/opere/madonna-di-ognissanti-di-giotto/ (accessed on 25 December 2021).
28. Buoninsegna, D. The Calling of the Apostles Peter and Andrew, 1308–1311. Available online: http://www.nga.gov/content/ngaweb/Collection/art-object-page.282.html (accessed on 25 December 2021).
29. Atlas of Battista Agnese. Available online: https://www.wdl.org/en/item/7336/ (accessed on 25 December 2021).
30. Available online: https://www.nationalgallery.org.uk/paintings/titian-bacchus-and-ariadne (accessed on 25 December 2021).
31. Available online: http://prints.rmg.co.uk/art/507034/The_Caribbean (accessed on 25 December 2021).
32. The Holy Family with Angels. Available online: https://www.wikidata.org/wiki/Q20176388#/media/File:Domencio_Beccafumi_-_The_Holy_Family_with_Angels.jpg (accessed on 25 December 2021).
33. Bassano, J. The Miraculous Draught of Fishes. 1545. Available online: https://www.nga.gov/collection/art-object-page.96688.html (accessed on 25 December 2021).
34. Mediterranean Sea Region 1569. Available online: https://www.wdl.org/en/item/6765/ (accessed on 25 December 2021).
35. Jesus among the Doctors. Available online: https://en.wikipedia.org/wiki/Christ_among_the_Doctors_(Veronese)#/media/File:Disputa_con_los_doctores_(El_Veron%C3%A9s)_grande.jpg (accessed on 25 December 2021).
36. Atlas. Available online: https://www.wdl.org/en/item/14159/ (accessed on 25 December 2021).
37. Atlas with Portolan Charts of the Old World and New World. 1580. Available online: https://www.wdl.org/en/item/8918/ (accessed on 25 December 2021).
38. Christ Healing the Blind. Available online: https://www.metmuseum.org/art/collection/search/436572 (accessed on 25 December 2021).
39. Available online: https://gallica.bnf.fr/ark:/12148/btv1b8447838j (accessed on 25 December 2021).
40. Atlas Sive Cosmographicae Meditationes de Fabrica Mvndi et Fabricati Figvra. Available online: https://www.loc.gov/item/map55000728/ (accessed on 25 December 2021).
41. Orrock, A. Homo ludens: Pieter Bruegel's Children's Games and the Humanist Educators. Available online: https://jhna.org/articles/homo-ludens-pieter-bruegels-childrens-games-humanist-educators/ (accessed on 25 December 2021).
42. Available online: https://www.raremaps.com/gallery/detail/49864/nova-totius-terrarum-orbis-geographica-ac-hydrographica-tabula-auct-guiljelmo-blaeuw-blaeu (accessed on 25 December 2021).
43. Enthroned Madonna with Child, Encircled by Saints. Available online: https://www.1000museums.com/art_works/peter-paul-rubens-enthroned-madonna-with-child-encircled-by-saints?from=artists (accessed on 25 December 2021).
44. Available online: https://www.raremaps.com/gallery/detail/51171/a-new-map-of-the-world-from-the-latest-observation-senex (accessed on 25 December 2021).
45. Available online: http://64.130.23.120/old-masters/jean-antoine-watteau.htm (accessed on 25 December 2021).
46. Neue Welt Karte Welche Auf Zwoo Kugelflaechen Die Haupt-Theile der Erde ... Ao. 1784. Available online: https://www.raremaps.com/gallery/detail/37267/neue-welt-karte-welche-auf-zwoo-kugelflaechen-die-homann-heirs (accessed on 25 December 2021).
47. The Death of General Wolfe. Available online: https://en.wikipedia.org/wiki/The_Death_of_General_Wolfe#/media/File:Benjamin_West_005.jpg (accessed on 25 December 2021).
48. Gilbert's New Map of the World 1839. Available online: https://www.davidrumsey.com/luna/servlet/detail/RUMSEY~{}8~{}1~{}306183~{}90076541:Gilbert-s-new-map-of-the-world-1839?sort=pub_list_no_initialsort%2Cpub_date%2Cpub_list_no%2Cseries_no&qvq=q:world_area%3D%22world%22%20;sort:pub_list_no_initialsort%2Cpub_date%2Cpub_list_no%2Cseries_no;lc:RUMSEY~{}8~{}1&mi=63&trs=2953 (accessed on 25 December 2021).
49. Wanderer above the Sea of Fog. Available online: https://germanculture.com.ua/famous-germans/wanderer-above-the-sea-of-fog/ (accessed on 25 December 2021).
50. The World in Hemispheres with Comparative Views of the Heights of the Principal Mountains Lengths of the Principal Rivers On The Globe. Available online: https://www.raremaps.com/gallery/detail/47413/the-world-in-hemispheres-with-comparative-views-of-johnston (accessed on 25 December 2021).

51. Geographical Distribution of Plants. Distribution of Plants in a Perpendicular Direction. Available online: https://www.davidrumsey.com/luna/servlet/detail/RUMSEY~{}8~{}1~{}308070~{}90077931:Geographical-Distribution-of-Plants?sort=pub_list_no_initialsort%2Cpub_date%2Cpub_list_no%2Cseries_no&qvq=q:physical%20atlas;sort:pub_list_no_initialsort%2Cpub_date%2Cpub_list_no%2Cseries_no;lc:RUMSEY~{}8~{}1&mi=50&trs=5987 (accessed on 25 December 2021).
52. Historical and Geographical Europe. Available online: https://gallica.bnf.fr/ark:/12148/btv1b53233030z (accessed on 22 January 2022).
53. Stanford's Double Hemisphere World Map. Available online: https://bryarsandbryars.co.uk/product/stanfords-double-hemisphere-world-map/ (accessed on 25 December 2021).
54. The Willows. Available online: https://www.claudemonetgallery.org/The-Willows.html (accessed on 25 December 2021).
55. Cezanne, P. House in Provence, 1885–86. Available online: https://www.paulcezanne.org/house-in-provence.jsp (accessed on 25 December 2021).
56. Cezanne, P. Quarry and Mont Sainte-Victoire. 1900. Available online: https://www.paulcezanne.org/quarry-and-mont-sainte-victoire.jsp (accessed on 25 December 2021).
57. Asia (Physical). Available online: https://www.antiquemapsandprints.com/asia-physical-relief-mountain-heights-ocean-depths-rivers-johnston-1900-map-353279-p.asp (accessed on 25 December 2021).
58. Mappemonde Coloniale Possessions Coloniales des Etats d'Europe avec les Cables Telgraphiques sous-Marins et les Lignes de Navigation Dressee D'Apres Les Documents Officiels Les Plus Recents par A. Dencede, Graveur et Dessinateur Geographe. 1897. Available online: https://www.raremaps.com/gallery/detail/56454/mappemonde-coloniale-possessions-coloniales-des-et-dencede (accessed on 25 December 2021).
59. Moet And Chandon Cremant Imperial. Available online: https://www.alfonsmucha.org/Moet-And-Chandon-Cremant-Imperial.html (accessed on 25 December 2021).
60. Le Petit Journal Mappemonde. Available online: http://nla.gov.au/nla.obj-232221880/view (accessed on 25 December 2021).
61. Image from www.wassilykandinsky.net. Available online: https://www.wassilykandinsky.net/work-370.php (accessed on 25 December 2021).
62. The Bauhaus at 100: Science by Design. Available online: https://www.nature.com/articles/d41586-019-02355-4?fbclid=IwAR0xeLFwsJXRGOYdluau02A0ODZKgq4fp4cTPnNZ2aXxxh1WZhlmV5k02mE (accessed on 25 December 2021).
63. W. & A.K. Johnston's "Effective" maps of the world. Available online: https://maps.nls.uk/world/rec/5846 (accessed on 25 December 2021).
64. Map of London's Underground Railways. Available online: https://www.davidrumsey.com/luna/servlet/detail/RUMSEY~{}8~{}1~{}274012~{}90047744:Map-of-London-s-Underground-Railway?sort=pub_date%2Cpub_list_no%2Cseries_no&qvq=sortid%3D%22batch016%22%20AND%20subject%3D%22pictorial%20map%22%20;sort:pub_date%2Cpub_list_no%2Cseries_no;lc:RUMSEY~{}8~{}1&mi=502&trs=2036 (accessed on 25 December 2021).
65. Mondrian, Composition with Red, Blue, and Yellow. Available online: https://www.khanacademy.org/humanities/ap-art-history/later-europe-and-americas/modernity-ap/a/mondrian-composition (accessed on 25 December 2021).
66. Available online: https://www.cia.gov/library/publications/the-world-factbook/attachments/images/large/world-political.jpg?1561571042 (accessed on 25 December 2021).
67. Available online: https://www.cia.gov/library/publications/the-world-factbook/attachments/images/large/world_phy.jpg?1558019809 (accessed on 25 December 2021).
68. Skopeliti, A.; Stamou, L. Online Map Services: Contemporary Cartography or a New Cartographic Culture? *Int. J. Geo-Inf.* **2019**, *8*, 215. [CrossRef]
69. Georges Seurat–Un dimanche après-midi à l'île de la Grande Jatte. Available online: https://commons.wikimedia.org/wiki/File:Georges_Seurat_-_Un_dimanche_apr%C3%A8s-midi_%C3%A0_l%27%C3%AEle_de_la_Grande_Jatte.jpg (accessed on 25 December 2021).
70. Halftoningcolor. Available online: https://en.wikipedia.org/wiki/File:Halftoningcolor.svg (accessed on 25 December 2021).
71. Itten, J. *The Art of Color: The Subjective Experience and Objective Rationale of Color*, 2nd ed.; Van Nostrand Reinhold: New York, NY, USA, 1973; ISBN 0442240376.
72. USA Shaded Relief Map from USGS. Available online: https://www.reddit.com/r/MapPorn/comments/5oc7y2/usa_shaded_relief_map_from_usgs_3700x2610/ (accessed on 25 December 2021).
73. The Delphic Sibyl by Michelangelo. Available online: https://www.michelangelo.org/the-delphic-sibyl.jsp (accessed on 25 December 2021).
74. Nova Totius Terrarum Orbis Geographica Ac Hydrographica Tabula Auct. Henr: Hondio. 1663. Available online: https://www.raremaps.com/gallery/detail/41764/nova-totius-terrarum-orbis-geographica-ac-hydrogra-hondius (accessed on 25 December 2021).
75. Available online: https://www.openstreetmap.org/#map=2/31.4/66.4 (accessed on 25 December 2021).
76. Carte japonaise du monde en 1840. Available online: https://www.laboiteverte.fr/carte-japonaise-du-monde-en-1840/1840_ryukei_tajima_carte-monde-japon-1840/ (accessed on 25 December 2021).
77. Irises. 1890. Available online: https://www.metmuseum.org/art/collection/search/436528 (accessed on 25 December 2021).

Article

Spatial Modelling and Geovisualization of House Prices in the Greater Athens Region, Greece

Polixeni Iliopoulou [1,*] and Elissavet Feloni [1,2]

[1] Department of Surveying & Geoinformatics Engineering, Egaleo Park Campus, University of West Attica, Ag. Spyridonos Str., 12243 Athens, Greece; feloni@chi.civil.ntua.gr
[2] Department of Water Resources and Environmental Engineering, School of Civil Engineering, National Technical University of Athens, Heroon Polytechniou 9, 15780 Athens, Greece
* Correspondence: piliop@uniwa.gr

Abstract: In this article, geovisualization is used for the presentation and interpretation of spatial analysis results concerning several house attributes. For that purpose, point data for houses in the region of Attica, Greece are analyzed. The data concern houses for sale and comprise structural characteristics, such as size, age and floor, as well as locational attributes. Geovisualization of house characteristics is performed employing spatial interpolation techniques, kriging techniques, in particular. Spatial autocorrelation in the data is examined through the calculation of the Moran's I coefficient, while spatial clusters of houses with similar characteristics are identified using the Getis-Ord Gi^* local spatial autocorrelation coefficient. Finally, a model is developed in order to predict house prices according to several structural and locational characteristics. In that respect, a classic hedonic pricing model is constructed, which is consequently developed as a geographically weighted regression (GWR) model in a GIS environment. The results of this model indicate that two characteristics, i.e., size and age, account for most of the variability in house prices in the study region. Since GWR is a local model producing different regression parameters for each observation, it is possible to obtain the spatial distribution of the regression parameters, which indicate the significance of the house characteristics for price determination in different locations in the study area.

Keywords: housing prices; kriging; spatial autocorrelation; local spatial autocorrelation; geographically weighted regression (GWR)

1. Introduction

The purpose of this article is to present spatial analysis results and suggest how geovisualization can contribute to their interpretation. For that purpose, spatial data concerning houses for sale in the Attica region, Greece are used. Statistical methods for the visualization of the data are employed instead of thematic cartography methods or deterministic interpolation techniques. Geostatistical methods (kriging analysis) and hot-spot analysis are used to depict statistically significant spatial clustering. In this way, areas within the study region with high and low values of certain variables are identified. In addition, a spatial regression model (Geographically Weighted Regression—GWR) is presented for estimating house prices according to several house characteristics. One main purpose for building up this model is to show ways to visualize the results of regression analysis, since this is important for their interpretation. The model is developed in a geographic information systems (GIS) environment and it is possible to map the importance of the factors influencing house prices in terms of mapping the regression coefficients. The regression coefficients vary over the study region and their geographical distribution can be interpreted according to the characteristics of different areas. In order to build the spatial regression model, a conventional multiple regression model (ordinary least squares–OLS) is the starting point. If the residuals of the OLS model are clustered, there is good chance that the results will be improved by a GWR model.

The data in this study include several characteristics, such as price, size, age and locational attributes. Several characteristics were derived from publicly available webpages, while some locational attributes were calculated through GIS operations. There is great differentiation in prices and house characteristics in the study region, as previous research has suggested [1–3]. Apart from the structural characteristics of the houses, such as size, age, condition etc., location is a very important factor for housing prices and geovisualization is necessary in order to explore the spatial variation in prices and the other house characteristics.

Geovisualization of house data is carried out using spatial analysis techniques, which incorporate the statistical properties of spatial data. Thematic maps are the first exploratory step in order to present the spatial variation of house characteristics. For point data, dot maps are common [2], although choropleth maps can be used, because they present clearer spatial patterns [1]. Spatial interpolation techniques, which create surfaces of values for a given characteristic, are also used in some studies for the visualization of house data [4].

Beyond data description, spatial analysis methods can identify spatial clusters of observations sharing similar characteristics, which are also statistically significant. For that purpose, the concept of spatial autocorrelation is important, indicating that observations at small distances from each other will share similar characteristics relative to observations far apart. Spatial autocorrelation is a common characteristic of spatial data; it is obvious for meteorological measurement or air pollution, but it is also observed for house characteristics.

There are indices that measure spatial autocorrelation for s whole region, including all observations, such as the Moran's I coefficient, and indices that can identify spatial clusters of observations with similar characteristics. These are the indices of local spatial autocorrelation, such as the local Moran's I and the Getis–Ord Gi^* coefficients. In this way, spatial clusters are identified, which are tested with inferential statistics and presented according to their statistical significance [5]. In this study, house characteristics are depicted using geostatistical techniques. Kriging analysis, in particular, is used in order to produce statistical surfaces for selected house characteristics. In order to measure spatial autocorrelation for these variables, the global Moran's I indicator is calculated, while the Getis–Ord Gi^* coefficient is used in order to identify spatial clusters.

Differences in housing prices across geographical regions can be attributed to a large variety of house characteristics, which can be organized in three groups: structural attributes, neighborhood characteristics and locational influences [6–8]. Structural attributes describe the physical structure of the property, such as size, age, floor and type of dwelling. Neighborhood characteristics refer to the socioeconomic conditions, such as crime, quality of schools, etc. Locational influences mainly describe proximity to locations of interest, such as parks, recreation areas and transportation [9–14].

In order to explore the factors that contribute to property values, hedonic regression is the most common technique [1,6,15]. These are regression models, in which house price is the dependent variable and a set of house characteristics the explanatory factors. Usually, linear regression models are used, however, there are variations, such as the transformations of the dependent and/or the independent variables [16]. On the other hand, several studies employ spatial regression models in order to study the spatial variation of housing prices [1,4,17–20]. In these models, the relative location of the observations is incorporated in the model, therefore, spatial autocorrelation is accounted for.

The main reason for using spatial regression models is that classic regression models are misspecified due to the presence of spatial autocorrelation and, therefore, the description of the data and the calculation of the regression parameters are not accurate [21,22]. For that same reason, several studies indicate the better fit of the spatial regression models when compared with the classic ones, although this is not the case for all datasets [1,23]. In addition, since spatial regression models capture the spatial variation of house characteristics, it is possible to achieve the more accurate prediction of the dependent variable when entering a smaller number of independent variables.

In this study, first, a classic linear regression model is constructed and the results are examined in terms of problems in the specification of the model resulting from spatial autocorrelation. Since spatial autocorrelation is detected in the error term, it is recommended that a hedonic pricing model is developed in a GIS environment, namely, a geographically weighted regression (GWR) model. This method produces local regression models, allowing spatial variation of the regression coefficients [22]. In this way, it is possible to identify areas where individual regression coefficients, for example, the regression coefficient of the independent variable "size" of the house, indicate a greater or lower impact on house prices.

2. Materials and Methods

2.1. The Study Region and the Data

The study area is the Greater Athens region and consists of 57 municipal units, in which the greater number of houses for sale are concentrated. House data were obtained by entries concerning property for sale, published on the internet by real estate agencies (www.xe.gr, accessed on 28 March 2020). However, only houses for which the approximate location on a map was available were included in the sample. The location was recorded in Google maps and the resulting map was exported into a geodatabase. The sample comprises 4995 dwellings for sale in the first quarter of the year 2020 and the selection of the sample is proportionate to the number of houses in each municipal unit (Figure 1). Only residential property was included in the sample and all types of houses were recorded (apartments and single family houses). Several structural characteristics were derived from the real estate web pages, such as price, size, age, floor, number of bedrooms, bathrooms, parking, view and fireplace.

In addition, some locational characteristics were created in a GIS environment, as follows: distance from the center of the city, distance from the closest metro station and distance from the beach. The first two variables are common in the relevant literature [6–8,11,13,15], while distance from the beach is important for the study region since some of the most expensive areas are close to the sea. Locational attributes represent the desirability of each neighborhood; therefore, they can be considered as neighborhood characteristics as well [6,7]. Other neighborhood characteristics, such as crime, would be important for the analysis, especially for the center of Athens, however they are not available for the entire study region. Furthermore, socioeconomic characteristics were not incorporated in the analysis, although they are highly correlated to property values [1]. Socioeconomic data, such as educational attainment, sector of economic activity, occupational status and unemployment, are available for municipalities, which are quite large areas. If values to each house were attributed through GIS operations, they would be identical for all houses in the same municipality and they would not be very useful for statistical analysis.

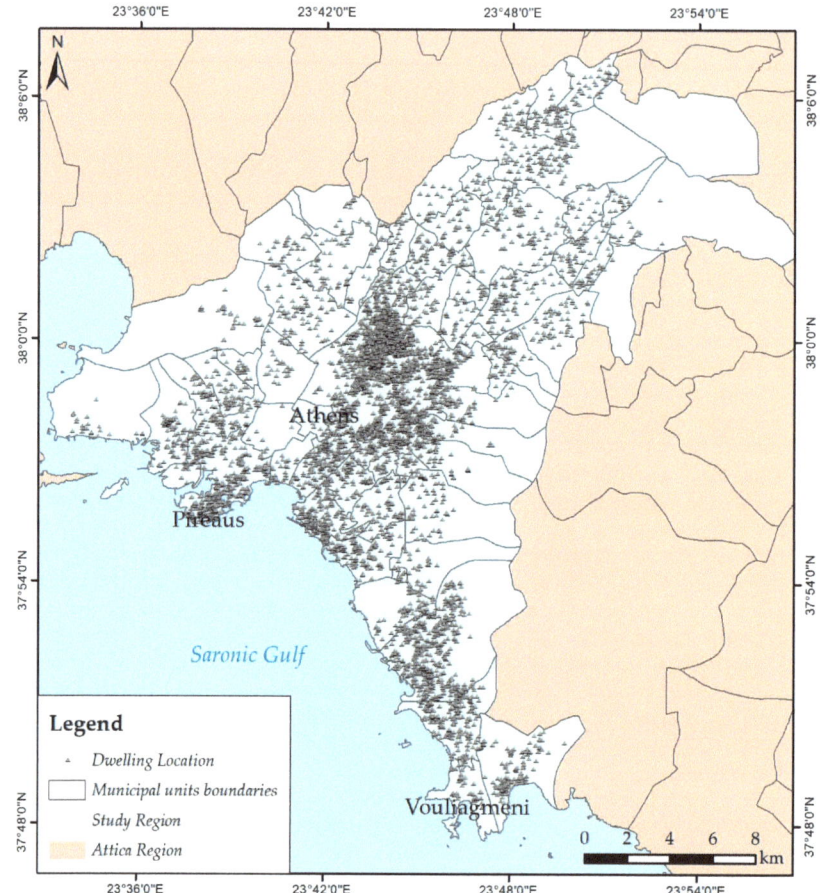

Figure 1. The study region and the sample of houses for sale.

2.2. Geovisualization of the Data with Kriging Analysis

At first, a description of the houses in the sample is presented, in terms of their structural characteristics. Since we are dealing with point data, a kriging interpolation analysis [24] was considered appropriate for geovisualization and was carried out for selected variables.

Spatial interpolation is the prediction of values of attributes at unsampled locations from measurements made at sample points in the same area. Therefore, interpolation is a type of spatial prediction and results in a continuous surface. The principle underlying spatial interpolation is the first law of geography. Formulated by Waldo Tobler [25], this law states that everything is related to everything else, but near things are more related than distant things. This is also the classic definition of spatial autocorrelation.

There are several methods of interpolation that can be classified into two groups: deterministic and geostatistical. Deterministic techniques assume no measurement error and use mathematical functions for interpolation, while geostatistical methods rely on both statistical and mathematical methods, which, apart from creating surfaces, can assess the uncertainty of the predictions [5]. In spatial interpolation methods, the values of attributes at certain locations are calculated employing a set of weights. For example, inverse distance weighting (IDW) is a common deterministic method and the weights are calculated as a function of distance. To predict a value for any unmeasured location, IDW uses the measured values surrounding the prediction location. In principle, the measured values closest to the prediction location have more influence on the predicted value than those farther away. IDW assumes that each measured point has a local influence that diminishes with distance. It gives greater weights to points closest to the prediction location, and the weights diminish as a function of distance. On the other hand, geostatistical interpolation techniques, i.e., kriging, utilize the statistical properties of the measured points. Kriging is a statistical interpolation method which assumes that at least some of the spatial variation observed in the data can be modelled by random processes and requires that spatial autocorrelation is explicitly modelled. Kriging techniques can be used to describe and model spatial patterns, predict values at unmeasured locations and create prediction surfaces but, also, they calculate the error associated with them.

Kriging analysis has been used in several studies for the analysis of house prices [26,27]. Due to the uncertainty as to the location of the house data in this study, a kriging interpolation technique is used in order to describe the spatial patterns of house characteristics. Kriging involves quantifying the spatial structure of the data by creating the semivariogram, which is a plot of the squared differences in the values of the sample points against the distance between them. To make a prediction for an unknown value for a specific location, kriging will use a fitted model from variography, the spatial data configuration, and the values of the measured sample points around the prediction location. There are several different types of kriging, according to the assumptions about the properties of the field being interpolated [28,29]. In this study, ordinary kriging is employed, which is one of the most often used types of kriging.

2.3. Mapping Spatial Clusters

The second procedure is the identification of spatial clusters through the measurement of spatial autocorrelation. There are several indices of spatial autocorrelation, such as the Moran's *I* and the Geary's *C*. In order to measure spatial autocorrelation, the spatial structure of the data has to be described and, for that purpose, a matrix of spatial weights is constructed. Locations at smaller distances are expected to share similar values for the attributes in question and this property is accounted for in the construction of spatial weights. There is a wide variety of methods to define spatial weights. For point data, some function of distance is used, such as the inverse distance. In this study, the inverse distance squared method is used. The most widely used measure of spatial autocorrelation is the Moran's *I* coefficient, which employs a covariance term between each spatial unit and its neighbors. Spatial autocorrelation can be positive or negative, indicating clustering or dispersion. In that case, the values of the Moran's index are positive and negative, respectively. Values are in the range of −1 to +1 and a value of zero indicates a random spatial pattern. The calculation of the values of Geary's *C* coefficient are different, but the interpretation of the results is similar [5]. These coefficients are the global ones, measuring spatial autocorrelation for the whole dataset.

The statistical significance of the autocorrelation coefficients is tested through randomization tests or resampling [30]. The values of the observations are randomly rearranged in order to create different spatial arrangements, for 1000 or 10,000 times, and the spatial autocorrelation coefficient is calculated for each dataset. The result is an experimental distribution from which an inference about the observed distribution can be derived. If the coefficient based on the observed distribution is sufficiently distant from the mean of the experimental distribution, it is plausible to conclude that the spatial distribution of the observed data is highly unlikely to have arisen from a random process. Conversely, if the coefficient for the observed distribution is not sufficiently far from the mean of the experimental distribution, it is concluded that a random process is in operation.

On the other hand, local measures of spatial autocorrelation, such as the Local Moran's *I* and the Getis–Ord Gi^*, can indicate the location of clusters of observations with high or low values [5,21,22]. The local coefficient Moran's *I* is derived in a similar way as the global statistic, but for smaller areas within the study region. The Getis–Ord Gi^* statistic aims to detect local concentrations of high or low values in an attribute, so spatial clusters of low or high values can be identified in the dataset. It is also referred to as hot-spot analysis. The calculation of the Getis–Ord Gi^* index involves the spatial weights and the values at different locations in the neighborhood of the location of interest. In a location where high values are clustered, Gi^* will be relatively high; conversely, in a location where low values are concentrated, Gi^* will be low.

In this study, the global Moran's I is used as a means to test global spatial autocorrelation for selected variables and, if a positive spatial autocorrelation is detected, the Getis–Ord Gi^* index is used to map the clusters of high or low values for selected variables. The resulting spatial patterns are compared with the kriging interpolation maps.

2.4. Regression Models

The final step of the analysis is the construction of a regression model in order to predict house prices from a series of house characteristics. Regression analysis involves one independent variable and one or more independent variables, the covariates or explanatory factors. The purpose of regression analysis is to create a model in order to predict values of the dependent variable for observations where there is no measurement. For hedonic pricing models, regression analysis is extremely important, because it makes it possible to estimate house prices given that the house characteristics are known. Regression analysis includes a great variety of models, but the model to begin with is linear regression. In linear regression, the dependent variable is a linear function of the independent variables. Simple linear regression involves only one independent variable, while multiple regression two or more independent variables. The equation for multiple linear regression is as follows:

$$Y = a + b_1 * X_1 + b_2 * X_2 + \ldots + b_n * X_n + e \qquad (1)$$

where Y is the dependent variable, X_i are the independent variables, a is a constant, b_i are the regression coefficients and e is the error term. The quantities a and b_i are the parameters that define the model and are estimated from the data. The regression coefficients measure the impact of each independent variable on the dependent variable. However, if the regression coefficients are going to be compared in terms of their impact, then the independent variables have to be standardized. In that case, the regression coefficients are transformed to beta coefficients. This model is global, in the sense that the regression equation is the same for all the study region and all the data have been used for its estimation. The error term (or residuals), however, is different for each observation and is the difference between the observed and the estimated value of the dependent variable for each observation. Linear regression uses the minimization of the sum of the squared residuals as the condition for the calculation of the regression parameters, hence the term ordinary least squares (OLS) model [31]. For geographical datasets, residuals can be mapped and reveal spatial patterns.

Many assumptions are associated with linear regression, the most important one being the linear relationship between the dependent and the independent variables. This hypothesis can be tested through bivariate scatter diagrams and correlation analysis, i.e., the calculation of the Pearson correlation coefficient. The most important measure to evaluate the goodness of fit of the model is the coefficient of determination, which is the proportion of the variance of the dependent variable explained by the independent variables. This is reported as R square (R^2) and is the squared Pearson correlation coefficient, with values ranging between 0 and 1. Therefore, if there is a strong linear relationship between the dependent and the independent variables, the coefficient of determination will be close to 1, indicating an accurate prediction of the dependent variable. Through correlation analysis, the relationship among the independent variables can be tested and multicollinearity can be identified, when two or more independent variables are related to each other. Another important assumption for regression analysis is the independence of the residuals. This assumption is very often violated for geographical problems, since data are spatially autocorrelated. Therefore, the regression model is misspecified and, in order to remedy this situation, spatial regression models have been developed that analyze spatial data. The spatial dependency of the residuals is tested through a measure of spatial autocorrelation, such as the Moran's I.

There is a variety of spatial regression models, which all engage spatial autocorrelation in the calculations of the parameters. In order to account for spatial autocorrelation in the data, there are two basic approaches [31]. The first approach is to include an independent variable, which is created by the values of the dependent variable for all the neighboring observations of each target location. This is a spatially lagged variable and is a weighted sum or a weighted average of the neighboring values for that variable [21]. The second approach is to create a model that allows spatial variation of the regression parameters and this is the geographically weighted regression (GWR) model [22]. The basic principle in this approach is that a global model is not representative for all the locations in the study area. GWR is a local regression model, since it constructs a separate regression equation for every location in the dataset. The equation incorporates the dependent variable and the explanatory variables of locations falling within the bandwidth of each target location. The regression coefficients vary across the study region and it is possible to evaluate the importance of each independent variable in different parts of the study region.

In this study, an OLS model is initially estimated incorporating quantitative variables as well as some binary variables. In the case of a large number of independent variables, there are methods for selecting the variables so that multicollinearity is avoided [32]. The stepwise elimination method is used in this analysis. The OLS residuals are tested for randomness using the Moran autocorrelation coefficient and, if they are clustered, a GWR regression model is estimated.

3. Results

The dataset includes several variables concerning the following house characteristics:

1. Price;
2. Price per m^2;
3. Size;
4. Age;
5. Floor number;
6. Number of rooms;
7. Number of bathrooms;
8. Existence of parking;
9. Existence of view;
10. Existence of fireplace;
11. Distance from the center;
12. Distance from the nearest metro station;
13. Distance from the beach.

Variables 1–7 and 11–13 are quantitative, while the rest (i.e., parking, view and fireplace) indicate the presence or absence of certain amenities. In addition, variables 5–7 represent quantitative characteristics but they have a small number of discrete values. Only continuous quantitative variables describing prices, and two structural characteristics (size and age) were examined in terms of spatial clustering. This selection is based on the importance of these characteristics and, also, the data properties, which affect the results of kriging and hot-spot analyses. In the regression models, all variables were introduced, with the exception of three variables, i.e., "price per m^2", "number of rooms" and "number of bathrooms", due to redundant information in these independent variables (see Section 3.3). Data analysis was carried out employing ArcGIS v.10.8 for geostatistical, hot-spot and GWR analysis, while IBM SPSS v.27 was used for OLS analysis.

3.1. Kriging Analysis and Measures of Spatial Autocorrelation

Ordinary kriging results for the variables "price", "price per m^2", "size" and "age" are shown in Figures 2 and 3 and Table 1. The results for each variable comprise the interpolation map, the empirical semivariogram and the diagnostics for the fit of the model.

The classification applied in the interpolation map was carried out by using the optimization method of classes' distribution natural breaks. The Jenks optimization method, also called the "Jenks natural breaks classification method", is a data classification method designed to determine the best arrangement of values into different classes. This is performed by seeking to minimize each class's average deviation from the class mean, while maximizing each class's deviation from the means of the other groups. In other words, the method seeks to reduce the variance within classes and maximize the variance between classes [33].

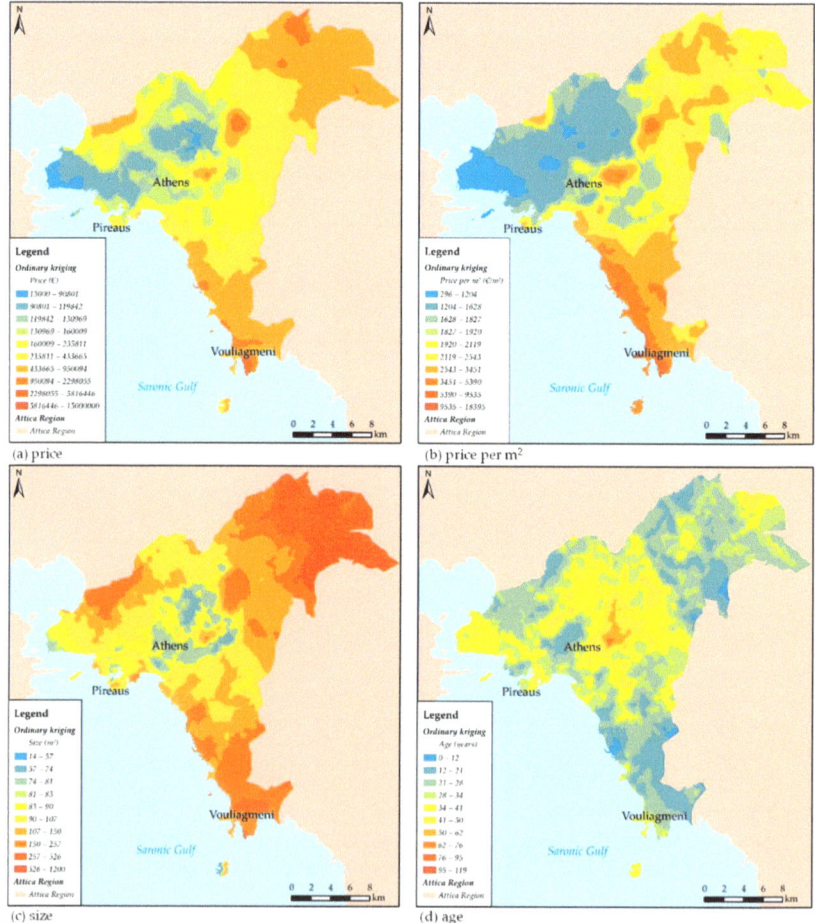

Figure 2. Ordinary kriging prediction maps for all four variables.

Each dot in the semivariogram (Figure 3) represents a group of locations at small distances. This is the binning process, which is applied for large datasets. If data are spatially dependent, the points that are close together should have smaller differences. As points become farther away from each other, in general, the difference squared should be greater. There is a certain distance beyond which the squared difference levels out and the locations beyond this distance are considered to be uncorrelated. In addition, a fitted model is presented, which is used to create the prediction surface. Two are the most important diagnostics for kriging analysis: the mean standardized (MS), which has to be close to zero, and the root mean square standardized (RMSS), which has to be close to 1. The results indicate a very good fit for all variables, with the exception of the variables "price" and "size", for which RMSS > 1.

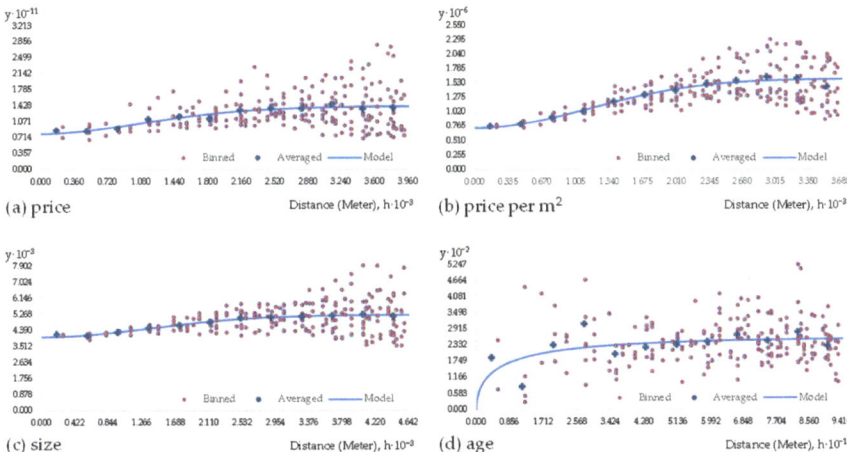

Figure 3. Semivariograms for all four variables.

Table 1. Ordinary kriging diagnostics (prediction errors).

	Price	Price Per m²	Size	Age
Mean	418.34	1.75	−0.02	−0.04
Root Mean Square	393,947.31	974.07	81.16	17.03
Mean Standardized	0.001	0.002	−0.000	−0.002
Root Mean Square Standardized	1.335	1.094	1.241	1.016
Average Standard Error	292,605.18	889.11	65.24	16.76

For the better interpretation of the kriging analysis, the global Moran's I index of spatial autocorrelation for the selected variables was calculated and the results are shown in Figure 4. The values of the Moran's index are in the range of −1 to +1, with an index score greater than 0.3 being an indication of relatively strong autocorrelation. The empirical distributions of Figure 4 are interpreted as in classic inference with normal distribution, calculating the z-values of the coefficient and the associated p-value. The results for all variables indicate a clustered spatial pattern at a 0.01 significance level.

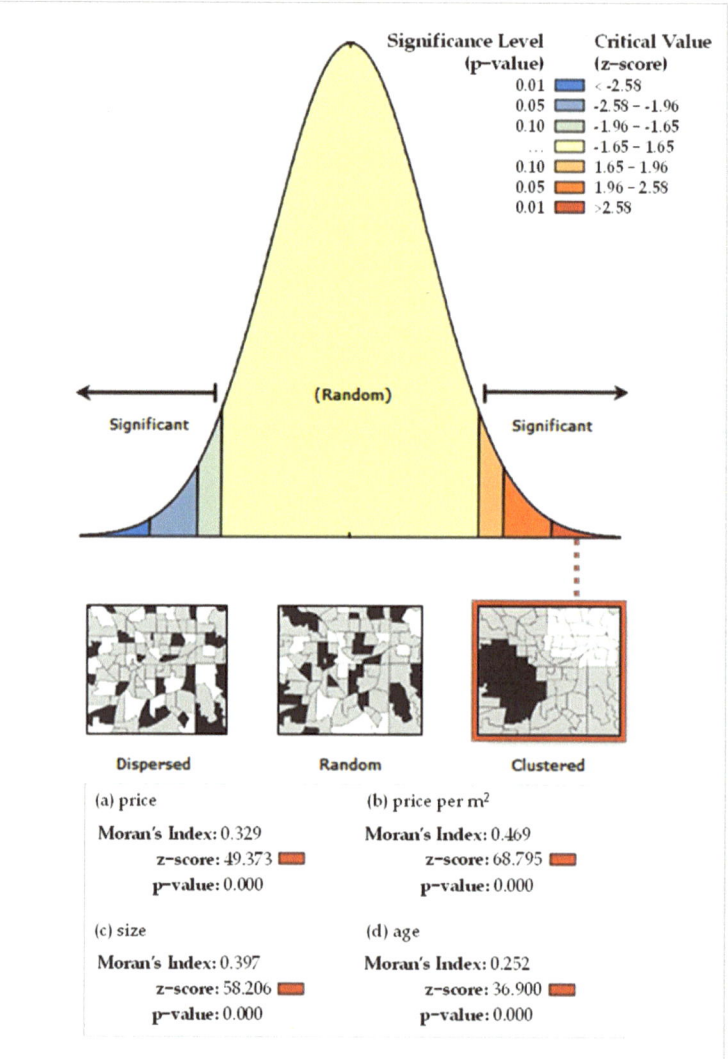

Figure 4. Moran's I for all four variables.

3.2. Mapping Spatial Clusters

The Getis–Ord Gi^* coefficient was calculated for the variables "price", "price per m^2", "size" and "age" in order to identify hot spots and cold spots, i.e., clusters of houses with high or low values for these characteristics. For the conceptualization of spatial relationships, the inverse distance squared option was selected, which results in decreasing the influence of neighboring observations with distance. The results of this procedure are presented in Figures 5–8, in which the significance of the Gi^* statistic is mapped.

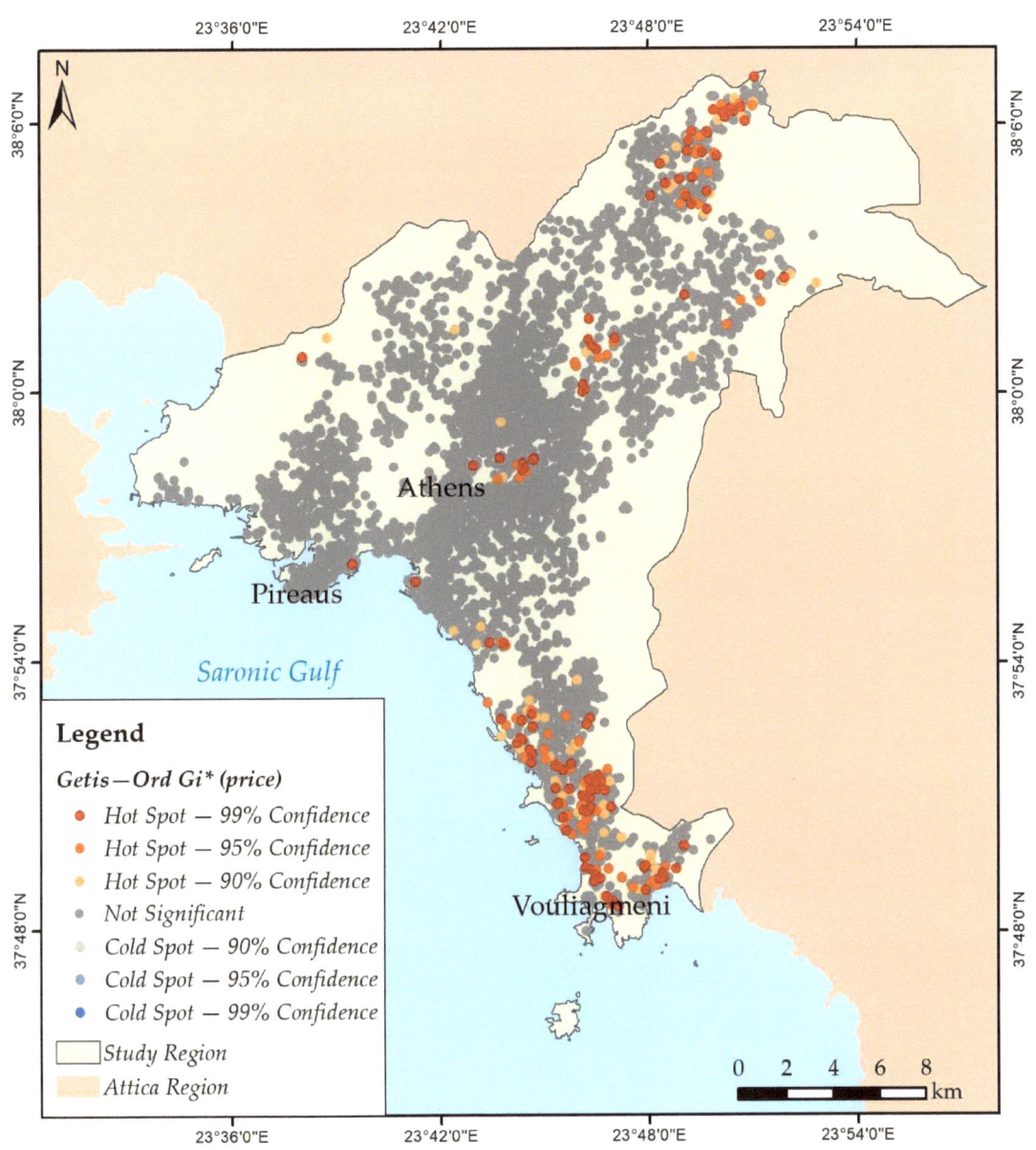

Figure 5. Getis–Ord Gi^*: "price".

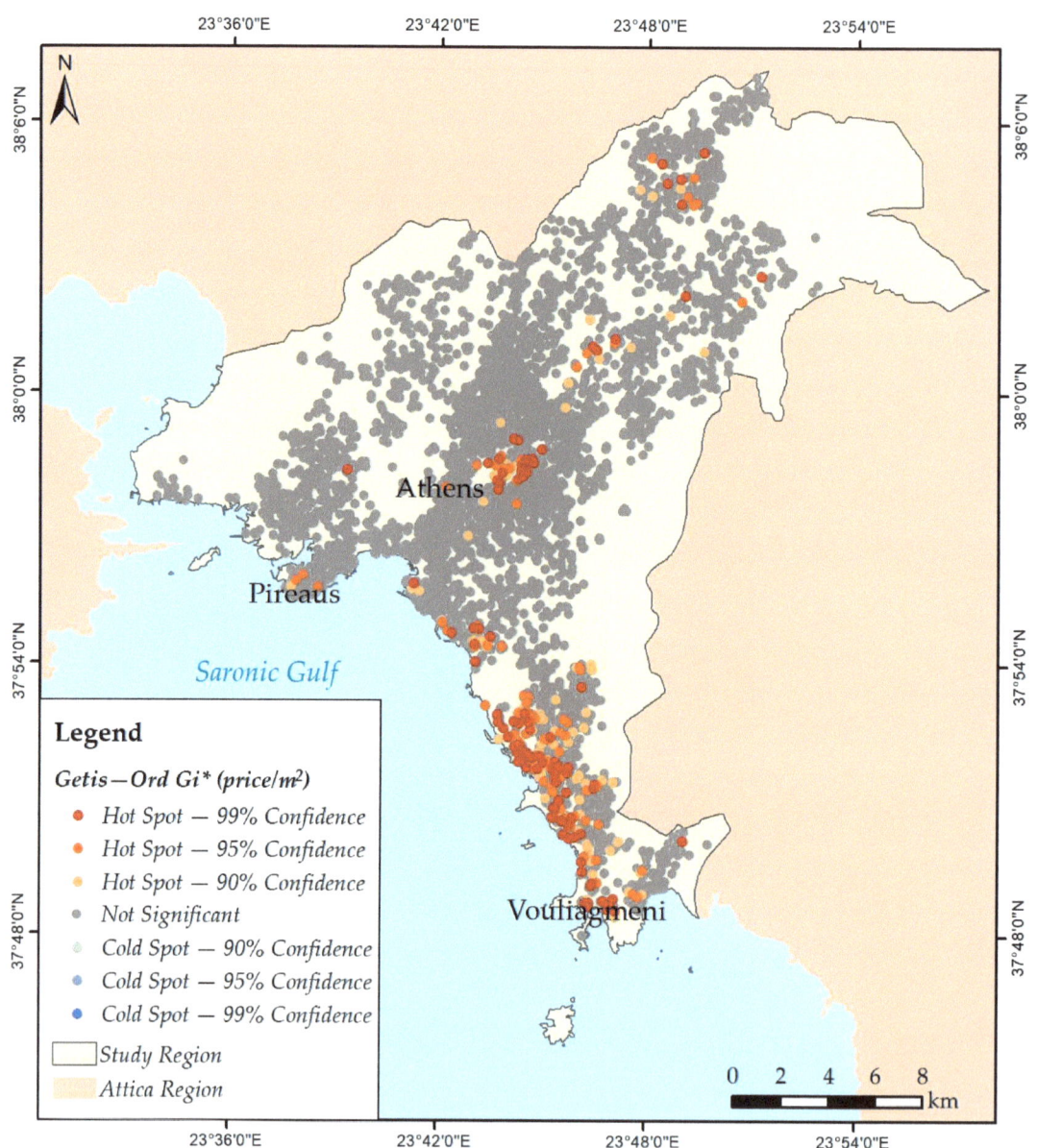

Figure 6. Getis–Ord Gi^*: price per m^2.

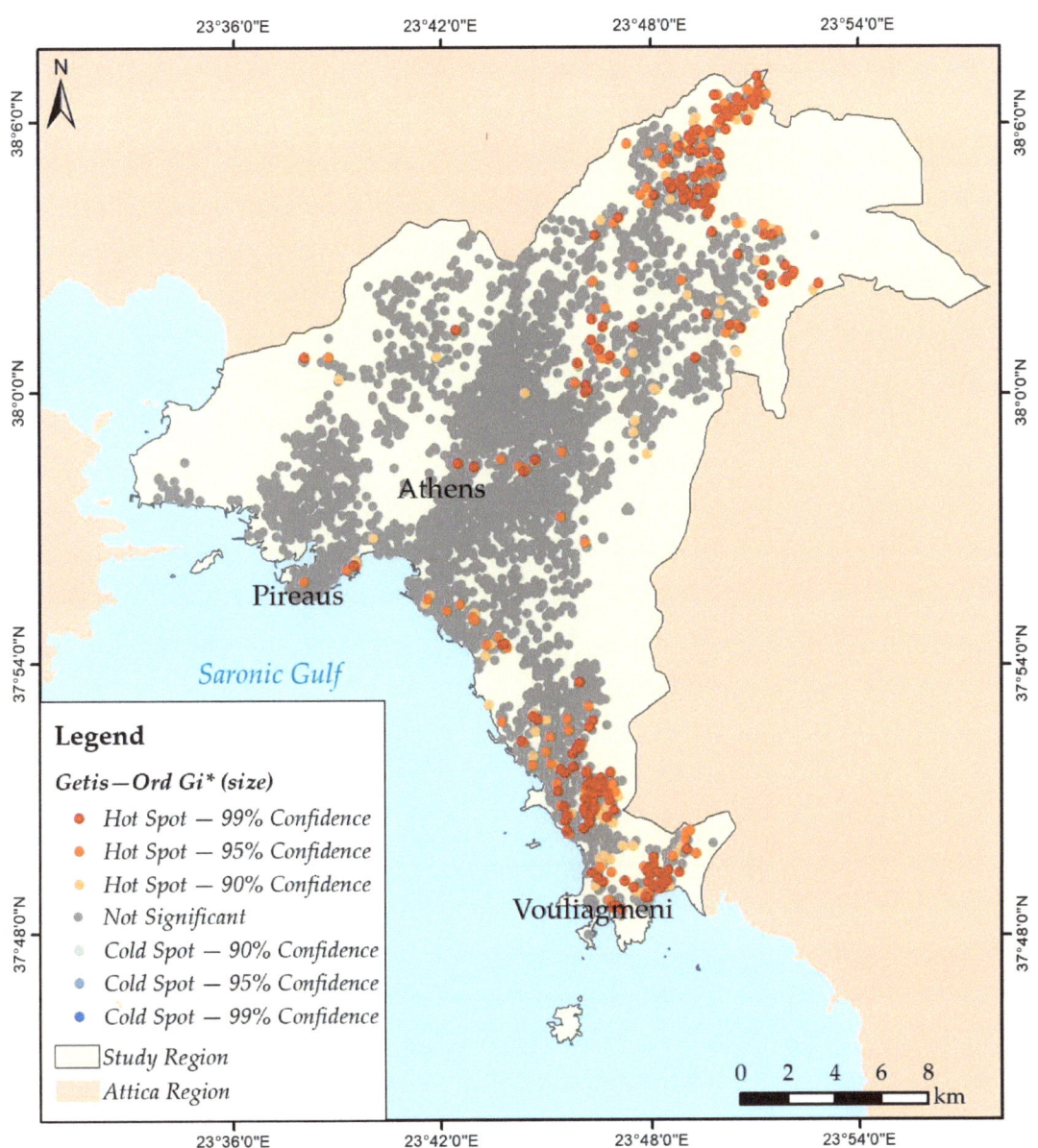

Figure 7. Getis–Ord Gi*: "size".

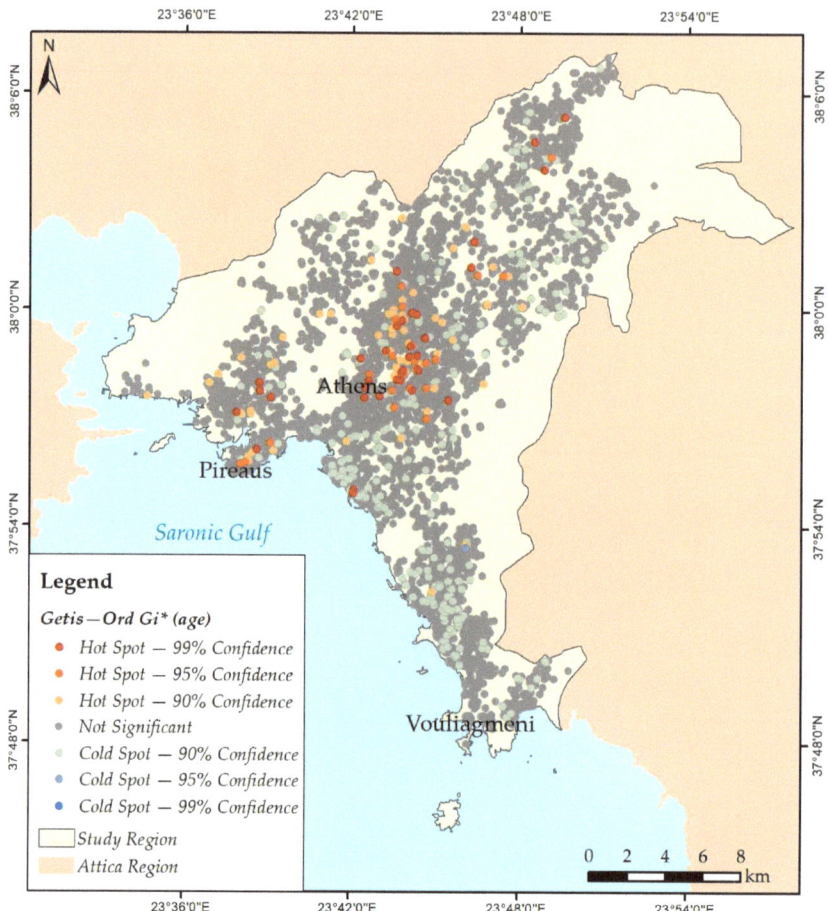

Figure 8. Getis–Ord Gi^*: "age".

3.3. Modelling Spatial Relationships

The final part of the analysis concerns a regression model that will explain the spatial variation in house prices and predict house prices for locations outside the sample data. As spatial data are analyzed, the aim is a spatial regression (GWR) model. The starting point, however, is a linear regression model (OLS) and if spatial autocorrelation causes misspecification problems, a spatial regression model would be more appropriate [21]. The OLS model can be calculated with conventional statistical analysis software but also in a GIS environment. However, when using statistical analysis software for the OLS model, it is easier to address multicollinearity problems and select independent variables that are not correlated with each other. In this way, only data without multicollinearity will enter the GWR model. For the OLS model, the dependent variable is house price ("price") and all variables listed in Section 3 were included as independent variables, with the exception of "price per m^2", "number of rooms" and "number of bathrooms". "Price per m^2" is derived from the variables "price" and "size" and it could be a dependent variable, while the number of rooms and bathrooms represent similar information as size. Three binary variables were entered as well: "parking", "fireplace" and "view". Therefore, nine independent variables were included in the analysis.

The initial linear regression model with all variables indicated several not significant regression coefficients. For that reason, a stepwise procedure was applied, which produced a model with five independent variables (Table 2). In Table 2, the regression coefficients and their significance are presented, together with the beta coefficients. The goodness of fit of the model is determined by the adjusted R^2, which has a value of 0.583, indicating a moderate fit.

In order to improve the fitting of the model, several procedures can be followed. A common procedure is to transform the dependent and/or the independent variables, usually employing a logarithmic transformation [34]. Other studies apply spatial regression models which are calculated in a GIS environment and they take into consideration the location of the observations and the property of spatial autocorrelation [1,35].

Table 2. Results of ordinary least squares regression model dependent variable "price": stepwise method (using SPSS).

Variables	Coefficients	Sig.	Standardized Coefficients (Beta)
Constant	−39,796.64	0.008	-
Size	3349.71	0.000	0.725
Age	−695.80	0.014	−0.028
Distance from the beach	−9.80	0.000	−0.098
Parking	34,899.72	0.003	0.037
View	54,540.50	0.000	0.053

Subsequently, the residuals of the OLS procedure were tested for spatial autocorrelation. The Moran's I indicated that the residuals are clustered at the 0.01 significance level. Therefore, an improvement in the model can be expected when taking into consideration the spatial autocorrelation in the data. Initially, all five independent variables of the OLS procedure were introduced into a GWR model, but this yielded no results, due to spatial multicollinearity issues [36,37]. Accordingly, different combinations of variables were tested for building a GWR model starting with "size" and gradually adding variables, so that R^2 would be maximized (Table 3). The variable with the highest adjusted R^2 in bivariate regression is "size" and then "age", "view", "parking" and "distance from the beach". The adjusted R^2 for different GWR models is presented in Table 3. In the end, the best fit is for the model with "price" as the dependent variable and "size" and "age" as the independent variables. This model has a high explanatory power with an adjusted R^2 of 84.8%. The variable "distance from the beach" was not, finally, included because of local multicollinearity problems and the binary variables did not increase the explanatory power of the model, when more than one variable was introduced. However, it has to be noted that the contribution of "age" in the explanatory power of the model is quite small (3.6%).

Table 3. Different GWR models.

Variables	Adj. R^2
Size	0.812
Size–age	0.848
Size–distance from the beach	0.652
Size–view	0.812
Size–parking	0.761
Size–age–view	0.411
Size–age–parking	0.799
Size –age–distance from the beach	error
Size–age–view–parking	0.776
Size–age–view–parking–distance from the beach	error

The results of this model indicated a much higher explanatory power in comparison to OLS (Table 4). In addition, the Akaike information criterion (AIC) decreased, indicating a better fir of the GWR regression model [38].

Table 4. Comparison of OLS and GWR models.

Model	Adj.R^2	AIC
OLS	0.583	140,247.45
GWR	0.848	136,454.30

The GWR model calculates a regression equation for each observation, a house in this study. As observed, there is a spatial variation of the coefficients, which can be interpreted as the spatial variation of the impact of each factor for the determination of house prices. In Figures 9 and 10 the spatial variation of the coefficients for the independent variables "size" and "age" are presented, respectively.

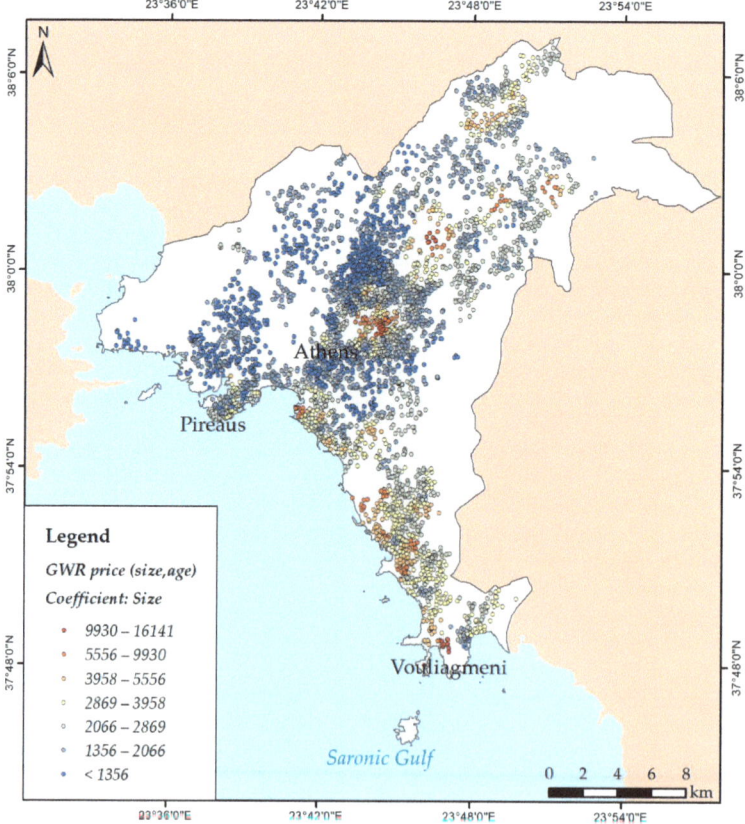

Figure 9. Geographically weighted regression (GWR): spatial variation in the size coefficient.

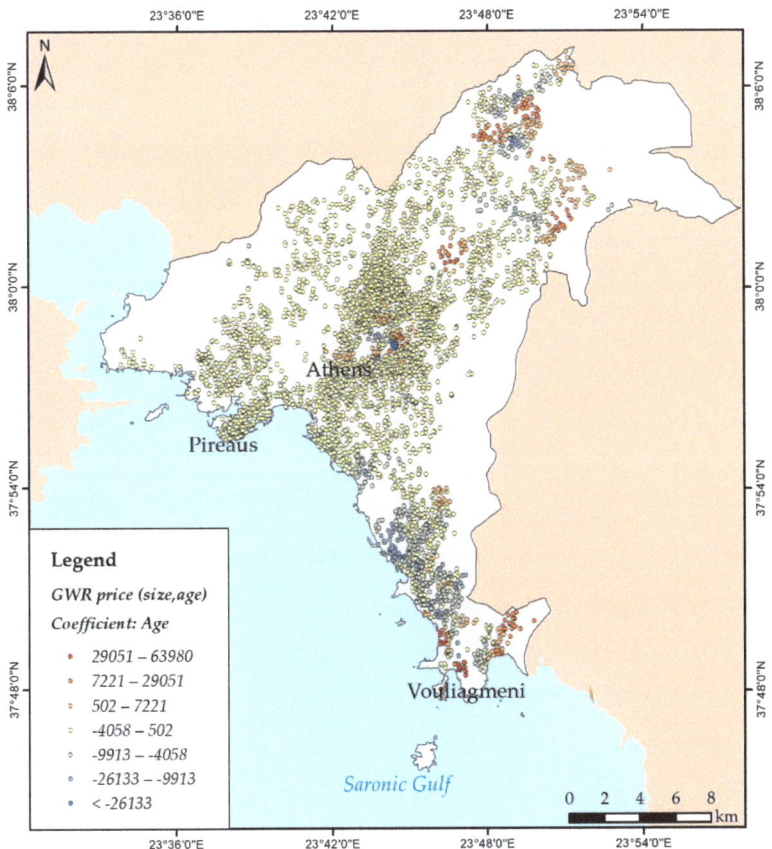

Figure 10. Geographically weighted regression (GWR): spatial variation in the age coefficient.

4. Discussion

The results of the kriging analysis in Section 3.1 present the spatial patterns for four house characteristics: price, price per m^2, size and age. For all these variables, the semivariograms model spatial autocorrelation, while the Moran's I index (Figure 4) suggests quite strong spatial autocorrelation and a clustered spatial pattern. In addition, the diagnostics for ordinary kriging indicate a good fit of the model.

Figure 2a shows the spatial distribution of house prices in the study region. There is a pattern which has been reported in other studies for the Athens region [1,3] indicating low prices at the western parts of the city and higher prices at the northern and southern suburbs. In addition, expensive houses are found at the center of the city and in some municipal units (Filothei and Psychiko) close to the center. Figure 2b presents the price per m^2 and the resulting spatial pattern is similar to the previous one for "price"; however, the distinction between the western suburbs, on the one hand, and the southern and northern suburbs, on the other, is more obvious. The spatial pattern for the variable "size" suggests that smaller houses are mostly concentrated in some neighborhoods of Athens. The municipality of Athens includes several neighborhoods with quite different characteristics, which mostly reflect socioeconomic differences and not differences in building regulations or the age of the buildings. Therefore, apartment buildings are the prevailing type of housing, however, the quality of buildings and the structural characteristics, such as size, are different, resulting in differences in house prices as well. On the other hand, large houses are found in several areas, but the larger houses are in the northern and southern suburbs, where the house prices are also high (see Figure 2a–c). Therefore, price and size of the houses seem to be spatially correlated. Finally, the spatial pattern for the age of the houses indicates that the older houses are found in the municipality of Athens and this is reasonable since the center is the oldest part of the study region, with the urban expansion towards the suburbs being implemented in subsequent time periods.

In terms of mapping spatial clusters, the Getis–Ord Gi^* produced maps of hot spots, and no cold spots, with the exception of the variable "age," for which cold spots of lower significance (90%) are detected. For the variable "price" (Figure 5), two main clusters of high prices (hot spots) are identified, at the northern and southern suburbs of Athens. In addition, high prices are found at the center of Athens and in two municipal units close to the center (Psychiko and Filothei). For the variables "price per m^2" and "size", similar clusters of high prices (hot spots) are observed as for "price". The spatial clusters for "age" indicate hot spots of old buildings at the center of Athens and Piraeus and cold spots mostly at the southern suburbs of Athens.

Therefore, two geovisualization methods, i.e., kriging analysis and hot-spot analysis produced similar results, indicating a quite clear spatial differentiation in the study region. The northern and southern suburbs are characterized by high house prices and larger properties, relatively new in age. In addition, some parts of the center of the city have high prices, although in general the houses are older and of smaller size. Finally, two municipal units, Psychiko and Filothei, are characterized by high prices and large properties. These findings are related to the socioeconomic characteristics in the study region [1]. In the center of the city, some of the most expensive areas in the study region are traditionally located in close proximity to the parliament and the central square of the city, named Syntagma Square. The northern suburbs are characterized by large properties and extended private or public green areas, which, for several decades, have been the residence of entrepreneurs and, in general, of higher status population groups. The southern suburbs are characterized by more recent growth and house prices are high due to the proximity to the sea and the construction of the new airport in the early 2000s. Psychiko and the neighboring Filothei have been built according to town plans characterized by a circular road pattern and the presence of green areas. Several embassies are located in Psychiko and the socioeconomic status of the residents is related to high house prices. The rest of the study region is in general characterized by lower prices, while the differences in size and age are not important.

In terms of creating a hedonic model for estimating house prices, two models were presented: the ordinary least squares model and the geographically weighted regression (GWR) model. For the OLS model, the dependent variable was "price" and the independent variables were five structural characteristics (size, age, floor, parking and fireplace) and four locational attributes, including view and distances from the city center, the metro stations and the beach. However, due to multicollinearity issues, five independent variables remained in the model: "size", "age", "distance from the beach", "parking" and "view". The results of the OLS regression model, especially the standardized beta coefficients, indicate that size is the most important factor for estimating house prices. This result is consistent with the findings of other studies [1,39,40]. Only one of the variables describing distances from points of interest was included in the OLS model (distance from the beach). Locational attributes although extremely important for house prices do not have a linear relationship with prices, especially for a large area such as the study region. After some critical distance, for example a walking distance or a short drive, it does not matter if the distance increases. In that case, statistical testing can show the effect on house prices [3].

The goodness of fit for this model is rather moderate, as indicated by an adjusted R^2 with a value of 0.583. In addition, the OLS residuals proved to be spatially clustered, suggesting misspecification of the regression parameters. Therefore, a spatial regression model (GWR) was investigated in order to improve the results. After several trials, the proposed GWR model has "price" as the dependent variable and "size" and "age" as the independent variables, however the results indicate that the variable "size" accounts for most of the variability in "price". The locational attributes were not useful in the GWR context, because of local multicollinearity issues. The explanatory power of the model is significantly higher relative to the OLS model, with an adjusted R^2 of 0.848. It is remarkable that the increased explanatory power is obtained with only two independent variables, instead of five in OLS. This is very useful for estimating house prices, since fewer house characteristics are needed for a mass appraisal model. In several studies, spatial regression models are used for the creation of the hedonic models [1,3,4,17,20,23], since they can capture the spatial autocorrelation properties of spatial data.

A very important advantage of GWR is that it creates local regression models and allows for the spatial variation of regression coefficients. The results produce regression coefficient surfaces and can lead to conclusions as to the importance of an explanatory factor in different parts of the study region. In Figure 9, the GWR regression coefficient for "size" is mapped, resulting to a quite clear spatial pattern. The smaller regression coefficients for size are observed mostly in the western parts of the study region, but also in several neighborhoods of Athens, where lower prices are prevailing (see Figure 2). On the contrary, larger regression coefficients are observed in the areas with high prices, especially Vouliagmeni, which is the most expensive region in Attica. In these areas, large sizes are accompanied by other amenities, such as the existence of a swimming pool. In Figure 10, the GWR regression coefficient for "age" is mapped. In most parts of the study region, negative coefficients for age are observed, as expected. The largest negative coefficients are observed in an expensive neighborhood at the center of Athens (Rigillis). On the other hand, positive coefficients for "age" are found in the expensive areas of the city, which were previously identified, although negative coefficients are observed there as well. For the interpretation of positive age coefficients specific knowledge for these houses is required, if, for example, they are houses of certain historical or architectural value.

In this study, the spatial patterns for house characteristics were presented using statistical techniques: kriging and hot-spot analyses. This type of visualization engages all points in the dataset and produces detailed spatial patterns, while the statistical significance of the results is presented. The regression models showed that working with spatial data, and especially a GWR model, can significantly increase the explanatory power of an OLS model. Since house data are inherently spatial, it seems that if hedonic models incorporate spatial regression techniques, they can improve the accuracy of prediction employing fewer house characteristics as independent variables.

Author Contributions: Conceptualization, P.I.; methodology, P.I.; formal analysis, P.I. and E.F.; investigation, P.I.; writing—original draft preparation, P.I.; writing—review and editing, P.I. and E.F.; supervision, P.I.; visualization, E.F. All authors have read and agreed to the published version of the manuscript.

Funding: This research received no external funding.

Data Availability Statement: The data presented in this study are available on request from the corresponding author. The data are not publicly available due to copyright restrictions. The open data used in this study are provided in the website: http://geodata.gov.gr/dataset (accessed on 11 November 2021).

Acknowledgments: The authors would like to thank the Geospatial Technology Research Lab (GAEA) of the University of West Attica for the provision of the house data.

Conflicts of Interest: The authors declare no conflict of interest.

References

1. Iliopoulou, P.; Stratakis, P. The geography of housing prices in the Greater Athens Region, Greece: Patterns, Correlations and trends. In *Innovative Geographies: Understanding and Connecting Our World, Proceedings of the 11th International Conference of the Hellenic Geographical Society, Lavrion, Greece, 12–15 April, 2018*; Govostis Publisher Co.: Athens, Greece, 2018. Available online: http://www.geochoros.survey.ntua.gr/hgs/el/11th-conference-proceedings?field_topic_tid=All&title=&title_field_value_1=iliopoulou (accessed on 8 December 2021).
2. Stamou, M.; Mimis, A.; Rovolis, A. House Price Determinants in Athens: A Spatial Econometric Approach. *J. Prop. Res.* **2017**, *34*, 269–284. [CrossRef]
3. Iliopoulou, P.; Stratakis, P. Spatial Analysis of Housing Prices in the Athens Region, Greece. *RELAND Int. J. Real Estate Land Plan.* **2018**, *1*, 304–313.
4. Fotheringham, A.S.; Crespo, R.; Yao, J. Exploring, Modelling and Predicting Spatiotemporal Variations in House Prices. *Ann. Reg. Sci.* **2015**, *54*, 417–436. [CrossRef]
5. O'Sullivan, D.; Unwin, D. *Geographic Information Analysis*; John Wiley & Sons: Hoboken, NJ, USA, 2003; ISBN 978-0-471-21176-1.
6. Baranzini, A.; Ramirez, J.; Schaerer, C.; Thalmann, P. *Hedonic Methods in Housing Markets: Pricing Environmental Amenities and Segregation*; Springer Science & Business Media: New York, NY, USA, 2008; ISBN 978-0-387-76815-1.
7. Bhattacharjee, A.; Castro, E.; Marques, J. Spatial Interactions in Hedonic Pricing Models: The Urban Housing Market of Aveiro, Portugal. *Spat. Econ. Anal.* **2012**, *7*, 133–167. [CrossRef]
8. Xiao, Y. *Urban Morphology and Housing Market*; Springer Geography: Singapore, 2017; ISBN 978-981-10-2761-1.
9. Anderson, S.T.; West, S.E. Open Space, Residential Property Values, and Spatial Context. *Reg. Sci. Urban Econ.* **2006**, *36*, 773–789. [CrossRef]
10. Cho, S.-H.; Poudyal, N.C.; Roberts, R.K. Spatial Analysis of the Amenity Value of Green Open Space. *Ecol. Econ.* **2008**, *66*, 403–416. [CrossRef]
11. Efthymiou, D.; Antoniou, C. How Do Transport Infrastructure and Policies Affect House Prices and Rents? Evidence from Athens, Greece. *Transp. Res. Part A Policy Pract.* **2013**, *52*, 1–22. [CrossRef]
12. Luttik, J. The Value of Trees, Water and Open Space as Reflected by House Prices in the Netherlands. *Landsc. Urban Plan.* **2000**, *48*, 161–167. [CrossRef]
13. McMillen, D.P.; McDonald, J. Reaction of House Prices to a New Rapid Transit Line: Chicago's Midway Line, 1983–1999. *Real Estate Econ.* **2004**, *32*, 463–486. [CrossRef]
14. Sander, H.A.; Polasky, S. The Value of Views and Open Space: Estimates from a Hedonic Pricing Model for Ramsey County, Minnesota, USA. *Land Use Policy* **2009**, *26*, 837–845. [CrossRef]
15. Raslanas, S.; Tupenaite, L.; Šteinbergas, T. Research on the Prices of Flats in the South East London and Vilnius. *Int. J. Strateg. Prop. Manag.* **2006**, *10*, 51–63. [CrossRef]
16. Pek, J.; Wong, O.; Wong, A. Data Transformations for Inference with Linear Regression: Clarifications and Recommendations. *Pract. Assess. Res. Eval.* **2019**, *22*, 9. [CrossRef]
17. De Bruyne, K.; Van Hove, J. Explaining the Spatial Variation in Housing Prices: An Economic Geography Approach. *Appl. Econ.* **2013**, *45*, 1673–1689. [CrossRef]
18. Lake, I.R.; Lovett, A.A.; Bateman, I.J.; Day, B. Using GIS and Large-Scale Digital Data to Implement Hedonic Pricing Studies. *Int. J. Geogr. Inf. Sci.* **2000**, *14*, 521–541. [CrossRef]
19. Mimis, A.; Rovolis, A.; Stamou, M. Property Valuation with Artificial Neural Network: The Case of Athens. *J. Prop. Res.* **2013**, *30*, 128–143. [CrossRef]
20. Pace, R.K.; Barry, R.; Sirmans, C.F. Spatial Statistics and Real Estate. *J. Real Estate Financ. Econ.* **1998**, *17*, 5–13. [CrossRef]
21. Anselin, L.; Rey, S.J. *Modern Spatial Econometrics in Practice: A Guide to GeoDa, GeoDaSpace and PySAL*; GeoDa Press LLC: Chicago, IL, USA, 2014.
22. Fotheringham, A.S.; Brunsdon, C.; Charlton, M. *Geographically Weighted Regression: The Analysis of Spatially Varying Relationships Wiley Wiltshire*; John Wiley & Sons: New York, NY, USA, 2002.
23. Herath, S.; Choumert, J.; Maier, G. The Value of the Greenbelt in Vienna: A Spatial Hedonic Analysis. *Ann. Reg. Sci.* **2015**, *54*, 349–374. [CrossRef]
24. Iliopoulou, P.; Kitsos, C. Kriging Analysis for Atmosphere Pollutants and House Prices: The case of Athens. In *Economics of Natural Resources & the Environment, Proceedings of the 6th ENVECON Conference, Volos, Greece, 11–12 June 2021*; Springer Science & Business Media: New York, NY, USA, 2012; pp. 233–247. Available online: http://envecon.econ.uth.gr/main/eng/images/6th_conference/6th_Conference_Proceedings.pdf (accessed on 12 December 2021).
25. Tobler, W.R. A Computer Movie Simulating Urban Growth in the Detroit Region. *Econ. Geogr.* **1970**, *46*, 234–240. [CrossRef]
26. Kuntz, M.; Helbich, M. Geostatistical Mapping of Real Estate Prices: An Empirical Comparison of Kriging and Cokriging. *Int. J. Geogr. Inf. Sci.* **2014**, *28*, 1904–1921. [CrossRef]
27. Chica-Olmo, J.; Cano-Guervos, R.; Chica-Rivas, M. Estimation of Housing Price Variations Using Spatio-Temporal Data. *Sustainability* **2019**, *11*, 1551. [CrossRef]
28. Cressie, N.A. *Statistics for Spatial Data*; John Willey & Sons, Inc.: New York, NY, USA, 1993.
29. Isaaks, E.H.; Srivastava, R.M. *Applied Geostatistics*; Oxford Univ. Press: New York, NY, USA, 1989.

30. Fotheringham, A.S.; Brunsdon, C. Some Thoughts on Inference in the Analysis of Spatial Data. *Int. J. Geogr. Inf. Sci.* **2004**, *18*, 447–457. [CrossRef]
31. Rogerson, P.A. *Statistical Methods for Geography: A Student's Guide*; SAGE: Southern Oaks, CA, USA, 2019; ISBN 978-1-5297-0023-7.
32. Draper, N.R.; Smith, H. *Applied Regression Analysis*; John Wiley & Sons: New York, NY, USA, 1998; ISBN 978-0-471-17082-2.
33. Jenks, G.F. The Data Model Concept in Statistical Mapping. *Int. Yearb. Cartogr.* **1967**, *7*, 186–190.
34. Osborne, J. Improving Your Data Transformations: Applying the Box-Cox Transformation. *Pract. Assess. Res. Eval.* **2019**, *15*, 12. [CrossRef]
35. Mankad, M.D. Analysis of Impact of Accessibility on Residential Property Values in Gotri Area of Vadodara City, India Using OLS and GWR. *Int. J. Sci. Res. Sci. Eng. Technol.* **2018**, *4*, 1118–1127. [CrossRef]
36. Wheeler, D.C. Diagnostic Tools and a Remedial Method for Collinearity in Geographically Weighted Regression. *Environ. Plan. A* **2007**, *39*, 2464–2481. [CrossRef]
37. Brunsdon, C.; Charlton, M.; Harris, P. Living with Collinearity in Local Regression Models. In Proceedings of the 10th International Symposium on Spatial Accuracy Assessment in Natural Resources and Environmental Sciences, Florianópolis, Brazil, 10–13 July 2012.
38. Portet, S. A Primer on Model Selection Using the Akaike Information Criterion. *Infect. Dis. Model.* **2020**, *5*, 111–128. [CrossRef]
39. Rodriguez, M.; Sirmans, C.F. Quantifying the value of a view in single family housing markets. *Apprais. J.* **1994**, *62*, 600–603.
40. Ozgur, C.; Hughes, Z.; Rogers, G.; Parveen, S. Multiple Linear Regression Applications in Real Estate Pricing. *Int. J. Math. Stat. Invent.* **2016**, *4*, 39–50.

Technical Note

Mapping Construction Costs at the National Level

Su Zhang [1,2,*], Christopher D. Lippitt [1], Susan M. Bogus [2], Tammira D. Taylor [1] and Renee Haley [1]

[1] Department of Geography and Environmental Studies, University of New Mexico, Albuquerque, NM 87131, USA; clippitt@unm.edu (C.D.L.); tammira.taylor@aps.edu (T.D.T.); renyay@gmail.com (R.H.)
[2] Department of Civil, Construction, and Environmental Engineering, University of New Mexico, Albuquerque, NM 87131, USA; sbogus@unm.edu
* Correspondence: suzhang@unm.edu

Abstract: The construction industry relies on construction cost indexes to prepare cost estimate benchmarks and develop cost estimates. Subsequently, government agencies, non-profit organizations, and private companies routinely publish construction cost indexes for cities. Currently, all construction cost indexes are released in a tabular format for 649 cities across the conterminous United States, which is not effective in illustrating construction cost variations at the national level. This study explored the utility of various established interpolation methods and mapping techniques to visualize construction cost indexes at the national level. Geovisualization techniques such as thematic mapping provide a visual representation of construction cost data in addition to traditional tabular formats. This study explored the utility of Thiessen polygon and inverse distance weighted (IDW) methods to create thematic maps which can be used to interactively visualize construction costs at the national level. A qualitative comparison revealed that the IDW method can produce the most intuitive, interactive, and continuous surface maps to identify dynamic and previously unrecognized patterns. These continuous surface maps allow construction practitioners and academics, real estate developers, and the public to locate the geographic proximity of high or low construction costs while cost change maps allow investors and businesses to identify patterns in changing construction costs over a certain period. This work contributes to the body of knowledge by introducing interpolated maps for visualizing any construction cost-related indexes at a large scale such as the national level.

Keywords: construction costs; mapping; national level; interpolation

1. Introduction

The construction industry plays a key role in a country's economy, in addition to producing physical structures that increase productivity and quality of life [1,2]. Construction is one of the largest industries in the United States, and it is the country's largest single production economic activity in terms of dollar value of the output produced within the borders of the nation [3]. According to the Bureau of Labor Statistics of the United States, the industry employs 8.3 million people and represents 5 percent of the workforce [4].

Therefore, construction is an important sector that contributes greatly to a nation's economic growth. Consequently, construction costs are a critical indicator of economic conditions because the construction market tends to follow the condition of the overall economy [5]. Generally, construction costs tend to decrease in times of recession because demand for new construction is low, while construction costs tend to increase in times of economic boom because demand is high [5].

In the construction industry, one of the common practices is to conduct project feasibility studies to assess the viability of a construction project prior to site acquisition or entering into a building commitment [6]. It should be noted that early and accurate construction cost forecasting is needed in such studies. Such forecasting, which is commonly known as construction cost estimating, is the process of forecasting the cost of building a physical structure such as a building or a bridge. Construction cost estimating can be used to assist project stakeholders in many ways, including, but not limited to, predicting costs, setting a budget, and managing design to meet budget restrictions [6].

In general, construction cost estimates are developed by using historical cost data and applying various adjustment factors to reflect the local costs of labor, material, equipment, project size, and project complexity. For example, the most common practice for estimating the total cost to construct a project at a specific location is to adjust standardized costs by applying a construction cost index for that location. That being said, the construction industry relies on location-based construction cost indexes to prepare cost estimate benchmarks and develop cost estimates. Subsequently, government agencies, non-profit organizations, and even private companies routinely (i.e., weekly, monthly, semi-annually, or annually) publish location-based construction cost indexes on a national scale to assist the construction industry with cost estimation. These cost indexes are also commonly used by investors and businesses to evaluate economic health and adjust their perspectives on economic growth and profitability.

In the United States, the most widely used location-based construction cost index is the RSMeans city cost index (CCI). Table 1 shows the 2010 CCI for cities in the states of Alabama and Arizona as an example; although, the CCI information is available for all 50 U.S. states. It should be noted that the construction cost for a city includes two components: material costs and installation costs (including both labor costs and equipment rental costs). The "Total" is the weighted average composite index, which reflects both material and installation costs, and it is the index referred to as the CCI. The weighted average for a city is a total of the divisional components weighted to reflect typical usage, but it does not include the productivity variations between trades or cities [7]. Additionally, the CCI does not take into account factors such as managerial efficiency, local competitive conditions, construction automation, restrictive union practices, unique local requirements, and local building codes [7].

Table 1. City cost indexes for cities in the states of Alabama and Arizona.

State	City	Material	Installation	Total
Alabama	Birmingham	97.4	75.2	87.6
	Tuscaloosa	96.0	60.2	80.2
	Jasper	96.3	58.5	79.6
	Decatur	96.0	61.8	80.9
	Huntsville	96.0	70.1	84.6
	Gadsden	95.9	59.2	79.7
	Montgomery	97.1	58.3	80.0
	Anniston	95.2	67.0	82.8
	Dothan	95.9	53.7	77.3
	Evergreen	95.4	55.6	77.8
	Mobile	97.1	67.4	84.0
	Selma	95.6	53.5	77.0
	Phoenix City	96.4	57.2	79.1
	Butler	95.8	53.9	77.3
Arizona	Phoenix	99.9	74.6	88.7
	Mesa/Tempe	99.4	64.4	83.9
	Globe	99.5	60.5	82.3
	Tucson	98.2	69.9	85.7
	Show Low	99.6	61.6	82.8
	Flagstaff	101.6	70.4	87.9
	Prescott	99.1	61.1	82.4
	Kingman	97.2	67.9	84.3
	Chambers	97.3	61.8	81.6

It should be noted that CCI values are also available for cities in U.S. territories and Canada. The CCI is a percentage ratio of the construction cost of a given city to the national average construction cost at a stated period of time [7]. That said, these index figures represent relative construction factors (i.e., multipliers) for materials, installation, and total costs (i.e., CCI) at a specific location when compared to the national average, which is set at 100. The construction costs of thirty major U.S. cities (e.g., New York and Los Angeles) are used to calculate the national average. For example, if the CCI value of a city is 80 in 2005, it indicates the construction cost of that city is 80% of the national average in the year 2005.

Currently, all construction cost indexes from RSMeans are released in a tabular format, lacking a straightforward illustration of the variation of construction costs at the national level. In addition, construction cost indexes are not available for all locations across the United States. For example, in the conterminous United States (excluding the states of Hawaii and Alaska), RSMeans routinely surveys 649 cities out of over 19,000 cities listed by the U.S. Census Bureau, which means that less than 4% of U.S. cities have been surveyed on a regular basis [8].

Maps provide an effective representation of data where the individual values are traditionally contained in a matrix because maps are an intuitive and user-friendly medium for representing information visually [9,10]. Due to these unique features, maps hold the potential to more effectively and efficiently visualize construction costs at the national level. It should be noted that map creation involves the process of effectively and efficiently visualizing geospatial information known as geovisualization [11]. Traditional maps can be characterized as being static, which limits their exploratory capability. Geovisualization, on the other hand, leverages a set of tools and techniques (e.g., internet mapping) to permit the creation of more interactive and dynamic maps [11].

There have been steadily growing research interests and efforts in the cartographic and geographic information science community for the effective and efficient visualization of myriad geospatial data through the use of a variety of new technologies and techniques for the purposes of geographic knowledge discovery, information sharing, and decision-making processes [12]. Over the past four decades, remote sensing missions (e.g., satellite imagery) and field survey work have exponentially increased the volumes of geospatial data available [13]. In this context, geovisualization is both a process for leveraging these geospatial data to meet scientific and societal needs, and a research field that develops visual methods and tools to support a wide range of geospatial data applications [14].

In recent years, researchers and practitioners have found a variety of creative ways to use new technologies and techniques to advance geovisualization. However, challenges still remain. Some of the challenges include the presentation of multivariate geospatial data, visualization–computation integration, user interface–device integration, and usability and cognitive issues [11]. All these challenges can be attributed to a lack of methods for transforming the ever-increasing geospatial data into information and for combining information from diverse sources to construct knowledge [11].

Currently, there are no national-level construction cost maps available due to the lack of data for unsurveyed cities and geovisualization methods. From the perspective of the survey, it is impossible to survey every single city's construction cost due to limited resources (e.g., money and manpower). To estimate the construction cost for a city that does not have a CCI, the widely adopted method in the construction industry is to use the nearest (in terms of geographic proximity) city's CCI.

From the perspective of geovisualization, a review of the literature revealed that methods for visualizing the CCI are limited and present a significant gap in the research. Several recent studies have revealed that several interpolation methods can be effectively used to estimate the CCI for unknown locations [15,16]. These methods include the nearest neighbor (NN) method, the conditional nearest neighbor (CNN) method, and the inverse distance weighted (IDW) method. The NN method is the most widely adopted method in the construction industry to estimate the CCI for unsurveyed cities. The other two methods, CNN and IDW, have been identified by previous studies as better alternatives when compared to NN. The CNN method is very similar to the NN method, but state boundaries play a role in determining the nearest neighbor in CNN. In other words, when using the CCN method, a city's nearest neighbor has to be within the same state. The IDW method uses the weighted average of a known location's CCI within the neighborhood to estimate the CCI of an unknown location. More details regarding NN, CNN, and IDW are discussed in the methodology section.

These three methods hold the potential to effectively and efficiently visualize CCI values at the national level via a series of maps to reveal spatial-temporal patterns that have traditionally been impossible to reveal by a tabular format. This is because, fundamentally, the CCI is geospatial data, i.e., a combination of location information (coordinates that define a specific feature, in this case, a specific city); attribute information (the characteristics that define a specific feature, in this case, a specific city); and temporal information (when the data are being collected, edited, and distributed). The attribute information is essentially the construction cost information that describes a city with a specific location. The intellectual significance of this research lies in exploring the utility of three geovisualization methods, including NN, CNN, and IDW, to permit visualization of the CCI at the national level. Unlike the traditional presentation of a CCI in a tabular format, this study visualizes CCI data through a series of maps.

All the aforementioned methods, including NN, CNN, and IDW, are spatial interpolation methods that can be used to produce maps that illustrate the variation of national-level construction costs over time. These maps can be considered "heatmaps": a grid composed of pixels with different colors, each of which corresponds to a data value; the hotter the color is, the higher the pixel value is [17]. This study explores the utility of NN, CNN, and IDW methods for mapping construction costs at the national level. Specifically, the intent of this study is to examine whether construction cost data can be mapped from NN, CNN, and IDW methods to exhibit their spatial-temporal patterns, and if so, to determine which method produces the most intuitive and interactive maps to assist construction practitioners and academics, real estate developers, investors and businesses, and the public in identifying dynamic and previously unrecognized patterns.

2. Materials and Methods

2.1. Construction Cost Data Collection

Construction material, labor, and equipment costs are factors used for calculating the CCI. However, it should be noted that other elements such as weather, climate, transportation, and labor productivity are not considered in the CCI estimates. The CCI is surveyed, updated, and published on an annual basis. For the 649 cities surveyed across the conterminous United States, the CCI values from 2004 to 2015 were obtained from RSMeans. This study did not use the latest CCI data because the data used are irrelevant since this study is focused on demonstrating how to use NN, CNN, and IDW methods to create construction cost maps at the national level.

These 2004 to 2015 CCI values were tabular-joined with a standard GIS point shapefile of cities obtained from ESRI [18] and saved for later processing. It should be noted that the cities in the states of Hawaii and Alaska were excluded because they do not have neighboring states to interpolate CCI values with the NN and IDW methods. This could be a future research topic which focuses on mapping construction costs at the state level.

Figure 1 shows the locations of these 649 cities using a color scheme to indicate each city's CCI value category in 2015. CCI values are represented via increasingly warm color hues (e.g., red color), which are prevalent in the construction field [19]. Users can identify a city's CCI from one of the seven categories as indicated in Figure 1. However, it is not possible for users to identify CCI values for cities that are not listed among the 649 cities.

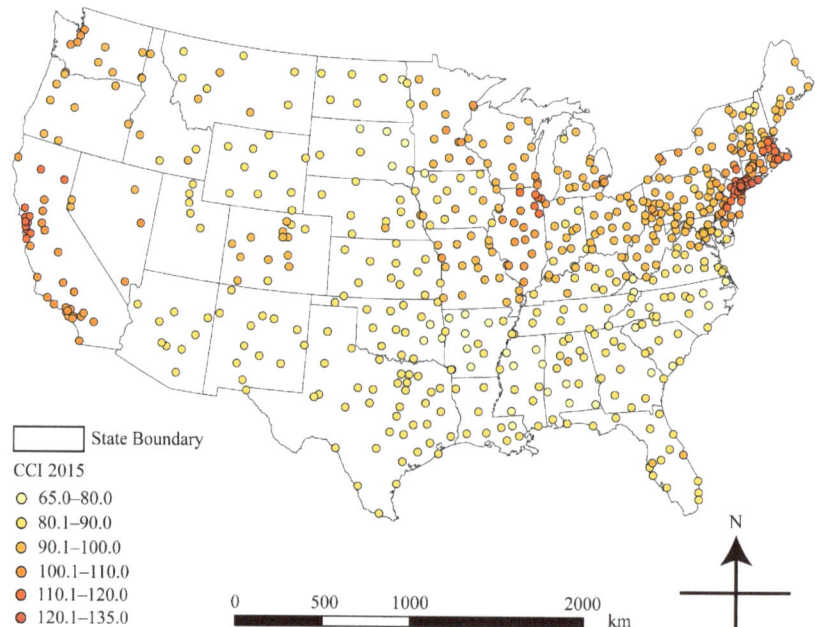

Figure 1. The 649 CCI cities in the conterminous U.S. and their CCI (city cost index) values in 2015.

Previous studies have proven that cities with CCI values are spatially auto-correlated [15,16], meaning that it is valid to perform interpolation for locations that do not have CCI values. As mentioned in the previous section, three methods, including NN, CNN, and IDW were selected as the interpolation techniques for estimating CCI values for cities not currently included in the index database.

2.2. Interpolation Methods

Interpolation allows users to estimate values at locations where they have not yet been measured [20]. These methods are commonly used when samples are limited, lost, incomplete, or when previously collected data may be dated and inaccurate [20]. When using the NN method, users select the value of the nearest surveyed city (in terms of Euclidean or linear distance, not actual travel distance over a road network) to estimate the CCI value for an unsurveyed location. The Thiessen polygon method was used to identify a zone closest to each of the 649 CCI sites (Figure 2); cities within the same zone were then assigned the same CCI value. However, when compared with alternative proximity-based interpolation methods such as CNN and IDW, NN has been proven to be less accurate [16].

The CNN method improves upon the NN method by selecting the value of the nearest surveyed city within the same state to estimate the CCI for an unsurveyed city. A previous study concluded that the CNN method outperforms the NN method in terms of accuracy because state boundaries are used concurrently with geographic proximity to select the nearest neighbor [16]. In addition, the CNN method is also the best method for creating a rough surface map of CCI (i.e., classified choropleth map) [16]. Figure 3 shows the use of the Thiessen polygon and state boundaries to implement the CNN method.

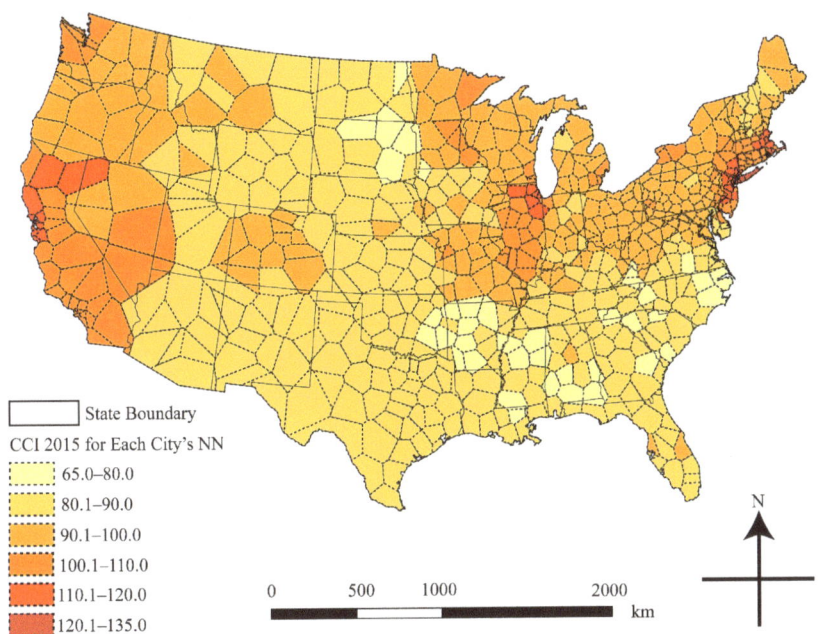

Figure 2. A 2015 construction cost map at the national level created by using the NN (nearest neighbor) method.

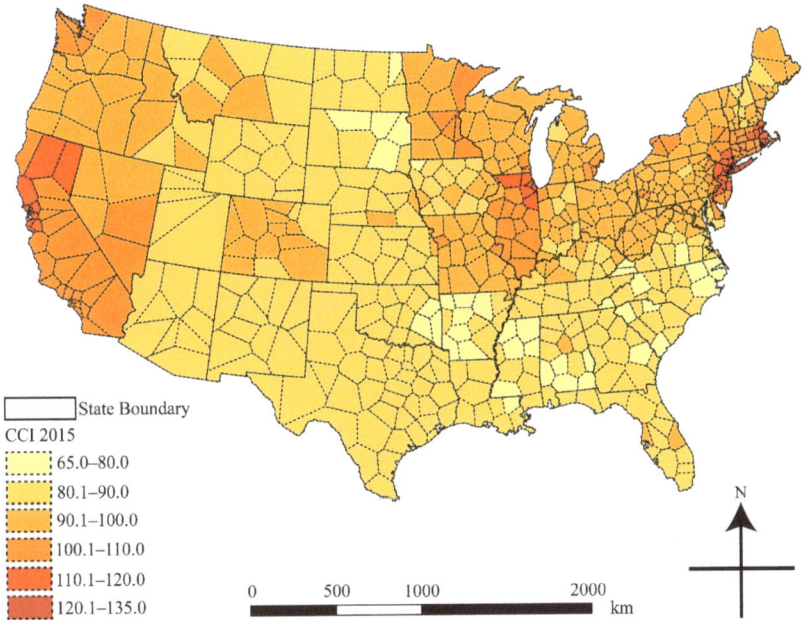

Figure 3. Construction cost map at the national level created by using the CNN (conditional nearest neighbor) method.

The IDW method is one of the most frequently used deterministic models in interpolation. This method evolved from the assumption that the attribute value of an unsurveyed point is the weighted average of known values within the neighborhood, and that those weights are inversely related to the distances between the unsurveyed and surveyed locations [21]. IDW is the best method for creating a smooth surface map of the CCI (i.e., stretched raster map) [16]. Equation (1) shows the algorithm of the IDW interpolation method. With IDW, values for unsurveyed points, Z_j, are estimated by:

$$Z_j = \frac{\sum_i \frac{Z_i}{d_{ij}^n}}{\sum_i \frac{1}{d_{ij}^n}} \tag{1}$$

where d_{ij} is the distance from known point i to unknown point j, Z_i is the value for the known point i, and n is a user defined exponent, which controls how quickly a point's influence decreases with distance [20]. According to the previous study, a value of 2 should be used for n, and the search radius should be limited to 10 neighboring points [16]. The output cell size (grid resolution) should be 1 km. Figure 4 shows an interpolated surface map produced by the IDW method.

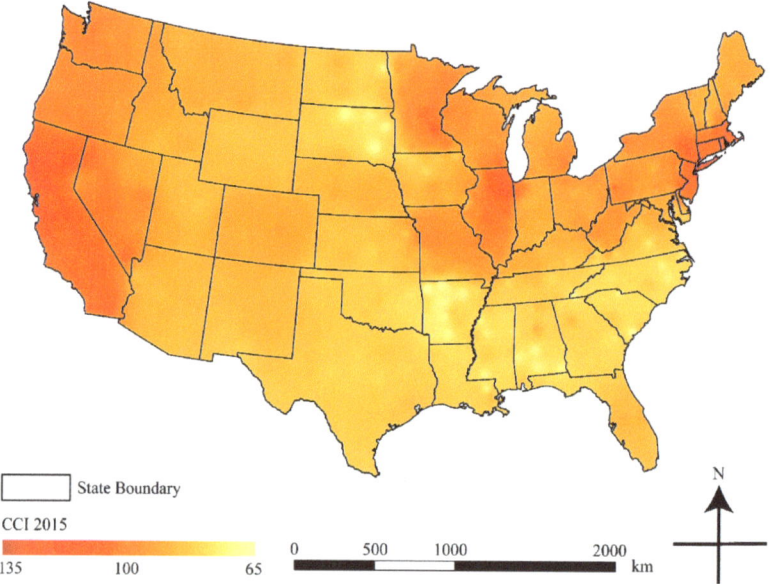

Figure 4. Construction cost map at the national level created by using the IDW (inverse distance weighted) method.

2.3. Selection of Interpolation Method for Mapping

As shown in Figures 2 and 3, both the NN and CNN methods can estimate CCI values for all cities at the national level. The color variation at the polygon level in these maps produces two-dimensional (2D) choropleth maps, which are only able to represent class membership per polygon [22]. If actual values are not available for reference units, unsurveyed cities can only be compared with class range values [22], which are very difficult if not impossible to interpret. A lack of variation within the polygons makes it more difficult for the viewers to assess the CCI values for unsurveyed cities, which can lead to difficulty in identifying any general patterns. Additionally, both NN and CCN methods will produce rough surfaces for the interpolated CCI values, which means that CCI values will change suddenly from one value to the next across certain boundaries creating a rough surface with jump discontinuities [16]. These discontinuities may greatly hinder CCI distribution pattern identification at the national level.

IDW methods, as shown in Figure 4, can also show CCI values for all cities at the national level. Previous studies have shown that the IDW method provides a more accurate interpolation of the CCI values; however, mathematically, IDW is slow and difficult to calculate [16]. However, modern spatial computing technologies have greatly alleviated this challenge. In addition, the IDW method involves many algorithm parameters and users need to identify the most appropriate ones to create the most accurate interpolation surface [16]. Unlike the polygon-based NN and CNN interpolation methods, IDW creates a smoother raster surface that can be used to assist in the comprehension of demographic or economic data more effectively than polygon-based, classified choropleth maps [22]. Therefore, the IDW method generally produces smooth surface maps that are more intuitive, which aid viewers in identifying overall, dynamic, and previously unrecognized patterns. Therefore, the authors decided to use IDW to create maps for CCI values at the national level to reveal spatial-temporal patterns more effectively. Table 2 summarizes the advantages and disadvantages of the aforementioned methods.

Table 2. Advantages and disadvantages of each interpolation method.

Methods	Advantages	Disadvantages
NN	Fast and easy to calculate	Less accurate
	Widely adopted by the construction industry to conduct cost estimates	Lack of variation within the polygon; no use of state boundary
	Can estimate CCI values for all cities at the national level	Rough surfaces for the interpolated CCI values
CNN	More accurate	Slow and difficult to calculate
	Consider state policies' and regulations' impact on cost variation	Lack of variation within the polygon
	Can estimate CCI values for all cities at the national level	Rough surfaces for the interpolated CCI values
IDW	More accurate	Slow and difficult to calculate
	Smooth surfaces for the interpolated CCI values which provide a more intuitive look to identify patterns	More parameters such as power to consider and test prior to deployment
	Can estimate CCI values for all cities at the national level	Unable to consider state policies' impact on cost variation

2.4. Mapping Construction Cost

As mentioned in Section 2.2, the IDW interpolation method was selected as the most effective technique for interpolating and mapping construction costs at the national level. Figure 5 has been created to exhibit the overall pattern of construction costs from 2004 to 2015 using the IDW method [7,23–33]. All maps were projected into the U.S. Continuous Lambert Conformal Conic coordinate system. As shown in Figure 5, each year's construction cost is presented as a smooth surface. The continuous surface fills the voids where no construction cost data exist. IDW interpolated surface maps are also produced in the raster format; therefore, they can be overlaid, meaning values from one map can be compared to another to produce cost change maps at the national level. Figure 6 shows the construction cost differences in one year, two years, five years, and ten years to reveal construction cost variations over the years.

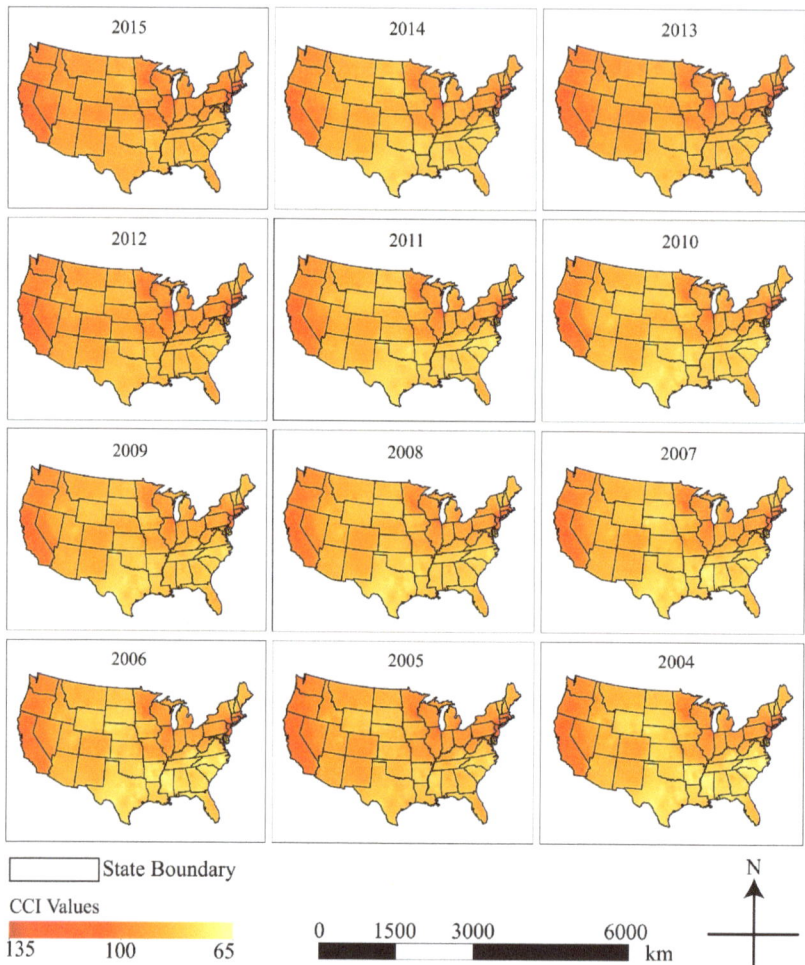

Figure 5. Multiple construction cost maps at the national level created using the IDW interpolation method.

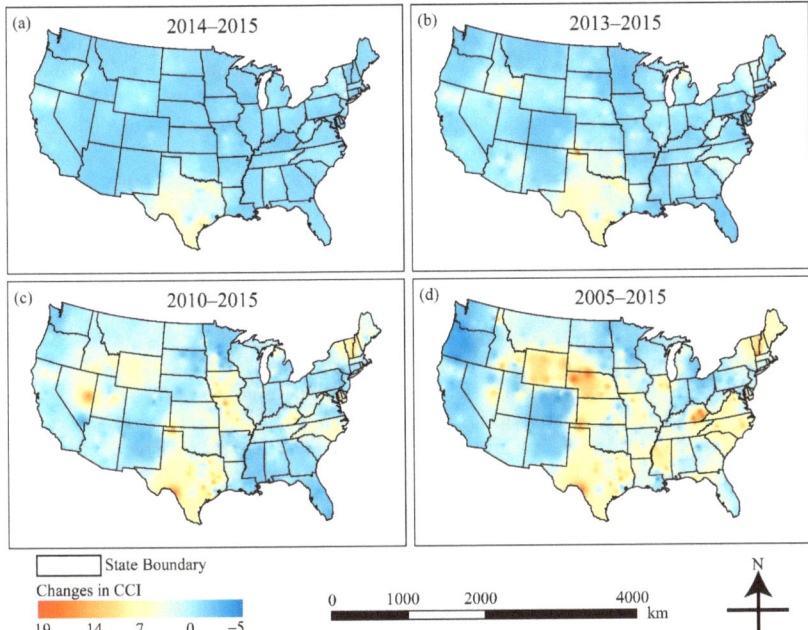

Figure 6. Multiple construction cost maps at the national level showing construction cost difference; (**a**) indicates construction cost difference in one year (2015 value minus 2014 value); (**b**) indicates construction cost difference in two years (2015 value minus 2013 value); (**c**) indicates construction cost difference in five years (2015 value minus 2010 value); (**d**) indicates construction cost difference in ten years (2015 value minus 2005 value).

3. Results and Discussion

Currently, construction cost data are released for a limited amount of cities as indexes in a tabular format, which fail to provide a straightforward illustration of national-level construction costs. With the help of the IDW interpolation method, construction cost maps at the national level have been created for multiple years (Figure 5).

Such smooth and continuous surface maps can be used to help construction practitioners, real estate developers, and the public to identify general patterns in the variation of construction costs across the conterminous United States. For example, a general pattern that can be identified from the maps in Figure 5 is that construction costs on the west coast are high, while the construction costs in the central United States are low. The aforementioned users can also identify hot or cold spots correlated with high or low-cost areas for a construction project. For example, construction costs in New York City and Chicago regions are relatively high, while construction costs in the state of Texas are relatively low.

Maps that show the changes in construction costs at the national level over a certain period have also been created for multiple years (Figure 6). It should be noted that the data used in this study are published CCI data from 2004 to 2015. As aforementioned, CCI values are being collected and published on an annual basis by RSMeans. Due to the proprietary nature of RSMeans' construction cost books, only a fraction of the published CCI data (2004 to 2015) was obtained. However, the data used in this study are irrelevant since this study focuses on demonstrating how to use interpolation methods to create construction cost maps at the national level, including the maps that exhibit changes in construction costs at the national level. The changes in CCI values are represented via increasingly colored hues from cold to warm (e.g., blue to red colors), which are prevalent in exhibiting changes [19]. These cost change maps can be used by investors and businesses to identify economic conditions over time. For example, a one-year construction cost change map (Figure 6a) indicates that construction activity grew remarkably in the state of Texas and in northern California from 2014 to 2015. The ten-year cost change map (Figure 6d) reveals that the states of Wyoming and Nebraska also experienced construction cost growth from 2005 to 2015. On the contrary, the state of Oregon experienced a recession in construction costs during the same period (2005 to 2015).

In a broader context, these maps can also assist with investment forecasting in the real estate industry. For example, a real estate investor might want to compare construction cost maps with home value maps to decide whether investing in existing properties or new construction would be more profitable. For example, cost change maps indicate that northern Ohio experienced a recession in construction costs from 2005 to 2015. If home values remained high, developing new buildings could compete with investment in existing properties. These maps can also provide the public with a quick view of overall economic conditions, which may inform general investment decisions. One future research topic could be exploring the relationship between the construction costs and economic cycles (e.g., recession and economic boom) via relative thematic maps, which hold the potential to provide an alternative and insightful perspective for construction practitioners and academics, real estate developers, investors and businesses, as well as the general public.

One of the robust applications of the national construction cost maps is via web mapping tools to further utilize the capability of geovisualization. Due to the rapid expansion of the internet and the development of web-based geographic information systems (GIS), access to geospatial data on various themes and of varying quality has become significantly easier [34]. When coupled with WebGIS technologies, national construction cost maps can be available to everyone, making accessible the construction cost knowledge that has been traditionally stored in paper-based books or publications. In addition, users can decide which method (NN, CNN, or IDW) to use when visualizing CCI values at the national level. Additionally, the visibility and color schemes of the layers on a web map application can be controlled by the users [35]. That said, the users can decide which method to use, which layers to present, and which color schemes and textures to use, allowing for interactive and dynamic visualization. These WebGIS technologies include not only commercial software programs but also free and open-source software programs, which provide flexibility for different users [36]. Lastly, recent advances in geovisualization provide new methods to visualize geospatial data in a three-dimensional (3D) environment [37]. Visualizing construction costs in a 3D environment holds the potential to identify many patterns that have been impossible in a traditional 2D environment.

Although this research used the CCI as an example of construction costs for mapping, other costs related to construction or costs that contribute to the CCI, such as equipment, material, or labor costs can also be interpolated and mapped at the national level. Construction cost indexes from other suppliers such as the Engineering News-Record (ENR) or highway construction cost index (HCCI) could also be interpolated and mapped at the national level. This research also revealed that interpolation methods can be applied to the geovisualization field to generate cost maps at a large scale.

4. Conclusions

This study investigated the potential of various interpolation methods to visualize construction costs at the national level. The results reveal that maps can provide an effective representation of data where individual values were traditionally represented in a matrix or table of construction costs. The results reveal that a map with a continuous surface provides a better representation of construction costs for cities not listed in the CCI database, and can be readily employed by agencies to visualize their construction cost indexes at the national level. Since construction costs are an indicator of economic conditions, construction cost maps can assist construction and real estate stakeholders, as well as the public, with adjusting their perspectives on economic growth and profitability. Although this research used the CCI as an example of construction costs for mapping, other costs related to construction, such as material or labor costs can also be interpolated and mapped at the national level. Although only a fraction of the published CCI values (i.e., 2004–2015) are used in this study to show the changes in construction costs at the national level, the geovisualization methods used in this study could be easily extended when the additional CCI data (e.g., prior to 2004 and after 2015) are available to reveal patterns over relatively longer temporal periods (e.g., a few decades). The overall contribution of this study to the body of knowledge is the introduction of interpolated maps in visualizing any construction cost-related indexes at a large scale.

Author Contributions: Conceptualization, S.Z., C.D.L. and S.M.B.; methodology, S.Z., C.D.L. and S.M.B.; software, S.Z. and T.D.T.; validation, S.Z.; formal analysis, S.Z. and T.D.T., and R.H.; investigation, S.Z.; resources, S.Z.; data curation, S.Z.; writing—original draft preparation, S.Z.; writing—review and editing, C.D.L., S.M.B., T.D.T. and R.H.; visualization, S.Z. and R.H.; supervision, S.Z.; project administration, S.Z. All authors have read and agreed to the published version of the manuscript.

Funding: This research received no external funding.

Institutional Review Board Statement: Not applicable.

Informed Consent Statement: Not applicable.

Data Availability Statement: This study used data collected by RSMeans. Data used in this study will be available upon request. Contact information is provided in this paper.

Acknowledgments: We would like to express our greatest gratitude to RSMeans. Without their enormous data support, it would not have been possible to complete this study. Thanks also go to the Geographies and anonymous reviewers for their valuable comments to improve this paper.

Conflicts of Interest: The authors declare no conflict of interest.

References

1. Dlamini, S. Relationship of Construction Sector to Economic Growth. In *Working Paper*; School of Construction Management and Engineering, University of Reading: Reading, UK, 2016. Available online: http://sitsabo.co.za/docs/misc/cib_paper2012.pdf (accessed on 5 April 2016).
2. Gould, P.E.; Joyce, N. *Construction Project Management*, 4th ed.; Prentice Hall: Columbus, OH, USA, 2014.
3. Sears, S.K.; Sears, G.A.; Clough, R.H.; Rounds, J.L.; Segner, R.O., Jr. *Construction Project Management—A Practical Guide to Field Construction Management*, 6th ed.; Wiley: New York, NY, USA, 2016.
4. U.S. Bureau of Labor Statistics. The Employment Situation—November 2016. In *News Release*; U.S. Bureau of Labor Statistics: Washington, DC, USA, 2016.
5. Dell'Isola, M.D. *Architect's Essentials of Cost Management*; John Wiley & Sons, Inc.: New York, NY, USA, 2002.
6. Lowe, D.J.; Emsley, M.W.; Harding, A. Predicting Construction Cost Using Multiple Regression Techniques. *J. Constr. Eng. Manag.* **2006**, *132*, 750–758. [CrossRef]
7. Waier, P.R. *Building Construction Cost Data 2014*; Robert S. Means Co.: Norwell, MA, USA, 2013.
8. Zhang, S.; Bogus, S.M.; Lippitt, C.D.; Migliaccio, G.C. Estimating Location-adjustment Factors for Conceptual Cost Estimating Based on Nighttime Satellite Imagery. *J. Constr. Eng. Manag.* **2017**, *143*, 04016087. [CrossRef]
9. Dransch, D.; Rotzoll, H.; Poser, K. The Contribution of Maps to the Challenges of Risk Communication to the Public. *Int. J. Digit. Earth.* **2010**, *3*, 292–311. [CrossRef]
10. Vexler, A.; Hutson, A.D.; Chen, X. *Statistical Testing Strategies in the Health Science*; CRC Press: Boca Raton, FL, USA, 2016.
11. MacEachren, A.M.; Kraak, M. Research Challenges in Geovisualization. *Cartogr. Geogr. Inf. Sci.* **2001**, *28*, 3–12. [CrossRef]
12. Jiang, B.; Li, Z. Geovisualization: Design, Enhanced Visual Tools and Application. *Cartogr. J.* **2005**, *42*, 3–4. [CrossRef]
13. Craglia, M.; Shanley, L. Data Democracy—Increased Supply of Geospatial Information and Expanded Participatory Processes in the Production of Data. *Int. J. Digit. Earth* **2015**, *8*, 679–693. [CrossRef]
14. MacEachren, A.M.; Gahegan, M.; Pike, W.; Brewer, I.; Cai, G.; Lengerich, E.; Hardisty, F. Geovisualization for Knowledge Construction and Decision Support. *IEEE Comput. Graph.* **2004**, *24*, 13–17. [CrossRef] [PubMed]
15. Migliaccio, G.C.; Zandbergen, P.A.; Martinez, A.A. Empirical Comparison of Methods for Estimating Location Cost Adjustment Factors. *J. Manag. Eng.* **2013**, *31*, 04014037. [CrossRef]
16. Zhang, S.; Migliaccio, G.C.; Zandbergen, P.A.; Guindani, M. Empirical Assessment of Geographically Based Surface Interpolation for Adjusting Construction Cost Estimates by Project Location. *J. Constr. Eng. Manag.* **2014**, *140*, 04014015. [CrossRef]
17. Busygin, S.; Prokopyev, O.; Pardalos, P.M. Biclustering in Data Mining. *J. Comput. Oper. Res.* **2008**, *35*, 2964–2987. [CrossRef]

18. ESRI Data & Maps. Available online: https://www.esri.com/arcgis-blog/products/product/mapping/esri-data-maps/ (accessed on 5 April 2016).
19. MacEachren, A.M.; Taylor, D.R.F. *Visualization in Modern Cartography*; Elsevier Science: Tarrytown, NY, USA, 1994.
20. Bolstad, P. *GIS Fundamentals, a First Text on Geographic Information Systems*, 2nd ed.; Eider Press: White Bear Lake, MN, USA, 2005.
21. Lu, G.; Wong, D. An Adaptive Inverse-Distance Weighting Spatial Interpolation Technique. *J. Comput. Geosci.* **2008**, *34*, 1044–1055. [CrossRef]
22. Rase, W. *Visualization of Polygon-Based Data as a Continuous Surface*; Federal Office for Building and Regional Planning: Bonn, Germany, 2009. Available online: http://www.wdrase.de/VisualPycnoInterEngl.pdf (accessed on 16 April 2016).
23. Chiang, J.H.; Plotner, S.C. *Building Construction Cost Data 2004*; Robert S. Means Co.: Norwell, MA, USA, 2003.
24. Balboni, B.; Bastoni, R.A. *Building Construction Cost Data 2005*; Robert S. Means Co.: Norwell, MA, USA, 2004.
25. Waier, P.R. *Building Construction Cost Data 2006*; Robert S. Means Co.: Norwell, MA, USA, 2005.
26. Waier, P.R. *Building Construction Cost Data 2007*; Robert S. Means Co.: Norwell, MA, USA, 2006.
27. Waier, P.R. *Building Construction Cost Data 2008*; Robert S. Means Co.: Norwell, MA, USA, 2007.
28. Waier, P.R. *Building Construction Cost Data 2009*; Robert S. Means Co.: Norwell, MA, USA, 2008.
29. Waier, P.R.; Babbitt, C.; Baker, T.; Balboni, B.; Bastoni, R.A. *Building Construction Cost Data 2010*; Robert S. Means Co.: Norwell, MA, USA, 2009.
30. Waier, P.R.; Babbitt, C.; Baker, T. *Building Construction Cost Data 2011*; Robert S. Means Co.: Norwell, MA, USA, 2010.
31. Waier, P.R.; Charest, A.C.; Babbitt, C.; Baker, T.; Balboni, T. *Building Construction Cost Data 2012*; Robert S. Means Co.: Norwell, MA, USA, 2011.
32. Waier, P.R.; Charest, A.C. *Building Construction Cost Data 2013*; Robert S. Means Co.: Norwell, MA, USA, 2012.
33. Waier, P.R. *Building Construction Cost Data 2015*; Robert S. Means Co.: Norwell, MA, USA, 2014.
34. Kiss, E.; Zichar, M.; Fazekas, I.; Karancsi, G.; Balla, D. Categorization and Geovisualization of Climate Change Strategies Using an Open-Access WebGIS Tool. *Infocommun. J.* **2020**, *12*, 32–37. [CrossRef]
35. Hoarau, C.; Christophe, S. Cartographic Continuum Rendering Based on Color and Texture Interpolation to Enhance Photo-Realism Perception. *ISPRS J. Photogramm. Remote Sens.* **2017**, *127*, 27–38. [CrossRef]
36. Balla, D.; Zichar, M.; Toth, R.; Kiss, E.; Karancsi, G.; Mester, T. Geovisualization Techniques of Spatial Environmental Data Using Different Visualization Tools. *Appl. Sci.* **2020**, *10*, 6701. [CrossRef]
37. Hildebrandt, D. A Software Reference Architecture for Service-Oriented 3D Geovisualization Systems. *ISPRS Int. J. Geo-Inf.* **2014**, *3*, 1445–1490. [CrossRef]

Article

Geovisualization of Hydrological Flow in Hexagonal Grid Systems

Mingke Li [1,*], Heather McGrath [2] and Emmanuel Stefanakis [1]

1. Department of Geomatics Engineering, Schulich School of Engineering, University of Calgary, Calgary, AB T2N 1N4, Canada; emmanuel.stefanakis@ucalgary.ca
2. Canada Centre of Mapping and Earth Observation, Natural Resources Canada, Ottawa, ON K1A 0E4, Canada; heather.mcgrath@canada.ca
* Correspondence: mingke.li@ucalgary.ca

Abstract: Recent research has extended conventional hydrological algorithms into a hexagonal grid and noted that hydrological modeling on a hexagonal mesh grid outperformed that on a rectangular grid. Among the hydrological products, flow routing grids are the base of many other hydrological simulations, such as flow accumulation, watershed delineation, and stream networks. However, most of the previous research adopted the D6 algorithm, which is analogous to the D8 algorithm over a rectangular grid, to produce flow routing. This paper explored another four methods regarding generating flow directions in a hexagonal grid, based on four algorithms of slope aspect computation. We also developed and visualized hexagonal-grid-based hydrological operations, including flow accumulation, watershed delineation, and hydrological indices computation. Experiments were carried out across multiple grid resolutions with various terrain roughness. The results showed that flow direction can vary among different approaches, and the impact of such variation can propagate to flow accumulation, watershed delineation, and hydrological indices production, which was reflected by the cell-wise comparison and visualization. This research is practical for hydrological analysis in hexagonal, hierarchical grids, such as Discrete Global Grid Systems, and the developed operations can be used in flood modeling in the real world.

Keywords: discrete global grid systems; hydrological analysis; multi-resolution; terrain data; geovisualization

1. Introduction

Recently, hydrological modeling on hexagonal mesh grids has gained popularity among researchers. Compared to other regular tessellation grids, such as square and triangular meshes, hexagonal cell geometry has noticeable merits in terms of hydrological modeling. First, hexagons eliminate the ambiguity of the cell neighborhood due to its uniform adjacency, and therefore, various weighting schemes and assumptions can be avoided in the cells' neighborhood. Consequently, hexagonal grids remove the island effect which is an obstacle when modeling watersheds in square grids with both direct and diagonal neighbors [1,2]. Additionally, the cell size is frequently approximated as the flow width in hydrological studies, and this approximation is more sound in hexagonal sampling than rectangular sampling due to its higher compactness, namely the higher area-to-perimeter ratio [3,4].

Research has been carried out to investigate algorithms to compute hydrological geomorphometry parameters in hexagonal meshes. For example, watershed delineation on a hexagonal grid was investigated by Liao, Tesfa, Duan, and Leung [2], where a group of hydrological functions on hexagonal meshes were explored, including flow direction and accumulation, watershed boundary extraction, stream networks, stream order, etc. The study evaluated their algorithm performance by comparing the hexagonal-mesh-based outputs to the square-mesh-based results and observed that the hexagonal mesh grid can contribute to an equivalent and even better performance than traditional methods [2]. The work was further improved in their latest research by adopting hybrid breaching-filling stream burning techniques [5]. In another study, valley lines were modeled based on hexagonal grids, and such a process was shown to maintain a more detailed shape and location accuracy compared to traditional square grids [6]. Wright [4] developed a regular hierarchical surface model where hydrological computation was generalized on hexagonal and triangular grids. The model also offered a pyramid framework to produce coarser values by a scaling function [4].

These existing algorithms can be easily migrated to hexagonal Discrete Global Grid Systems (DGGS), a spatial reference system that hierarchically partitions the Earth's surface by almost identical hexagonal cells [7]. In fact, researchers have shown increasing interest in managing multi-source geospatial data and developing environmental models to solve real-world problems by using open-sourced DGGS [8–11]. The proposed analytical operations on hexagonal meshes are useful in the development of hydrological analysis in the DGGS context. In particular, flow routing grids are fundamental in hydrological analysis, which is the basic grid for producing flow accumulation, flow networks, watersheds, etc. However, most of the current research accepted the D6 algorithm, which is analogous to the D8 algorithm over a square grid, to produce flow routing [2,4]. With D6 or D8 algorithms, the flow of a center cell is always routed to the neighboring cell with the lowest elevation [4]. In this study, we explored the other four methods to compute flow direction, essentially following multiple understanding and computations of the slope aspect, in the hexagonal DGGS environment. We evaluated the results by quantitively comparing the consequent flow accumulation and hydrological indices and visualizing the upslope area and watersheds.

The remainder of this paper is arranged as follows: Section 2 shows the quantization process of terrain data as the baseline of this paper. In Section 3, we explain the developed algorithms of hydrological operations in detail. Section 4 introduces three study areas and the experimental environment. Section 5 presents the experiment results. Section 6 discusses the results and points out the directions for future study.

2. Terrain Data Quantization

In this study, the Icosahedral Snyder Equal Area Aperture 3 Hexagonal Grid (ISEA3H) DGGS was adopted as the modeling grid system, and the source terrain data were the Canadian Digital Elevation Model (CDEM), gained from the Canadian Open Government Portal with a resolution of 0.75 arcsec in a south-north direction (https://open.canada.ca/data/en/dataset/7f245e4d-76c2-4caa-951a-45d1d2051333, accessed on 4 August 2021). We followed the quantization method of converting square grid to hexagonal grid elevations proposed by Li, McGrath and Stefanakis [9] who managed to resample elevations at centroid locations of hexagonal cells using bilinear interpolation. Elevation values at the cell centroid locations represent the elevation of a certain hexagonal cell. R library dggridR was used to locate grid cell centroids during this process [12]. Considering the CDEM data were at a resolution of about 400 m^2, the finest resolution of the ISEA3H DGGS was chosen as level 24 where the cell area is around 180.6 m^2. This was based on the Nyquist–Shannon sampling theorem, which states that the sample rate should be at least double the frequency of the signal component with the highest frequency [13]. By comparing the elevations of ground control points, previous research has shown that the difference between pre-DGGS and post-DGGS elevations was minor at the finest resolution level following the Nyquist–Shannon sampling theorem [9]. Another four successively coarser levels, namely levels 20 to 23, were also examined, where the cell area was 14,628.5, 4876.2, 1625.4, and 541.8 m^2, respectively. At coarser levels, we progressively degrade the elevation precision to maintain a rough ratio of horizontal to vertical resolution [9]. During the quantization process, the Quadrilateral 2-Dimensional Integer (Q2DI) indices, which have been implemented in the dggridR library, were also populated for each hexagonal cell. Q2DI is a coordinate-based cell indexing mechanism that is practical in locating neighboring cells around a center cell [14]. To avoid the edge effect, we assigned the edge cells without valid interpolation inputs void elevations.

3. Hydrological Operations

3.1. Pit Filling and Flat Removal

As suggested by previous studies, pits are usually spurious depressions and should be removed during the hydrological analysis [15,16]. In addition, flats are areas of cells with zero slope where flow direction cannot be determined merely with reference to its neighbors [17]. Thus, pits and flats need to be treated before computing flow directions [17]. This study adopted the Priority-flood depression-filling algorithm proposed by Barnes, et al. [18] and adjusted it in the ISEA3H DGGS context to remove pits and flat areas. The algorithm essentially starts from the study area boundary and progressively searches toward the interior, based on the ascending order of elevations in the Priority Queue, to assure that flows cannot be terminated and are along the path where elevations have the smallest changes [18]. This algorithm outperformed other alternatives and showed its feasibility on hexagonal grids [2,5,18]. In our implementation, we applied a small slope (1%) when filling the depression to avoid flat areas, as suggested by Barnes, Lehman and Mulla [18] and Liao, Tesfa, Duan and Leung [2]. Figure 1 shows an example of elevation changes and flow-direction updates after applying the Priority-flood depression-filling algorithm (cell spacing = 5 m). The central cell is considered a pit that does not have a lower neighbor (Figure 1). Flow directions are computed by the D6 algorithm, where the flow of a certain cell is always routed to its lowest neighboring cell [19]. The D6 algorithm is equivalent to the Maximum Downward Gradient (MDG) algorithm in this study, which will be explained more in the following sections. An elevation of 0.05 m is added to form a 1% slope to avoid flat areas after the pit-filling process. More details and step-by-step illustrations can be found in the previous studies [2,18].

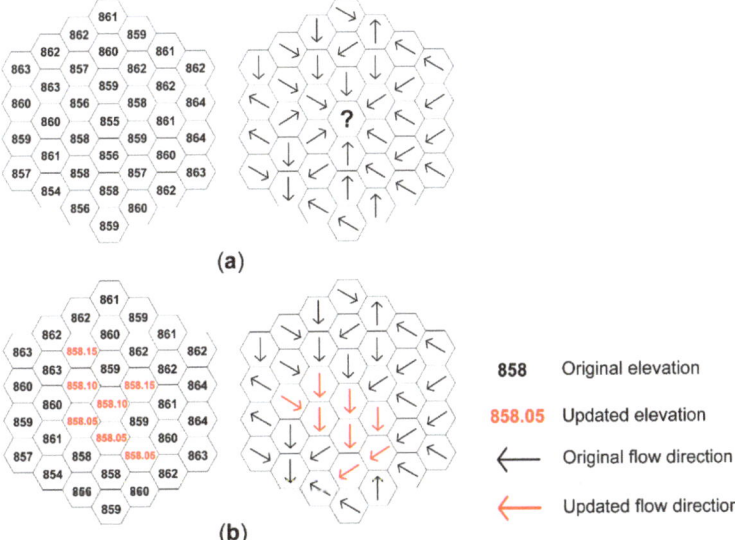

Figure 1. Illustration of elevation changes and flow direction updates after applying the Priority-flood depression-filling algorithm on hexagonal grids (cell spacing = 5 m; [18]): (**a**) original elevations and flow directions based on the D6 algorithm where the central cell is a pit [19]; (**b**) elevations and flow direction after pit-filling process where updated elevations and flow directions are marked as red.

3.2. Flow Direction

In this study, flow direction was computed based on five approaches to calculating the slope aspect in the ISEA3H DGGS: Maximum Adjacent Gradient (MAG), Maximum Downward Gradient (MDG), Multiple Downhill Neighbors (MDN), Finite-Difference Algorithm (FDA), and Best-Fit Plane (BFP) methods. The MAG and MDG methods describe the slope aspect as the direction of the first neighboring cell with the maximum absolute elevation difference or the lowest elevation value scanned clockwise from the north, respectively [20,21]. For the MAG method, if the aspect direction is toward an uphill cell, then its directly opposite direction will be assigned to the center cell as the aspect direction [22]. The MDN method examines all downhill neighbors and uses a 'mean vector' to represent the orientation of the 'mean surface' [23]. The FDA method calculates the finite difference of elevations, and the slope aspect is computed by combining partial derivatives along axes [20,23]. The BFP method fits a local plane surface for each center cell, and the normal vector of the local plane surface is used to calculate the aspect direction [20,23]. Among the five methods, the MAG and MDG lead to six restricted aspect angles, while the other three can result in arbitrary aspect angles ranging from 0 to 360°.

With the aspect angle computed by one of the five methods, the flow direction code 1–6 is assigned to the cell depending on which direction bin it falls in, no matter if the aspect angle is restricted or not (Figure 2). The direction code corresponds to six equally divided direction bins clockwise from north. Because a relative 30° shift of the hexagonal grids' orientation exists between every two successive resolutions in the ISEA3H DGGS, the specific direction code one cell takes depends on whether it is at an odd-resolution level or an even-resolution level (Figure 2).

Flow direction based on the MDG method on a hexagonal grid is essentially the D6 algorithm, adjusted from the D8 algorithm, applied to rectangular rasters, where the flow always travels along the path of the steepest descent [2,19]. However, flow directions computed by the other four methods, namely MAG, MDN, FDA, and BFP, can potentially cause close loops which will lead to the infinite upstream area [4]. To break the close loops, we adjusted the outlet-breaching methodology used by Jones [16] and extended it into the ISEA3H DGGS context. The specific algorithm has the following steps:

1. Populate all cells with their flow directions according to one of four methods: MAG, MDN, FDA, and BFP.
2. Scan all cells following their existing flow directions and record all close loops in a list.
3. Find out the lowest cell in each of the close loops, which is defined as the 'head' of the loop. Sort the close loops ascendingly by elevations of their 'head' cells.
4. Construct a 'tree' for the 'head' cell in the first close loop by viewing this cell as the tree root.
5. Deepen the tree by one level by adding the first-ring neighbors as the leaf nodes clockwise from north. Extend each of the leaf nodes by adding their first-ring neighbors as the new leaf nodes clockwise from the north. Duplicated leaf nodes are removed after all neighbors are added. At this point, the tree is deepened to three levels having all of its second-ring neighbors as the new leaf nodes.
6. Continuously deepen the tree until the first candidate outlet is found, where an outlet is defined as an edge cell or a cell with a lower elevation than the tree root. Examine if the candidate outlet flows back to the target 'head' cell. If it does, continue to enlarge the search ring until a legit outlet is found.
7. Trace the path from the root cell to the outlet cell and update the flow directions and elevations along the tracing path. New elevations of cells forming the tracing path are an arithmetic sequence with elevations of the root cell and the outlet cell as the first and last term.
8. Remove the broken close loop from the list. If the tracing path passes any cell in any unbroken close loop, remove this close loop from the list as well.
9. Repeat Steps 4–8 until all close loops in the list are broken sequentially.

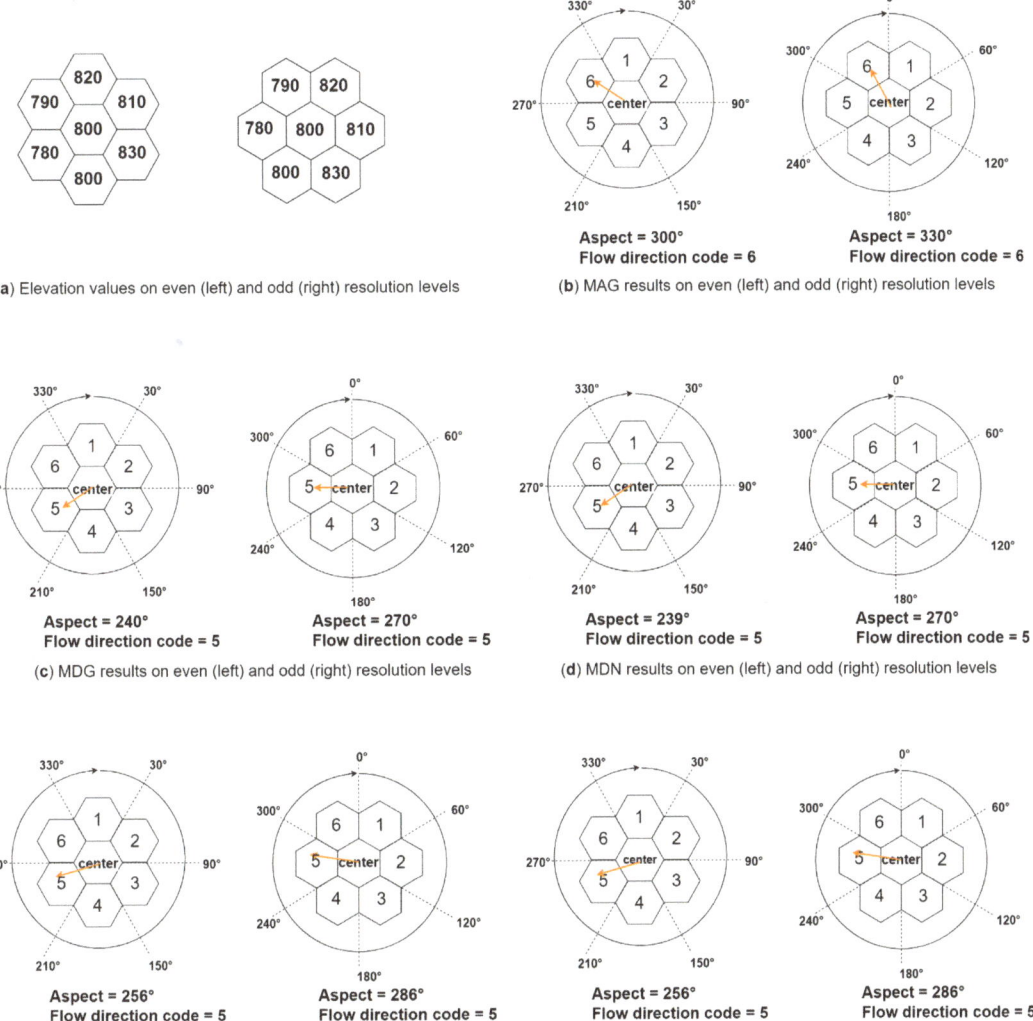

Figure 2. Illustration of flow direction code assignment an even and odd resolution levels based on (**b**) Maximum Adjacent Gradient (MAG), (**c**) Maximum Downward Gradient (MDG), (**d**) Multiple Downhill Neighbors (MDN), (**e**) Finite-Difference Algorithm (FDA), and (**f**) Best-Fit Plane (BFP) methods. Elevation values of cells are shown in (**a**).

Figure 3 presents an example of treating a 'head' cell in a close loop. Cells' Q2DI coordinates, elevation values, and flow direction are shown in Figure 3a, where the flow directions result from the MAG method. For example, the cell (58,55) has the highest absolute difference among six neighbors of the cell (57,54), and therefore, the cell (57,54) flows to (56,53) which is in the directly opposite direction of the cell (58,55). At this stage, there should not be any pits and flat areas. As shown in Figure 3a, cells (57,55), (56,54), and (56,55) form a close loop and the 'head' cell is (57,55). To break this close loop, a 'tree' is constructed and extended for this 'head' cell, and a candidate outlet cell (60,56) with a lower elevation of 854 m is found at Level 3 (Figure 3b–d). The outlet is finalized if confirmed not to flow back to the target 'head' cell. Then the flow directions and elevations along the tracing path from the 'head' cell to the outlet are updated accordingly. Figure 3 shows a case at an even-resolution level, and close loops at an odd-resolution level are broken with the same strategy.

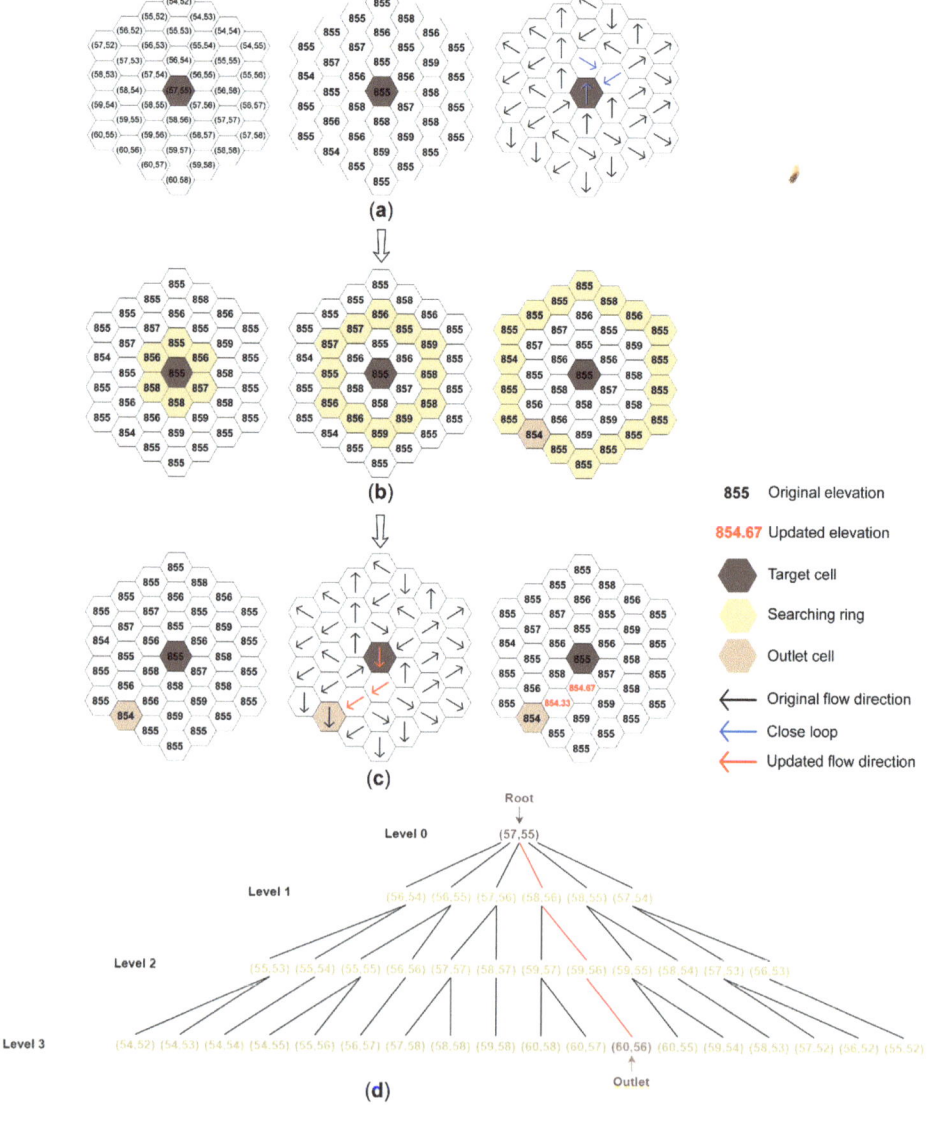

Figure 3. Illustration of the algorithm to break a close loop at an even-resolution level: (**a**) Coordinates, elevations, and flow directions of a sample group of cells with an existing close loop, where a 'head' cell with the lowest elevation within the loop is determined; (**b**) Search by enlarging rings around the target 'head' cell until a candidate outlet is found at the third ring; (**c**) Examine if the candidate outlet flows back to the target 'head' cell, if not, update the flow directions and elevation values along the tracing path; (**d**) A 'tree' structure is constructed during the search process.

3.3. Flow Accumulation

Flow accumulation, or upslope area, is the total catchment area above a point [15,24]. Flow accumulation algorithms typically count the number of cells contributing flow to the target cells and multiply the count by the cell area [15]. Computing flow accumulation employs a recursive flow climbing algorithm based on the given flow routing grid [15,25]. The algorithm of computing flow accumulation has the following steps [26]:

1. Initialize the inflow count as 0 and upslope count as 1 for all cells.
2. Iterate the cells and determine the inflow count with reference to the existing flow directions for each cell. In other words, the number of cells whose flow direction points to the center cell is saved as the inflow count for the center cell, ranging from 0 to 6.
3. Scan all cells and identify those whose inflow count is 0. For each of the zero-cells, determine which neighboring cell the zero-cell flows into and increase this neighboring cell's upslope count by the zero-cell's upslope count.
4. If this neighboring cell's inflow count is negative and it is not an edge cell, then reset it to 0 and decrease the zero-cell's inflow count by 1; if not, decrease the inflow count for all cells involved by 1.
5. Repeat Steps 3 and 4 until the inflow count for all cells are negative.
6. The flow accumulation is then calculated as the upslope count multiplying by the cell area.

3.4. Watersheds above Outlets

The watershed over a specific cell is determined by recursively identifying all the cells that contribute to this defined outlet cell according to the flow routing grid. The longitude–latitude coordinate of a potential outlet of interest can be converted to the corresponding cell using the dggridR library. The delineated watershed may differ when the flow routing grids are created by different methods.

3.5. Hydrological Indices

Two hydrological indices are produced, including the Topographic Wetness Index (TWI) and Stream Power Index (SPI). TWI is a geo-morphometric variable used to quantitatively measure the local relief and evaluate the runoff in flood studies, and SPI indicates the potential of the stream to cause erosion and the intensity of surface runoff [24,27]:

$$\text{TWI} = \ln\left(\frac{\alpha}{\tan \beta}\right) \quad (1)$$

$$\text{SPI} = \alpha \times \tan \beta \quad (2)$$

where α is the specific catchment area of a certain cell, and β is the slope gradient in radians at this cell location. The specific catchment area α is defined as the upslope area per unit width of contour and calculated as the upslope area divided by cell spacing [24].

4. Study Area and Experimental Environment

We tested our algorithms over three regions, each around 170 km^2 in area (Figure 4). Three study areas locate in Alberta, Canada, and were at different levels of roughness: the Canmore area is the roughest with elevations ranging from 1360 to 2919 m, the Calgary area is moderately rough where elevations range from 1043 to 1274 m, and the Buffalo Lake area has the smoothest terrain with 799 to 850 m elevations. CDEM data were quantized in ISEA3H DGGS at levels 20 to 24 within these study area extents, following the method described in Section 2. All developed functionalities were tested in the ISEA3H DGGS from level 20 to 24, by using the machine with 8 cores, 12 GB memory, and 2× Intel(R) Xeon(R) CPU L5520 @ 2.27GHz.

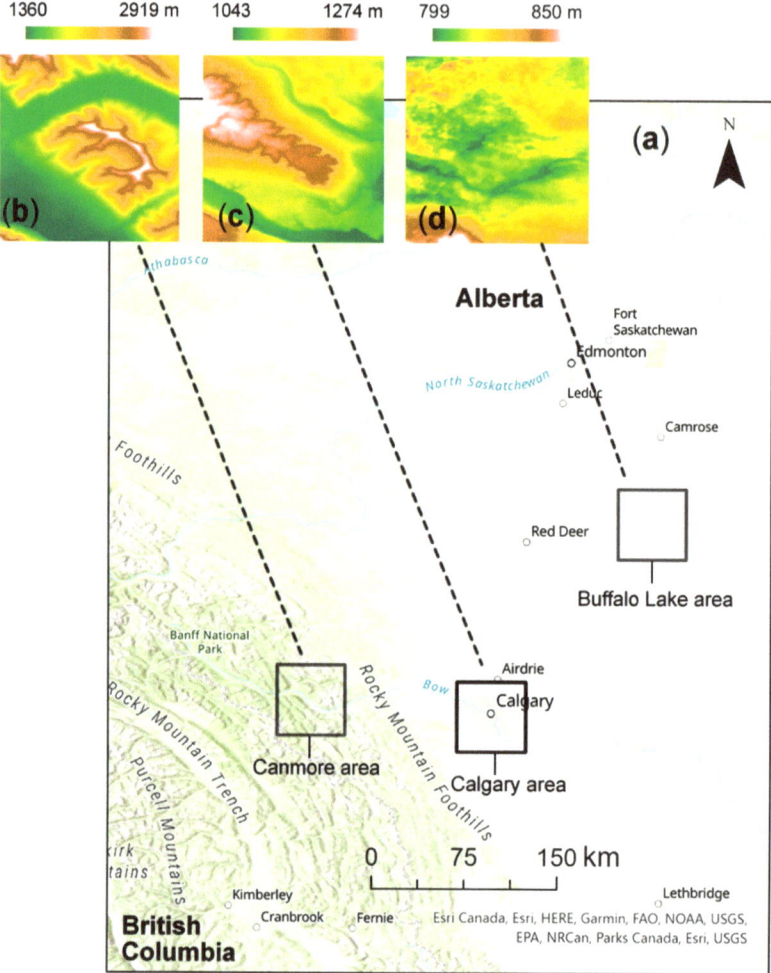

Figure 4. The spatial locations of three study areas (**a**) in Alberta, Canada, and the rendered elevations [28] in (**b**) Canmore area, (**c**) Calgary area, and (**d**) Buffalo Lake area.

5. Results

Flow directions computed by five algorithms were not directly and quantitatively compared because they were not linear measurements, while the different flow routing grids were reflected by the resulting flow accumulation, watershed delineation, and hydrological indices computation. We pair-wisely compared flow accumulation and hydrological indices derived from multiple flow routing grids and visualized the flow accumulation and watersheds above an outlet at the finest resolution level.

5.1. Flow Accumulation

Based on flow routing grids generated by five algorithms, flow accumulation was recursively computed over all tested areas and resolution levels and compared pair-wisely by Pearson correlation coefficients (r). The results showed that flow accumulation derived from different methods has positive correlation coefficients in all cases, while the coefficient values varied dramatically among resolution levels and study areas (Figure 5). The correlation between the MDG and MDN showed a pattern that r was lower at odd-resolution levels than that at even-resolution levels (Figure 5). It was also noticed that the coefficients between the FDA and BFP methods remained high ($r > 0.7$) among all resolutions in three areas (Figure 5).

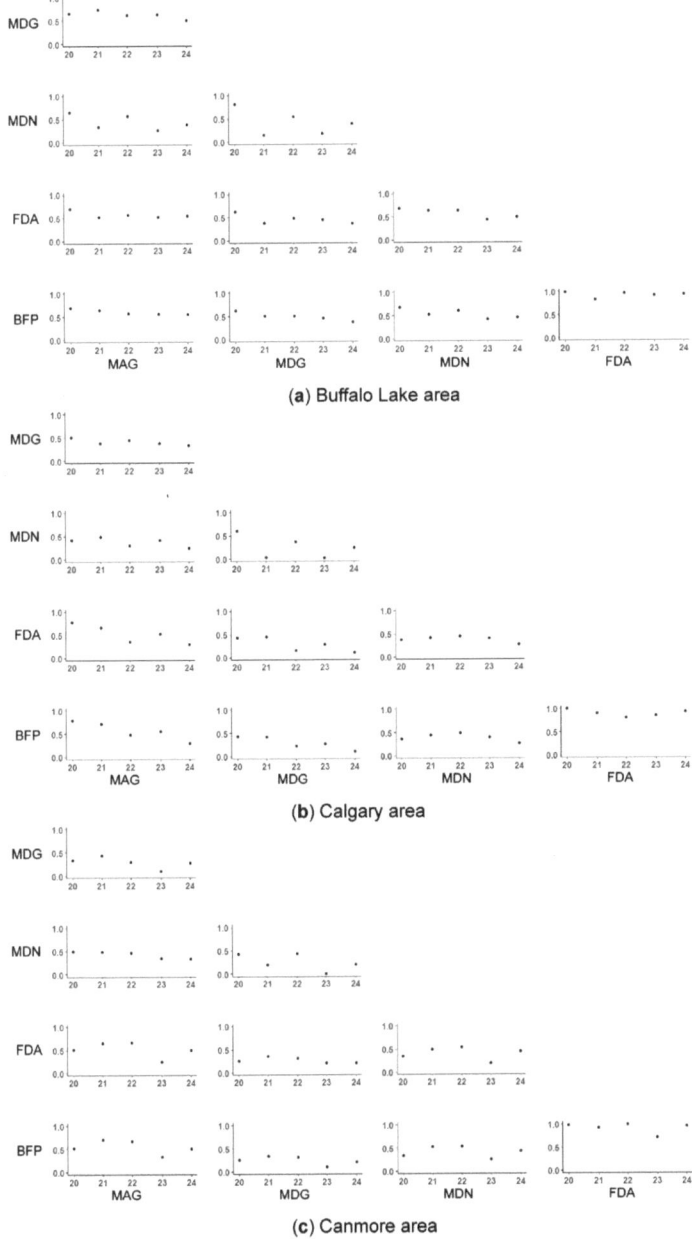

Figure 5. Correlation matrix of Pearson correlation coefficients of calculated flow accumulation by Maximum Adjacent Gradient (MAG), Maximum Downward Gradient (MDG), Multiple Downhill Neighbors (MDN), Finite-Difference Algorithm (FDA), and Best-Fit Plane (BFP) methods from level 20 to 24 in (a) Buffalo Lake area, (b) Calgary area, and (c) Canmore area ($p < 0.0001$).

Figure 6 visualizes the flow accumulation generated by five algorithms in three areas at level 24. The maximum flow accumulation of the major outlet within an area was different among various algorithms, most apparently in the Buffalo Lake area which has the smoothest terrain, where the MDN algorithm led to 3 km² flow accumulation while the MAG and MDG algorithms led to 9 km² (Figure 6). In the Canmore area, however, the MAG and MDG algorithm contributed to diverse flow routing scenarios, where the maximum flow accumulation was 12 and 20 km², respectively (Figure 6). We also computed flow directions and flow accumulation among three study areas by Hydrologic Engineering Center's Hydrologic Modeling System (HEC-HMS) model which adopts the D8 algorithm [29]. Figure 7 visualizes the difference in flow accumulation of a sample branch computed by the HEC-HMS model and the MDG method, namely the D6 algorithm, at the finest resolution.

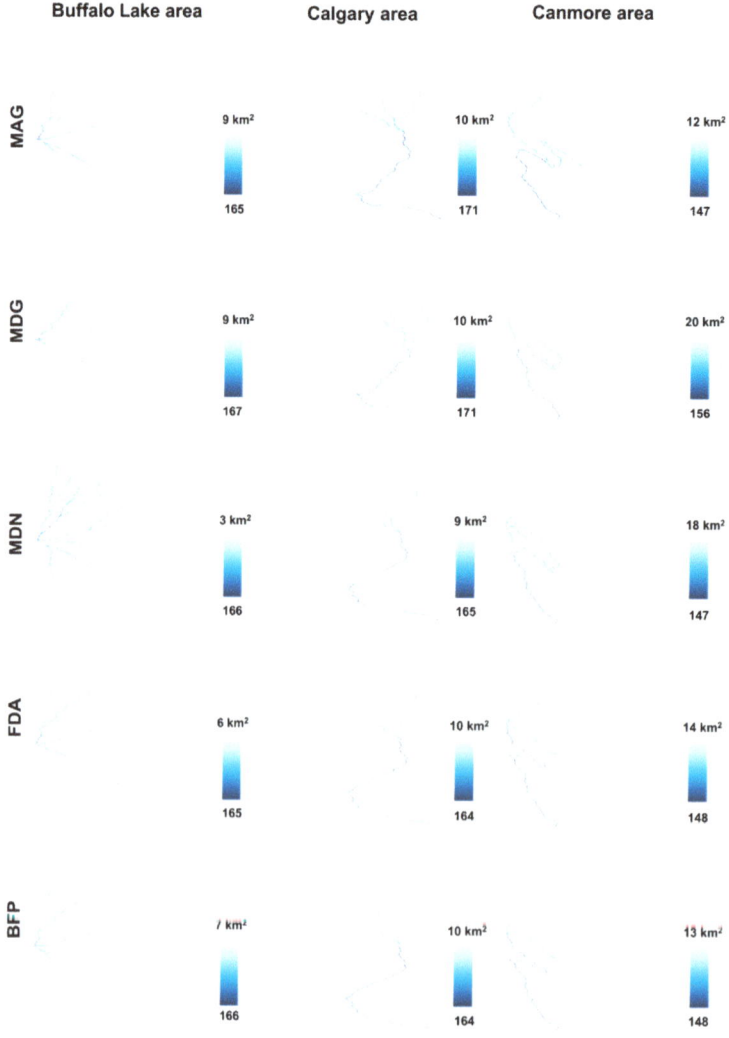

Figure 6. Visualization of flow accumulation in three study areas at level 24, derived from Maximum Adjacent Gradient (MAG), Maximum Downward Gradient (MDG), Multiple Downhill Neighbors (MDN), Finite-Difference Algorithm (FDA), and Best-Fit Plane (BFP) methods.

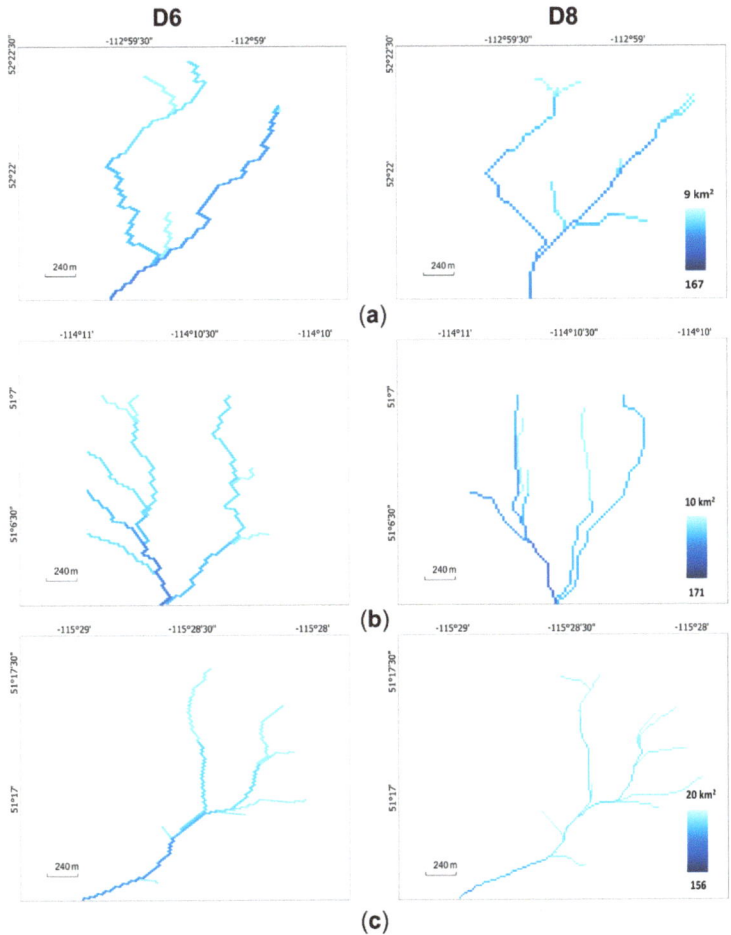

Figure 7. Visualized comparison of a zoom-in sample branch computed by D6 and D8 algorithms at level 24 in (**a**) Buffalo Lake area, (**b**) Calgary area, and (**c**) Canmore area.

5.2. Watershed Delineation

We defined a random point in each of the three study areas as an example to show the generation of the watershed above it, based on different flow routing grids resulting from multiple slope aspect calculation methods. The longitude–latitude coordinates of the defined outlets are (112.92°W, 52.34°N), (114.06°W, 51.09°N), and (115.46°W, 51.25°N) in the Buffalo Lake, Calgary, and Canmore areas, respectively. The visualization of the watersheds above the defined outlets at level 24 is shown in Figure 8. According to the visualization, created watersheds by the MAG and MDG algorithms in the Canmore area were evidently different from the watersheds created by the other three algorithms (Figure 8). Nonetheless, watersheds based on various flow routing grids in the Buffalo Lake and Calgary areas showed slight differences (Figure 8).

Figure 8. Visualization of the watersheds above a random point in each of three study areas at level 24, derived from Maximum Adjacent Gradient (MAG), Maximum Downward Gradient (MDG), Multiple Downhill Neighbors (MDN), Finite-Difference Algorithm (FDA), and Best-Fit Plane (BFP) methods.

5.3. Hydrological Indices

The Pearson correlation coefficients (r) comparing the TWI values resulting from different slope algorithms were greater than 0.7 in the Canmore area, and greater than 0.5 in the Calgary area, across all resolution levels (Figure 9b,c). The correlation coefficients (r) were relatively lower in the Buffalo Lake area, ranging from 0.3 to 0.9 across the levels (Figure 9a). A high positive correlation ($r > 0.7$) was observed between the FDA and BFP methods in all study areas (Figure 9). The SPI values derived from different slope aspect algorithms were diverse across resolution levels, which was reflected by highly varied coefficient values without a clear pattern in most cases (Figure 10), except that r remained high ($r > 0.9$) between the FDA and BFP algorithms in the Canmore area (Figure 10c).

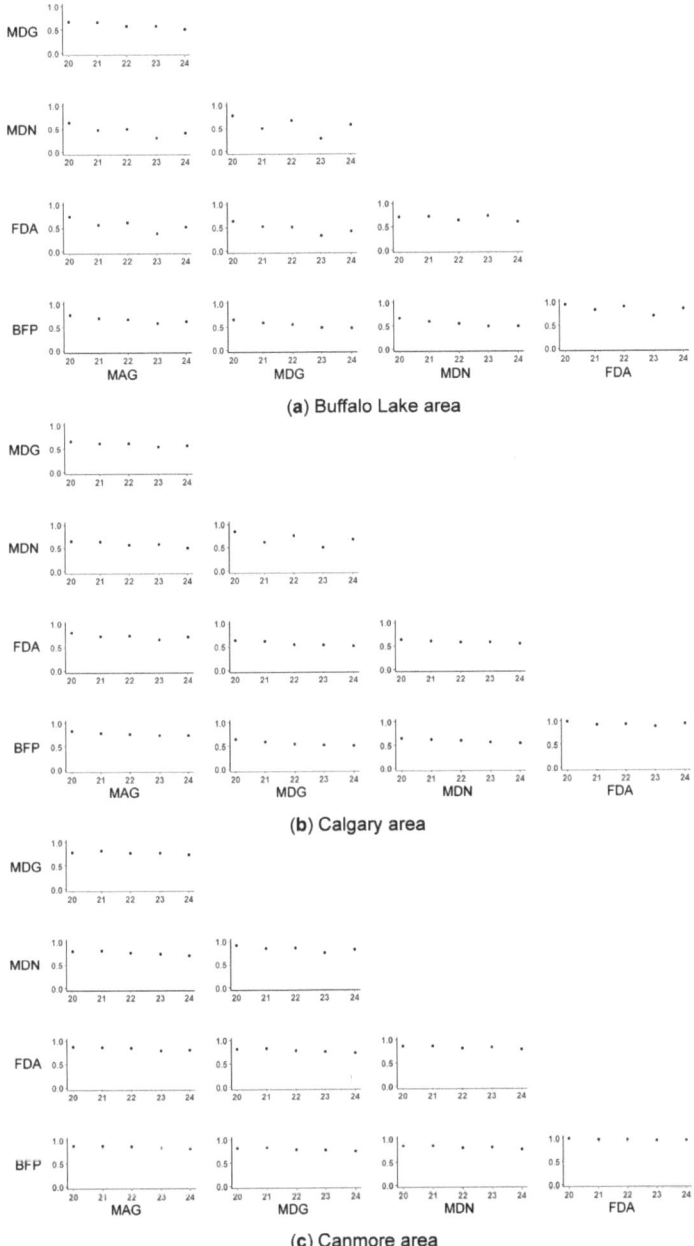

Figure 9. Correlation matrix of Pearson correlation coefficients of calculated Topographic Wetness Index (TWI) by Maximum Adjacent Gradient (MAG), Maximum Downward Gradient (MDG), Multiple Downhill Neighbors (MDN), Finite-Difference Algorithm (FDA), and Best-Fit Plane (BFP) methods from level 20 to 24 in (**a**) Buffalo Lake area, (**b**) Calgary area, and (**c**) Canmore area ($p < 0.0001$).

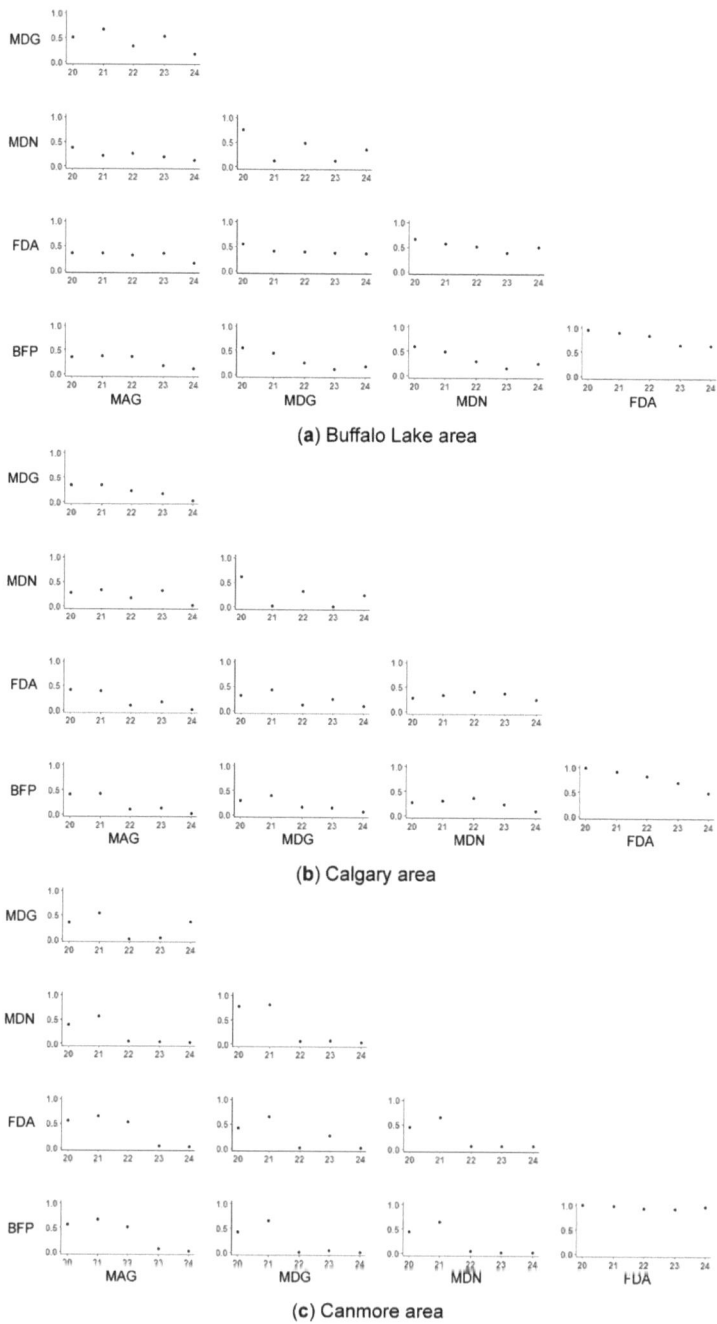

Figure 10. Correlation matrix of Pearson correlation coefficients of calculated Stream Power Index (SPI) by Maximum Adjacent Gradient (MAG), Maximum Downward Gradient (MDG), Multiple Downhill Neighbors (MDN), Finite-Difference Algorithm (FDA), and Best-Fit Plane (BFP) methods from level 20 to 24 in (**a**) Buffalo Lake area, (**b**) Calgary area, and (**c**) Canmore area ($p < 0.0001$).

6. Discussion

6.1. Comparison between Flow Routing Methods

The correlation of flow accumulation among five methods differed a lot at multiple granularities in three areas, which reflected that the slope aspect and caused flow routing grids can highly vary depending on the modeling resolution and study area. These uncertainties propagated to the computation of TWI and SPI. Nonetheless, it was observed that the FDA and BFP methods led to highly correlated flow accumulation, TWI, and SPI, in most cases of various modeling resolutions and study areas. This aligned with the conclusion on square grids where the slope and aspect values obtained by the third-order finite-difference algorithm without a weighting factor on eight neighboring cells were the same as those for a least-square linear surface fit to these eight neighboring cells [26]. Among five algorithms used in computing flow directions, the MDG, namely the D6 algorithm, is recommended, because it can avoid close loops after pit-filling processes [2,19,30]. Although we proposed an algorithm to break close loops, it took extra computation time, especially over large areas.

Although without a clear relationship, the differences between calculated flow accumulation and SPI caused by different algorithms, reflected by their pair-wise correlation coefficients, also depended on the resolution level. Such differences in slope gradient and TWI had less sensitivity to resolution, where the correlation coefficients generally remained at the same level across the resolutions.

6.2. Geovisualization in Hexagonal Discrete Global Grids

In this paper, geovisualization was used to convey differences in flow accumulation and watersheds delineation resulting from multiple methods of flow routing production. In terms of geovisualization, DGGS can avoid deformation of the content given that DGGS cells are almost uniform in size and shape at each resolution level [7]. Although geospatial objects in a DGGS need to be projected to be displayed, the expressed geospatial information does not depend on the chosen projection [31]. However, the current visualization of geospatial data modeled in a DGGS relies on existing approaches to display vector or raster data. In this study, modeled geospatial data in the hexagonal DGGS were exported to Esri shapefile to be visualized. Other examples of DGGS visualization include the linkage to PostgreSQL or Leaflet to enable geovisualization in static maps or interactive web maps, respectively [32–34]. Some remaining challenges of visualizing massive data modeled in a DGGS at fine resolutions are, for instance, data I/O, data interoperation, and data rendering [35].

6.3. Study Impact and Future Work

The outcome of this paper is useful for hydrological analysis in hexagonal grids, and the developed operations can be generalized in hexagonal DGGS with various aperture, for example, aperture 3, 4, or 7. In previous research, Chaudhuri, Gray and Robertson [10] managed to implement a height above nearest drainage (HAND) model in a hexagonal DGGS platform, while leaving the processes such as determining drainage directions, calculating drainage accumulation, and generating watershed boundaries as GIS-preprocessing based on traditional square Digital Elevation Model (DEM). Hydrological operations developed and compared in this paper are meaningful for flood inundation modeling, for instance, a HAND model, in a pure hexagonal DGGS environment. In addition, flood susceptibility modeling frequently required hydrological parameters as inputs to machine learning models such as a support vector machine, gradient boosting machine, and neural network [36–38]. Flood susceptibility predictions based on machine learning methods in hexagonal DGGS can be efficient taking advantage of its discrete nature and power of multi-source data integration [31].

One of the major future study directions is to parallelize the pit-filling and flow accumulation processes. One option is to decompose the dataset into regular tiles and solve each of the tiles independently, then combine adjacent tiles by joining their edges. For example, a linearly scaling algorithm was implemented by Barnes [39], which succeeded in partitioning DEM with regular tiles and parallelizing the Priority-flood depression filling process. Barnes [40] also proposed a parallel algorithm to produce flow accumulation by two sequential MapReduce operations via Message Passing Interface (MPI). On the other hand, the area can be decomposed as sub-basins as the independent units in line with the natural watershed boundaries, so that the stream networks can be connected merely at the watershed outlet points [41]. These parallelization algorithms can be potentially migrated to a hexagonal DGGS environment in the future. Other future directions include allowing flow dispersion when computing flow directions, for example, partitioning and assigning upslope counts to lower neighbors proportionally to their slope gradient [15].

7. Conclusions

This study examined five methods to compute flow directions in an ISEA3H DGGS and developed hydrological operations including flow accumulation, watershed delineation, and hydrological indices computation. An algorithm was also proposed to break the potential close loops created by flow routing. Flow accumulation and hydrological indices resulting from multiple methods were compared quantitatively and visually. It was revealed that the resulting flow routing grids can vary among different approaches, and the impact of such variation can propagate to the follow-up hydrological productions. Among five methods, the D6 algorithm is recommended because it can avoid close loops after pit-filling processes. This research can be a guide for future flood inundation modeling or susceptibility modeling in a pure hexagonal DGGS environment.

Author Contributions: Conceptualization, E.S., H.M. and M.L.; methodology, E.S., H.M. and M.L.; software, M.L.; validation, E.S., H.M. and M.L.; formal analysis, M.L.; investigation, M.L.; resources, E.S. and H.M.; writing—original draft preparation, M.L.; writing—review and editing, E.S., H.M.; visualization, M.L.; supervision, E.S., H.M. All authors have read and agreed to the published version of the manuscript.

Funding: This research was funded by Canadian Natural Sciences and Engineering Research Council (NSERC) Discovery Grant program, grant number RGPIN/03977-2019.

Data Availability Statement: Publicly available datasets were analyzed in this study. This data can be found here: https://open.canada.ca/data/en/dataset/7f245e4d-76c2-4caa-951a-45d1d2051333 (accessed on 4 August 2021).

Acknowledgments: We acknowledge the technical advice from the Research Computing Services at the University of Calgary.

Conflicts of Interest: The authors declare no conflict of interest.

References

1. Johnston, C.M.; Dewald, T.G.; Bondelid, T.R.; Worstell, B.B.; McKay, L.D.; Rea, A.; Moore, R.B.; Goodall, J.L. *Evaluation of Catchment Delineation Methods for the Medium-Resolution National Hydrography Dataset*; Scientific Investigations Report 2009–5233; U.S. Department of the Interior, U.S. Geological Survey: Reston, VA, USA, 2009.
2. Liao, C.; Tesfa, T.; Duan, Z.; Leung, L.R. Watershed delineation on a hexagonal mesh grid. *Environ. Model. Softw.* **2020**, *128*, 104702. [CrossRef]
3. Gallant, J.C.; Hutchinson, M.F. A differential equation for specific catchment area. *Water Resour. Res.* **2011**, *47*, W05535. [CrossRef]
4. Wright, J.W. Regular Hierarchical Surface Models: A Conceptual Model of Scale Variation in a GIS and its Application to Hydrological Geomorphometry. Ph.D. Thesis, University of Otago, Dunedin, Otago, New Zealand, August 2017.
5. Liao, C.; Zhou, T.; Xu, D.; Barnes, R.; Bisht, G.; Li, H.Y.; Tan, Z.; Tesfa, T.; Duan, Z.; Engwirda, D.; et al. Advances in hexagon mesh-based flow direction modeling. *Adv. Water Resour.* **2022**, *160*, 104099. [CrossRef]
6. Wang, L.; Ai, T.; Shen, Y.; Li, J. The isotropic organization of DEM structure and extraction of valley lines using hexagonal grid. *Trans. GIS* **2020**, *24*, 483–507. [CrossRef]
7. Alderson, T.; Purss, M.; Du, X.; Mahdavi-Amiri, A.; Samavati, F. Digital Earth Platforms. In *Manual of Digital Earth*; Guo, H., Goodchild, M., Annoni, A., Eds.; Springer: Singapore, 2020; pp. 25–54.
8. Hojati, M.; Robertson, C. Integrating Cellular Automata and Discrete Global Grid Systems: A Case Study into Wildfire Modelling. In Proceedings of the 23rd AGILE Conference on Geographic Information Science, Chania, Greece, 16–19 June 2020. [CrossRef]

9. Li, M.; McGrath, H.; Stefanakis, E. Integration of heterogeneous terrain data into Discrete Global Grid Systems. *Cartogr. Geogr. Inf. Sci.* **2021**, *48*, 546–564. [CrossRef]
10. Chaudhuri, C.; Gray, A.; Robertson, C. InundatEd-v1.0: A height above nearest drainage (HAND)-based flood risk modeling system using a discrete global grid system. *Geosci. Model Dev.* **2021**, *14*, 3295–3315. [CrossRef]
11. Robertson, C.; Chaudhuri, C.; Hojati, M.; Roberts, S.A. An integrated environmental analytics system (IDEAS) based on a DGGS. *ISPRS J. Photogramm. Remote Sens.* **2020**, *162*, 214–228. [CrossRef]
12. Barnes, R.; Sahr, K.; Evenden, G.; Johnson, A.; Warmerdam, F. dggridR: Discrete Global Grids for R. R Package Version 2.0.4. Available online: https://github.com/r-barnes/dggridR (accessed on 5 March 2020).
13. Shannon, C.E. Communication in the Presence of Noise. *Proc. IRE* **1949**, *37*, 10–21. [CrossRef]
14. Sahr, K. Location coding on icosahedral aperture 3 hexagon discrete global grids. *Comput. Environ. Urban Syst.* **2008**, *32*, 174–187. [CrossRef]
15. Tarboton, D.G. A new method for the determination of flow directions and upslope areas in grid digital elevation models. *Water Resour. Res.* **1997**, *33*, 309–319. [CrossRef]
16. Jones, R. Algorithms for using a DEM for mapping catchment areas of stream sediment samples. *Comput. Geosci.* **2002**, *28*, 1051–1060. [CrossRef]
17. Kenny, F.; Matthews, B.; Todd, K. Routing overland flow through sinks and flats in interpolated raster terrain surfaces. *Comput. Geosci.* **2008**, *34*, 1417–1430. [CrossRef]
18. Barnes, R.; Lehman, C.; Mulla, D. Priority-flood: An optimal depression-filling and watershed-labeling algorithm for digital elevation models. *Comput. Geosci.* **2014**, *62*, 117–127. [CrossRef]
19. Wright, J.W.; Moore, A.B.; Leonard, G.H. Flow direction algorithms in a hierarchical hexagonal surface model. *J. Spat. Sci.* **2014**, *59*, 333–346. [CrossRef]
20. Travis, M.R. *VIEWIT: Computation of Seen Areas, Slope, and Aspect for Land-Use Planning*; Department of Agriculture, Forest Service, Pacific Southwest Forest and Range Experiment Station: Albany, CA, USA, 1975; p. 70, Rep. PSW 11.
21. Shanholtz, V.O.; Desai, C.J.; Zhang, N.; Kleene, J.W.; Metz, C.D.; Flagg, J.M. Hydrologic/water quality modeling in a GIS environment. *ASAE* **1990**, *90*, 3033.
22. Skidmore, A.K. A comparison of techniques for calculating gradient and aspect from a gridded digital elevation model. *Int. J. Geogr. Inf. Syst.* **1989**, *3*, 323–334. [CrossRef]
23. Hodgson, M.E. Comparison of angles from surface slope/aspect algorithms. *Cartogr. Geogr. Inf. Syst.* **1998**, *25*, 173–185. [CrossRef]
24. Moore, I.D.; Grayson, R.B.; Ladson, A.R. Digital terrain modelling: A review of hydrological, geomorphological, and biological applications. *Hydrol. Process.* **1991**, *5*, 3–30. [CrossRef]
25. Freeman, T.G. Calculating catchment area with divergent flow based on a regular grid. *Comput. Geosci.* **1991**, *17*, 413–422. [CrossRef]
26. Raaflaub, L.D.; Collins, M.J. The effect of error in gridded digital elevation models on the estimation of topographic parameters. *Environ. Model. Softw.* **2006**, *21*, 710–732. [CrossRef]
27. Beven, K.J.; Kirkby, M.J. A physically based, variable contributing area model of basin hydrology/Un modèle à base physique de zone d'appel variable de l'hydrologie du bassin versant. *Hydrol. Sci. Bull.* **1979**, *24*, 43–69. [CrossRef]
28. NRCan. Canadian Digital Elevation Model, 1945–2011. Available online: https://ftp.maps.canada.ca/pub/nrcan_rncan/elevation/cdem_mnec/ (accessed on 4 August 2021).
29. HEC. Hydrologic Modeling System v.4.9.0. Available online: https://www.hec.usace.army.mil/software/hec-hms/default.aspx (accessed on 5 April 2022).
30. Wang, L.; Liu, H. An efficient method for identifying and filling surface depressions in digital elevation models for hydrologic analysis and modelling. *Int. J. Geogr. Inf. Sci.* **2006**, *20*, 193–213. [CrossRef]
31. Li, M.; Stefanakis, E. Geospatial operations of discrete global grid systems—A comparison with traditional GIS. *J. Geovis. Spat. Anal.* **2020**, *4*, 26. [CrossRef]
32. Leaflet. Leaflet: An Open-Source JavaScript Library for Mobile-Friendly Interactive Maps. Available online: https://leafletjs.com/ (accessed on 10 March 2020).
33. OpenEAGGR. Open Equal Area Global GRid. Available online: https://github.com/riskaware-ltd/open-eaggr (accessed on 26 November 2019).
34. PostgreSQL. PostgreSQL: The World's Most Advanced Open Source Relational Database. Available online: https://www.postgresql.org/ (accessed on 1 April 2022).
35. Hojati, M.; Robertson, C.; Roberts, S.; Chaudhuri, C. GIScience research challenges for realizing discrete global grid systems as a Digital Earth. *Big Earth Data* **2022**, 1–22, ahead-of-print. [CrossRef]
36. Tehrany, M.S.; Jones, S.; Shabani, F. Identifying the essential flood conditioning factors for flood prone area mapping using machine learning techniques. *Catena* **2019**, *175*, 174–192. [CrossRef]
37. Esfandiari, M.; Jabari, S.; McGrath, H.; Coleman, D. Flood mapping using random forest and identifying the essential conditioning factors: A case study in Fredericton, New Brunswick, Canada. *ISPRS Ann. Photogramm. Remote Sens. Spat. Inf. Sci.* **2020**, *V-3-2020*, 609–615. [CrossRef]
38. McGrath, H.; Gohl, P.N. Accessing the impact of meteorological variables on machine learning flood susceptibility mapping. *Remote Sens.* **2022**, *14*, 1656. [CrossRef]

39. Barnes, R. Parallel Priority-Flood depression filling for trillion cell digital elevation models on desktops or clusters. *Comput. Geosci.* **2016**, *96*, 56–68. [CrossRef]
40. Barnes, R. Parallel non-divergent flow accumulation for trillion cell digital elevation models on desktops or clusters. *Environ. Model. Softw.* **2017**, *92*, 202–212. [CrossRef]
41. Gong, J.; Xie, J. Extraction of drainage networks from large terrain datasets using high throughput computing. *Comput. Geosci.* **2009**, *35*, 337–346. [CrossRef]

Article

Studying the Utilization of a Map-Based Visualization with Vitality Datasets by Domain Experts

Kenji Wada [1,*], Günter Wallner [1,2] and Steven Vos [1,3]

1. Department of Industrial Design, Eindhoven University of Technology, 5600 MB Eindhoven, The Netherlands; g.wallner@tue.nl (G.W.); s.vos@tue.nl (S.V.)
2. Institute of Computer Graphics, Johannes Kepler University Linz, 4040 Linz, Austria
3. School of Sport Studies, Fontys University of Applied Sciences, 5644 HZ Eindhoven, The Netherlands
* Correspondence: k.wada@tue.nl

Abstract: With the rapid growth of information technology and geographic information science, many map-based visualization applications for decision-making have been proposed. These applications are used in various contexts. Our study provides empirical evidence of how domain experts utilize map-based data visualization for generating insights into vitality with respect to health-related concepts. We conducted a study to understand domain experts' knowledge, approach, and experience. Nine domain experts participated in the study, with three experts each from the fields of government, business, and research. The study followed a mixed-methods approach involving an online survey, open-ended tasks, and semi-structured interviews. For this purpose, a map-based data visualization application containing various vitality-related datasets was developed for the open-ended tasks. Our study confirms the importance of maps in this domain but also shows that vitality is strongly geographical. Furthermore, we found that map-based visualizations require multiple data sources and dimensions to enhance the utilization of them in the context of vitality. Therefore, our study suggests the necessity of a combination of multiple datasets as 'vitality themes' to efficiently communicate this particular subject to experts. As such, our results provide guidelines for designing map-based data visualizations that support the decision-making process across various domain experts in the field of vitality.

Keywords: geovisualization; map-based visualization; vitality; domain experts; open-ended tasks

1. Introduction

Visualizations offer great potential for uncovering information in data and efficiently communicating complex quantitative information [1,2]. Offering cognitive support for understanding a large amount of information [1,3], visualizations are increasingly used to assist in decision-making processes [4]. As such, information visualization is used to solve real-world problems in a variety of different formats [5], such as defining sources of contamination [6], reducing crime [7], and improving pedestrian safety [8]. These real-world problems are often complicated due to the various data sources and people involved [5]. Consequently, it remains challenging to make visualization applications useful to such diverse audiences [9]. Another challenge is that a majority of the data available today contain geographic references, such as geographic coordinates and postal addresses, which brings diverse information but also complexity [10]. Therefore, the consideration of spatial data is important in visualization. Geographic visualizations ("geovisualizations" for short) have the potential to represent such complicated data, including location attributes [10].

There is also an increasing interest in human factors in visualization research [3]. Tory and Möller [3] indicate several human–computer-interaction (HCI) methods for designing and evaluating visualization systems such as User- and Task-Based Design, Perception-

and Cognition-Based Design, and User-Centered Design. Among those HCI methods, our study considers "User- and Task-Based Design" to address users' preferences, knowledge, experience, and processes in a map-based data visualization containing various vitality datasets through qualitative research. We use a map as the format of information visualization in this study, considering its accessibility for both technical and non-technical users, as discussed by several open-data studies, such as [11,12].

1.1. Aim of This Study

This study is a part of an ongoing project to promote vitality (e.g., physical health, mental health, and social cohesion) among urban citizens. Different domains, such as health and physical activity research, have covered the concept of vitality [13]. In the domain of industrial design, there is an increased interest in data-enabled applications using users' behavioral data to improve people's vitality [14]. In the field of geography, Sui [15] discussed the importance of Geographic Information Systems (GISs) in public health, and vice versa. In our case, we are specifically interested in how a map-based data visualization similar to a GIS conveys information about vitality, which constitutes a multi-dimensionality construct [16] for different domain experts. GIS utilizes multiple datasets from different sources yet communicates subject matters effectively [17]. Furthermore, Public Participation Geographic Information Systems (PPGISs) have targeted a variety of stakeholders [17], an aspect in line with the purpose of our study.

Given these backgrounds, our main research question for this study is "How does a map-based visualization containing various vitality data support the visual analysis process among different domain experts?" To answer this question, we investigated the following user-related points:

1. Insight generation and approach of visual analysis by users;
2. Relationship between the selection of vitality datasets and participants' expertise;
3. Amount, details, and kinds of data preferred;
4. Preference and impression;
5. Applicability of this type of visualization to domain experts' projects in practice.

The goal of our study explores how domain experts utilize vitality-related datasets on a map-based data visualization. This study crosses different topics such as vitality, geovisualization, and human factors. Therefore, in the following subsection, we discuss related work by separating it into three subsections: vitality, map-based data visualization, and qualitative research in visualization.

1.2. Vitality

Vitality has its origins in vitalism: that living things have a life force to construct their organic processes [18]. With the advancement of science during the 19th century [13], the concept of vitalism became obsolete. However, in recent years, vitalism has once again garnered interest in many domains, such as in the humanities and social sciences [18]. Van Steenbergen et al. [19] define the three aspects of vitality as "energy", "motivation", and "resilience". In a study to differentiate vitality, well-being, and quality of life, Guérin [20] defines vitality as a "psychological sense of aliveness, enthusiasm, or energy". Several other articles discuss the phenomenological perspective of vitality, which individuals experience through their bodies [13,20,21]. Considering the aspect of phenomenology, physical activity is one of the key factors in vitality. According to the World Health Organization Global Observatory Data Repository 2011, about one-third of adults do not reach sufficient physical activity levels [22]. Physical inactivity can cause health disorders such as non-communicable diseases [23] and affect health-related quality of life [24]. Given this, there is growing interest in active and healthy lifestyles and vitality [25].

Not only physical activity but also the meaning of vitality can vary. Van Steenbergen et al. [19] discuss the mental aspects of vitality such as emotional well-being, in addition to physical aspects. Our previous study reported on the multi-dimensionality of vitality, which is perceived differently by individuals, including factors such as stamina, activeness, health, happiness, and social status [16]. This finding is in line with results from other studies that addressed (a) the multifactorial nature and the individuality of vitality [19,21] and (b) the influence of social contexts on vitality [19,26].

Furthermore, there is the concept of urban vitality, which considers how urban environments attract people and invite them to visit places in the city [27]. Urban vitality can be realized by many factors, such as the use of public green spaces [28] and walkability [29]. The study by Marquet and Miralles-Guasch [29] found that walkable environments increase physical activity levels among the elderly and that urban vitality is one important factor to promote public health. Including the case of urban vitality, the term vitality can be found in many diverse domains such as health sciences (including physiology and psychology), agriculture, and organizational studies [30]. Among those various aspects of vitality, we use vitality as a health-related concept, considering various data which could influence people's health (e.g., sports participation, mental health, green space, and alcohol consumption).

1.3. Map-Based Data Visualization

The usage of maps has a long history. The earliest forms of data visualization include geometric diagrams of tables and maps found in the 10th century [31]. Maps are used not only by researchers and experts but also by individuals for their daily lives, as maps require minimum visualization literacy to understand the information on them, such as the distribution of events, phenomena, and objects [32]. Additionally, one of the other several benefits regarding the function of maps is problem-solving [32]. A remarkable example of this in history is a map created by Dr. John Snow in 1855, which successfully demonstrated the source of a cholera outbreak in the Broad Street area of London [6]. As such, modern computer-based geovisualizations are based on cartographic knowledge and techniques [33]. This study aims to promote vitality in a city through a map-based data visualization, which can be utilized by multiple parties such as government, business, and researchers. We explore those studies addressing urban issues using maps in the following section.

First, we reviewed several articles from the field of PPGIS. PPGIS uses GIS for policymaking by involving various parties, such as non-governmental organizations and local agencies. Policy-related information is visualized in map formats in a manner easy to consume, regardless of the volume and disparate sources of data [17]. Kahila-Tani et al. [34] conducted a study to analyze over 200 real-life planning cases that use PPGIS in multiple countries to investigate their outcomes in terms of public participation and societal and environmental benefits. Their study indicated several benefits and drawbacks of the use of PPGIS methodologies. Regardless of the aforementioned advantages of the maps, Kahila-Tani et al. [34] found the digital divide and technical challenges to be drawbacks. Importantly, those authors also discussed the context dependency of PPGIS; context influenced the benefits and drawbacks of PPGIS on a case by case basis. The study by Bugs [35] assessed the available online PPGIS tools and concluded that there is a limitation of these tools due to the usage gap between non-expert users (such as citizens) and expert users (such as planners). A study to evaluate a PPGIS tool was conducted by Rinner and Bird [36] through a case study with a citizens' association in downtown Toronto, Canada, to understand their technical and engagement experience. The results showed the technical difficulties in using the PPGIS tool among users and the necessity of context for enhancing the engagement.

The studies mentioned above also recommend further studies to understand the usability of PPGIS among different types of users, considering the contexts. In terms of context, Gebre and Morales [37] highlight the importance of technical and social context for analyzing and understanding data. The San Francisco Municipal Transportation Agency developed a map-based data visualization system called TransBASE [8] to support identifying context-specific trends and evaluating pedestrian collision events for pedestrian safety improvement [38]. Crime mappings are another classic example of maps developed for a specific context and aimed to solve a specific social problem [7]. Psyllidis et al. [39] developed a platform called

Social Glass, which focuses on the utilization of social data—data generated through users' social contexts such as social networks, for urban planning and decision making. Sui and Holt [40] used health-related data, such as the percentage of obese adults in the United States, to investigate the cognitive and analytical aspects of cartograms to study their effectiveness in the context of public health.

Several aforementioned studies include evaluations of their application through user studies and interviews. Yet, evaluations in visualization research are still limited compared with the research in the field of human –computer interaction (HCI) [41]. Additionally, case-by-case evaluations may be required as visualizations are context-specific. The requirements and use of those visualizations by users likely differ depending on context, as addressed by Kahila-Tani et al. [34]. Therefore, we echo the necessity of evaluations of map-based visualization applications, especially through qualitative approaches such as performed by Brewer et al. [34] and Yang and Goodwin [42,43]. As such, we apply qualitative approaches in our study to holistically capture the contexts behind users' analysis of visualizations [44]. In the following, we discuss qualitative research in visualization more closely.

1.4. Human-Centered Visualization

The evaluation of visualizations remains challenging [41,45]. Some scholars discuss these challenges because visualizations are used outside of laboratory environments and utilized by practitioners [9]. Visualizations are applied in the real world environment to support the decision-making process among a variety of users [5]. It is considered that high-level cognitive activities occur when users interact with visualizations [41]. Additionally, users in the real world have different backgrounds, which makes it difficult to design proper quantitative metrics in addition to performance indicators such as completion time and error [41]. Considering those factors for the evaluations of visualization, we mainly focus on a qualitative approach for our visualization study—i.e., interview studies with domain experts. Such interview studies with domain experts are common in visualization research, e.g., [42,43,46,47]. However, those studies are conducted with different visualization outputs, such as Geographically-Embedded Flow Data [43] (e.g., spatial movement data displayed in the context of a map) and Collaborative Geographic Visualization, which allows multiple users to manipulate visualizations simultaneously as well as to communicate among them [42]. Additionally, these studies used different methodologies to analyze data, such as card sorting [47] and the "what-why-how" framework [43].

In cartography including the field of PPGIS and geovisualization, the importance of a human-centered approach has been discussed by scholars such as Roth et al. [48], Haklay and Tobón [49], and Lloyd and Dykes [50]. Considering the usefulness of qualitative studies for the evaluation of user-centered systems [51], several studies, including the one by Lloyd and Dykes [50], implemented interviews to evaluate geovisualizations and PPGIS systems. Suchan [52] conducted an interview study with experts to explore what types of data and tools they currently use and the requirements for geovisualization tools to support their work. The study by Bąkowska-Waldmann and Kaczmarek [53] involved in-depth interviews with local authorities and officials and the analysis of planning documents to investigate the role of PPGIS tools in the decision-making process. Lloyd and Dykes [50] conducted a series of studies following the ISO standard 13407 [54] for the human-centered design process to design geovisualization applications. Their studies were designed to understand use and requirements and to evaluate prototypes by using a variety of methods including qualitative studies such as interviews and observations at experts' workplaces.

Among the related studies, the following two studies are closest to ours. First, our study is in a similar stage as the one by Brewer et al. [42], who conducted a user task analysis to define guidelines for their future design of collaborative geographic visualization. However, our study differs from their study in that we are less focused on collaboration and more focused on the different requirements of domain experts in the specific context of vitality. Second, although our study is not as extensive as the study by Lloyd and

Dykes [50], our study also aims (1) to understand the context of use and the requirements regarding a map-based visualization application in experts' real work environments and (2) to evaluate the map-based visualization application through user studies by using a prototype for further development. In the following section, we discuss the materials and methods of our study.

2. Materials and Methods

Our study investigates how diverse domain experts utilize a map-based visualization containing various vitality-related data to analyze and generate insights. To address this research question, we conducted a mixed-methods study involving an online survey, open-ended tasks, and semi-structured interviews with nine domain experts from the fields of government, business, and research.

2.1. Material

A map-based data visualization application (shown in Figure 1), containing various vitality-related datasets, was developed for open-ended tasks conducted by domain experts (see Supplementary Materials). This application was built by the first author in Eindhoven, The Netherlands using the web application framework Angular (version 11.2.12) [55] with the integration of JavaScript libraries D3 (version 6) [56] and Leaflet (version 1.7.1) [56], which support the creation of interactive maps for web applications.

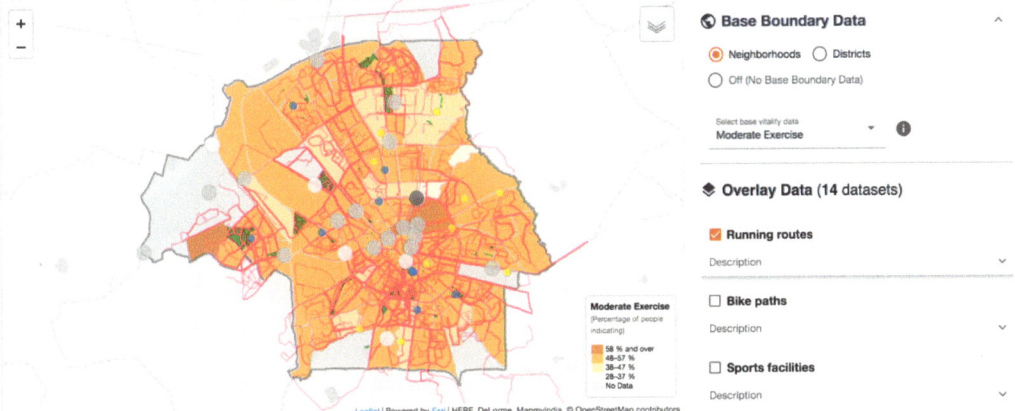

Figure 1. A screenshot of the map-based data visualization application with various vitality-related datasets used for our study to explore how domain experts utilize this type of information visualization for their visual analysis and insight generation.

In our previous study [16], we established the potential of data visualization to support domain experts' analysis on a data platform, as other open-data researchers such as [11,12] have discussed. Moreover, our focus is specifically on a map-based data visualization in this study. The advantages of maps have been addressed by the aforementioned open-data researchers, with the consideration of users with different backgrounds [11,12]. Some public health researchers such as Park et al. [57] also discuss the advantages of maps for the comparison and representation of multiple datasets. These advantages of maps addressed by scholars are in line with the concept of PPGIS, which includes a variety of stakeholders as target audiences and uses data from various sources [17]. Therefore, we applied the format of GIS for our particular use case and developed a map-based data visualization application, which enables spatial analysis by overlaying thematically different data (e.g., air quality, the percentage of smokers by neighborhood, bike paths) using different visual elements [58]—polygon (e.g., green area in the city), line (e.g., bike path), and point (e.g., locations of sports facilities)—to present spatial data.

Next to the potential of data visualization, our previous study [16] also found various perspectives on vitality, which include health (physical and mental), food, activities, loneliness, social status, and environment (e.g., air quality). We carefully selected datasets related to vitality covering those various aspects. In the map-based data visualization application, a total of nine base layers (e.g., the percentage of moderate exercise, smoker, and overweight population) are available for two different geographical boundaries: neighborhoods (116 entries) and districts (7 entries), as base boundary datasets. To create these boundary datasets, first, tabular data containing the aforementioned attributes was downloaded through CBS StatLine [59], the database of statistics in the Netherlands. Next, the tabular data were combined by using keys (the names of neighborhood in a city) and an open-source GIS application, QGIS [60], with neighborhood boundary polygon data (shapefile format) obtained through Eindhoven Open Data [61]—a local data portal. Afterward, the combined dataset was exported in GeoJSON [62] format, which is a JSON file with location attributes, enabling it to use in web applications. On top of these layers, there are fourteen overlay datasets, which consist of the polygon, line, and point data such as green area, running routes, sports facilities, public concerns, and air quality. Several data sources were used to obtain these overlay datasets, such as a local open data portal. Among these, one of the major data sources we used was OpenStreetMap (OSM)—a collaborative project to create an open license geographic database [63]. Since we could not find datasets that we considered as related to vitality from CBS StatLine and the local open data portal, we used the OSM's points of interest (POIs) data and extracted each interesting attribute (e.g., sports facilities, parks and playgrounds, and medical facilities) by using QGIS and exported it to GeoJSON files. Table 1 shows the spatial data used on the map-based data visualization application.

Table 1. Spatial data used on the map-based visualization application.

Type *	Name	Visual Element	Description	Source
Base	Moderate Exercise	Polygon	Percentage of people who exercise at least 150 min per week	CBS StatLine
Base	Healthy	Polygon	Percentage of people who indicate good or very good general health status	CBS StatLine
Base	Drinker	Polygon	Percentage of people who drink alcohol a maximum one glass per day	CBS StatLine
Base	Smoker	Polygon	Percentage of people who smoke	CBS StatLine
Base	Overweight	Polygon	Percentage of people whose body mass index is 25 kg/m^2 or above	CBS StatLine
Base	Illness	Polygon	Percentage of people who have one or more long-term (6 months or longer) illness or disorder	CBS StatLine
Base	Physical Unavailability	Polygon	Percentage of people who have physical difficulty or inability (e.g., not being able to carry an object of 5 kg for 10 m)	CBS StatLine
Base	Depression	Polygon	Percentage of people who have a high risk of anxiety or depression	CBS StatLine
Base	Loneliness	Polygon	Percentage of people who experience severe loneliness (emotional and social)	CBS StatLine
Overlay	Parks and playgrounds	Polygon	Parks and playgrounds extracted from point of interest data	OSM
Overlay	Local project (Bennekel)	Polygon	The results of a vitality related survey (e.g., barriers for sports and exercise) from a local project in a specific neighborhood (Bennekel)	Local project in Bennekel

Table 1. Cont.

Type *	Name	Visual Element	Description	Source
Overlay	Traffic	Line	Traffic (with speed limit) extracted from the point of interest data	OSM
Overlay	Running routes	Line	Anonymized running route data extracted from a running application (N = 500)	Hardlopen met Evy app
Overlay	Bike paths	Line	Bike path data	Eindhoven Open Data
Overlay	Sports facilities	Point	Sports facilities (e.g., sports center, swimming pool, and pitch) extracted from the point of interest data	OSM
Overlay	Medical facilities	Point	Medical facilities (doctors) extracted from the point of interest data	OSM
Overlay	Community centers	Point	Community centers extracted from the point of interest data	OSM
Overlay	Sports shops	Point	Sports shops (e.g., bicycle, outdoor shops) extracted from the point of interest data	OSM
Overlay	Grocery stores	Point	Grocery stores (supermarkets and butchers) extracted from the point of interest data provided	OSM
Overlay	Fast foods	Point	Fast foods extracted from the point of interest data	OSM
Overlay	Public concerns	Point	Public concerns data (e.g., noise, odor, and traffic)	Eindhoven Open Data
Overlay	Air quality	Point	The data of particulate matter (PM)1, PM2.5, and PM10	Eindhoven Open Data

* In the type column, "Base" refers to the base polygon layer showing information (e.g., sports participation rate by neighborhood) using a choropleth map. "Overlay" refers to layers, which can be either polygon, line, or point datasets (e.g., area of parks and playgrounds, running routes, and location of sports facilities), added on top of the base polygon layers.

In these overlay datasets, we also included specific data about a certain neighborhood to examine how users react to this type of context-specific information shown in Table 2 as "Local project (Bennekel)". This data contains the results of a survey asking questions such as "What are barriers for sports and exercise?" for residents in this neighborhood. As mentioned before, each neighborhood contains some demographic information, such as population (total and ratio of men and women), age (ratio of kids, adults, and seniors), residents (ratio of native and immigrants), income and household, and the percentage of travel mode (foot, bicycle, auto, and transit). This demographic information was obtained through a local open data portal, Eindhoven in Cijfers [64], in tabular format and then converted to a JSON file for use in our online visualization application. Each dataset was implemented as spatial data layers in the map-based data visualization used for this study.

Besides the spatial data layers, we considered the levels of information provided in different steps similar to the study by Prieto et al. [65] in our map-based data visualization application. The application provides an initial overview of the vitality data (the default dataset is the percentage of moderate exercise by each neighborhood in a city represented as polygons) as shown in Figure 2a. The participants could switch between different base polygon layers, which we refer to as "base boundary datasets", such as the percentage of healthy people, smokers, and loneliness. They could also add different types of polygon, line, or point data on top of the base boundary datasets as overlay datasets for their spatial analysis. Figure 2 shows the default base boundary datasets (polygon) and the example of overlay polygon, line, and point data used for our map-based data visualization.

Table 2. Participants' expertise, demographics, background, and domain knowledge of vitality.

Domain ID	Current Position	Gender	Age Range	Years of Experience	Knowledge of Vitality
G01	Area manager of a municipal park	Male	35–44 years	6 to 10 years	High
G02	Innovation manager at a municipality	Male	35–44 years	11 to 20 years	High
G03	Policy advisor for sports and active living at a municipality	Female	45–54 years	21 to 30 years	High
B01	Executive director at an innovation center for sports and vitality	Male	45–54 years	21 to 30 years	High
B02	Program manager at an independent non-profit foundation	Male	35–44 years	11 to 20 years	High
B03	Coordinator, neighborhood coach, and chairman a a local service	Male	45–54 years	21 to 30 years	High
R01	Teacher and researcher in the Public Health department of a university	Female	25–34 years	6 to 10 years	High
R02	Researcher about sports, society, and public health at a research institute	Female	25–34 years	6 to 10 years	High
R03	Project coordinator at the Public Health department of a university	Female	35–44 years	11 to 20 years	Moderate

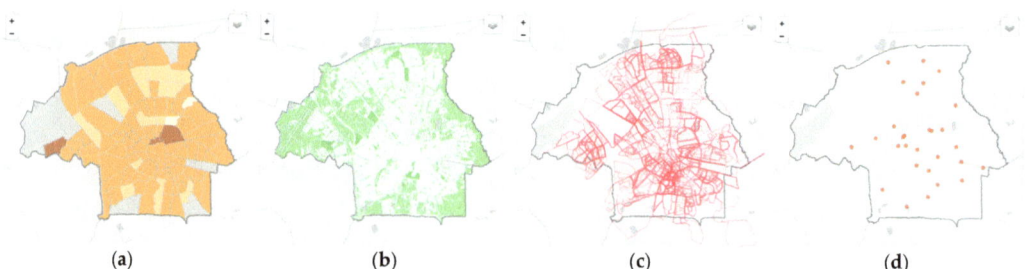

(a)　　　　　　　　(b)　　　　　　　　(c)　　　　　　　　(d)

Figure 2. Example of spatial data layers used for this study. (**a**) Default base polygon layer showing sports participation rate by neighborhood; (**b**) Polygon data showing green areas; (**c**) line data showing various runners' running routes; (**d**) Point data showing the location of sports facilities.

Additionally, the details of data can be viewed using interactions. When the participant hovered on the spatial data (either polygon, line, or point), the application returned detailed information through pop-ups. The general information about each neighborhood, such as total population, income levels, and the percentage of seniors, is shown with a click on each neighborhood polygon.

2.2. Participants

We recruited nine participants, three each from the field of government, business, and research, as shown in Table 1, to investigate the difference among these experts in terms of their approach, requirements, and analysis regarding the map-based data visualization, which also resembles vitality-related projects in the real world. We checked the participants for color blindness when we asked them to confirm their participation by means of a consent form. The consent form also explained the procedure of the study as well as how the personal data collected for this study will be processed (e.g., what data will be collected and how we store their data in compliance with the European General Data Protection Regulation). Each participant received a digital voucher, worth 15 Euros, as compensation for participation in this study. Five out of nine participants had some level of geographical familiarity with the area used in the map-based data visualization. The other participants (B02, B03, R01, and R03) weren't familiar with the geographical context. We obtained the participants' expertise, demographics (age range and gender), background, and domain knowledge of vitality through an online questionnaire prior to conducting the free tasks and the interviews.

2.3. Study Setup

This study was structured along three steps: (1) an online survey, (2) open-ended tasks, and (3) semi-structured interviews. We asked the participants to complete the online survey prior to the open-ended tasks and interview to understand their background and professional experience and domain knowledge about vitality. The open-ended tasks and semi-structured interviews were conducted by the first author at the participants' work environment remotely using an online meeting platform, Microsoft (MS) Teams, considering the COVID-19 pandemic during which this study took place.

After the introduction of the study, we sent a URL for the map-based data visualization, with which the participant conducted the open-ended tasks (exploring the visualization freely for 15 to 20 min for their analysis and insight generation) via the chat window on MS Teams. Open-ended tasks were implemented in this study to understand diverse experts' approaches, such as search behaviors, in the context close to the participants' real work [66,67]. We used open-ended tasks, with consideration of complexity in the real work environment, particularly in the field of vitality. As aforementioned, vitality is a multidimensional concept. Therefore, we consider that vitality-related issues likely have a variety of aspects, which results in complexity. To solve complex issues, high-level thinking and open-ended approaches are usually required [68]. Although domain-specific knowledge and general problem-solving skills are needed for open-ended tasks [69], we consider open-ended tasks to be appropriate for our study because all our participants are familiar with the subject matter of vitality due to their professional experience [70], as shown in Table 2.

During the open-ended tasks, the participants were asked to leave notes of their findings and insights in the chat window. The participants could ask the author when they encountered any problems or had questions during the open-ended tasks. The participants' behavioral data, specifically click events, were collected using Google Analytics [71] to understand which datasets in the map-based data visualization the participants used during the open-ended tasks.

Following the open-ended tasks, semi-structured interviews were conducted to address the domain experts' preferences (including requirements), knowledge, experience, and process (analysis and insight generation) with respect to the map-based data visualization. We applied one of the Human Factors Research approaches indicated by Tory and Möller [3], "User and Task-Based Design", to gain insights into designing a practical map-based data visualization application utilized by different domain experts in the context of vitality. Particularly, our interests were the domain experts' insights, visual analysis approach, data preference and requirements, overall impressions, required features, and work practice (applicability of our application to their work) regarding the map-based data visualization. Interview questions were prepared by referring to the scenarios of "understanding environments and work practice", "evaluating visual data analysis and reasoning", and "evaluating user experience" from the seven evaluation scenarios of information visualizations proposed by Lam et al. The interviews were video recorded for the case of discussions when participants pointed out some objects or elements on the visualization. The participants were asked to turn off their cameras before starting the video recording in order to not collect unnecessary personal data. Each interview lasted on average 30 min.

2.4. Analysis

The video recordings of the interviews were transcribed. The transcribed data was analyzed together with the notes the participants left in the chat window during the open-ended tasks. We implemented a deductive coding approach to guide the analysis based on the researchers' theoretical and analytical interests [72]. The first author created codes to address our research question, which are "insight", "approach", "data (amount)", "data (levels of detail)", "data (required)", "data (irrelevant)", "impression", "applicability", and "features." While familiarizing with the data by looking through transcriptions, mentions related to collaboration stood out. Therefore, we added the code "collaboration" to the set of codes. The transcriptions were coded based on the set of predefined codes.

The quantitative data (participants' click events) obtained through Google Analytics were analyzed by summary statistics to assess if there are any differences among participants and between domain groups (government, business, and research). Only the summary statistic was applied for the investigation due to the small sample size. Following this, participants' click events were visualized to investigate which datasets they used during the open-ended tasks and to see if there were any differences between the domain groups regarding click counts and the variety of datasets used.

3. Results

In this section, we present the results of the qualitative content analysis of the interview data and the analysis of the click events data described in the previous section; we indicate each participant as G = government, B = business, and R = research, based on the sector they are from.

3.1. Interview Data

The transcribed interview data and the participants' notes were coded using the aforementioned predefined codes. The summary of each coded theme is discussed below.

Insight. The majority of the participants (seven out of nine) mentioned the benefits of combining the datasets on the map. Four participants gained insights into how different vitality datasets are correlated and also uncorrelated by conducting spatial analysis with the combination of the spatial data on the map. For instance, "They would rather run on a big road or next to a big road than in the forest" (B02) and " ... doesn't seem to be a correlation between green areas and health" (G01). In addition, the color-coded base polygon datasets provided quick insight for some participants, such as "In the city center, which has a really high level of moderate exercise, and also in some of the neighborhoods in the southwestern part of the city" (R02).

However, we did not obtain as much insight from the participants as we expected. This may be due to the nature of open-ended tasks (no specific tasks were assigned), so that the participants tended to explore instead of searching for particular information. Additionally, four out of nine participants were not familiar with the geographical context used in this study. We did not gain any insights from three out of these four participants. Therefore, the geographical knowledge of the city is important as it has likely affected the insight generation process.

Approach. There were mainly two types of approaches found, which can be interpreted as a top-down and a bottom-up approaches. Five participants took the top-down approach, and three other participants took the bottom-up approach. We could not find a clear approach from one participant (R03).

Participants who took the top-down approach first explored the application and what was possible with it. Then, they started performing certain actions, such as clicking the base boundary datasets, overlay datasets, or neighborhoods on the map. Instead, the bottom-up approach was initiated by actions such as clicking through the overlay datasets and the neighborhood polygon data to get a grasp of the visualization almost by trial and error for their exploration and perhaps the analysis process at the same time. We did not find any patterns or orders in terms of the clicks on the base boundary, overlay datasets, and neighborhood on the map, and it was rather different for each participant.

Data (amount). We asked the participants if the amount of data used in the map-based application was appropriate. As discussed in Section 3.1, there were two different geographical boundaries used in the map, which are neighborhoods (116 entries) and districts (7 entries), and fourteen overlay datasets on top of these. Four out of nine participants found it was the right amount (two of them mentioned it could also have been more). Two participants clearly stated they expected more datasets. We were surprised by the fact that none of the participants was overwhelmed by the number of datasets. This may be partially because of the advantage of maps to present multiple datasets from different data sources effectively [17]. Seven participants showed their preference for the format of maps with comments such as "if you would have it in numbers or text, it is much harder to get a feel of the data ... this makes it a lot easier to get a feel of the data I think" (R03).

Data (levels of detail). The level of detail of the data was investigated to understand if the domain experts appreciate the dimensions of the datasets (e.g., showing the detailed data about the neighborhood when the participants click). Generally, the participants liked to have the level of detail of data for the reason that this prevents the overload of information at the first picture and users can access more information only when needed [73]. The detailed data are likely necessary when users need to conduct further and in-depth analysis. There were also mentions of the participants' preference over the neighborhood level or district level for the base polygon data. Four participants clearly mentioned they preferred the neighborhood level for their analysis, and the district level was not useful for that purpose. This is likely because the planning often happens at neighborhood levels, which was mentioned by two participants during the interview. Other than the neighborhood or district levels, one participant (B03) preferred even the zip code level, which was expected to have more data entries than the neighborhood level.

Data (irrelevant). As we implemented a wide variety of datasets related to vitality, and also because the participants had diverse backgrounds, we assumed not all datasets were relevant to each participant. Therefore, we asked the participants if there were any irrelevant datasets. We investigated the participants' thoughts on and how they dealt with those datasets. The majority of the participants (seven) answered there were some datasets that they were not interested in or that were not relevant to their expertise. However, those participants also showed an understanding of the presence of the irrelevant datasets as beneficial for the other domain experts, considering the multi-functional nature of vitality [16]. Interestingly, one participant (B02) mentioned that the participant had a chance to take a look at those datasets regardless of the irrelevancy. Similarly, another participant (R01) pointed out that those irrelevant datasets may have an opportunity to provide different perspectives not originally considered.

Data (required). With this coding theme, we addressed which data domain experts required the map-based data visualization. We learned that domain experts were looking for very specific datasets to support their work, such as data showing "what kind of (sports) programs are running in a certain neighborhood" (B02) and "the impact of sports facilities on the health of people" (G03). Two participants showed high interest in data from citizens in addition to those specific datasets.

Impression. The map-based data visualization developed for this study generally elicited a positive impression from the participants. This positive impression likely benefitted from the format of the map, as mentioned in such comments from the participants as "Visualization like the map itself is helpful" (R02), "Combining different overlays is really insightful" (R02), and "I like the options of the layers of the map that you can switch off and on easily" (G02). We found some concerns from the participants as well. However, they were mostly related to the datasets themselves (e.g., quality and content) and not to the design and functions of the map-based data visualization.

Applicability. We intend to assess the applicability of our application to the domain experts' own work practice. Unlike the overall impressions of the application, many participants (seven out of nine) were not fully positive about the applicability. The main reason for this was that domain experts' projects are often very specific, and the application was still too broad for this purpose, regardless of the focus on the context of vitality. A few participants explained the necessity of designing this type of application with a clear connection with a certain policy, such as "vitality in public space", which may be interpreted as themes or frames the domain experts work on during their analysis and insight generation process. Some specific datasets are also likely required for this purpose. At the same time, we had the impression that this type of application would still be useful for the domain experts when they define (vitality) issues in a city and also communicate them to their partners and citizens. We realized the gap between the general usability of a map-based data visualization and its use in practice in various domain experts' environments.

Features. There were several features suggested by the participants, such as "time-series data", "real-time data", "filtering", "data comparison by separate windows", "creation of reports", and "3D mapping". One participant (B03) was interested in obtaining other data by using an Application Programming Interface (API). The same participant also showed interest in a monitoring function using real-time data (or data updated automatically) to see the performance (e.g., if a certain neighborhood reaches the set goal of the percentage of moderate exercise). Two participants (B01 and G01) indicated a preference for a customized dashboard. Among them, one participant (G01) explained the dashboard as a vital dashboard showing a vitality indicator aggregated by different parameters (e.g., mental, physical, and social). One participant (B02) showed interest in an annotation feature, which could be used to exchange ideas with other users as a part of a collaborative process.

Collaborations. Lastly, collaborative aspects of this type of visualization application were investigated due to the frequent mentions related to collaboration throughout the interviews. This appears very understandable, as vitality contains multiple perspectives. Thus, experts from many different domains (e.g., sports, health, and environment) work in the context of vitality with different goals. Six out of nine participants made mentions that likely related to collaboration, including the annotation feature discussed above. In particular, the participants from the field of research (R01 and R03; both work in public health) clearly stated, regarding their collaborative work with other partners and also residents, that "together we did that with the concept mapping session with professionals and residents" and "we have quite a large research consortium with a lot of different expertise".

3.2. Click Event Data

We looked at the summary statistics of the click events obtained through Google Analytics (Table 3) to grasp if there are any differences between the participants and also between the domain groups in terms of their approach (click counts and the datasets they used). Due to the low sample size, no statistical analysis was performed. We couldn't collect the click events data from one participant (G01) due to a technical difficulty. The participants' click events were also visualized for conducting visual analysis to better understand the distribution of the datasets used by each participant and domain group as well as the frequency of clicks on each dataset to understand which datasets the participants were more or less interested in.

As shown in Table 3, the domain experts from the field of research clicked the datasets the most (both in terms of times and variety). In contrast, the domain experts from the government had the least clicks. It is important to note that two domain experts from research were not familiar with the geography presented in the map used for this study. Instead, both experts from the government work for the municipality that was shown on the map. The difference in background knowledge might have affected their click actions in terms of the necessity for exploration for learning.

Table 3. Summary statistics of the participants' click events during the free task.

Domain ID	Number of Datasets	Total Clicks	Number of Datasets *	Total Clicks *
G02	9	16	12	26
G03	14	36		
B01	18	26	18	30
B02	12	24		
B03	23	39		
R01	20	39	20	39
R02	18	41		
R03	23	37		

* Domain group average.

Figure 3 shows the clicked datasets by all participants, with the frequency of clicks on each dataset. Except for the base boundary datasets by the participants G02 and B02, all datasets were used by all participants. Although participant R03 explained her approach to focus on a particular area and the datasets on the map-based data visualization, she clicked through all the available datasets. One participant (B02) stated during the interview regarding irrelevant datasets that "sports facilities is one that I would always use, whereas medical facilities ... but ... could be of interest later on" and "it's good that it's there and then to see whether it would help you find a solution for the problem ... ". We see that the participants tended to explore different datasets regardless of their focus or interests. These results may be partially due to the nature of the open-ended tasks that we used for this study. However, as the comments above show, the majority of the participants were at least positive about having various datasets on the map-based data visualization in the context of vitality.

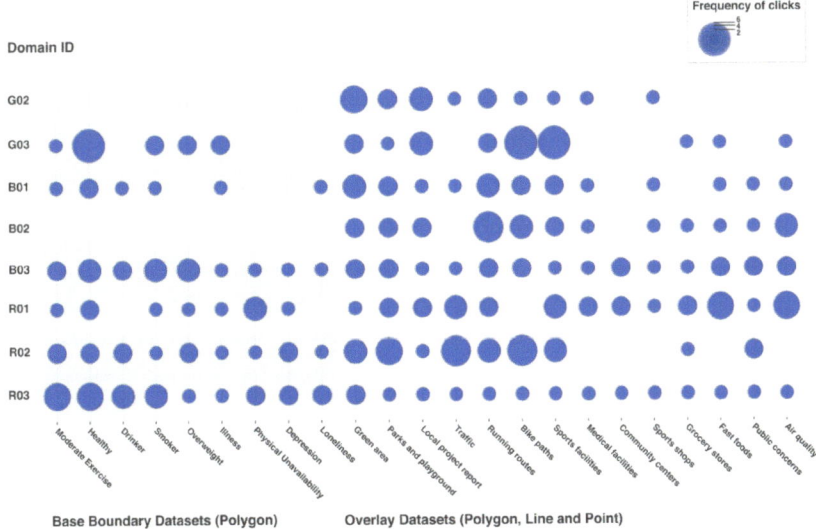

Figure 3. The participants' click events and frequency with the base boundary datasets (polygon) and overlay datasets (polygon, line, and point).

4. Discussion

Our study investigated how domain experts utilize a map-based visualization containing various vitality data for their analysis and insight generation. We conducted a mixed-methods study consisting of an online survey, open-ended tasks, and semi-structured interviews with nine domain experts from the field of government, business, and research. Both qualitative data (the participants' notes during the open-ended tasks and the interviews) and quantitative data (click events data during the open-ended tasks) were obtained and analyzed to answer our research question: "How does a map-based visualization containing various vitality data support the visual analysis process among different domain experts?" We particularly investigated the participants' overall impression, insights and visual analysis approach, preference on datasets depending on their expertise, amount and types of data preferred in general, and applicability of this to their real projects.

Our study confirmed several benefits of map-based data visualization targeting diverse domain experts in the context of vitality. First of all, the majority of interview participants expressed a positive impression of the map-based visualization in the sense that it can contain many datasets without getting cluttered with information. Secondly, we also found the participants appreciated the data layers they could choose on the map to conduct spatial analysis for their insight generation. Seven out of nine participants made comments that showed their preference in this regard. There was only one participant (B03) who did not appreciate the map-based visualization. This participant also mentioned using data tables for discussions and decision-making processes with other agencies. We also learned that map-based data visualizations are not necessary for all kinds of domain experts. However, we believe they still have substantial benefits for users with different levels of related literacies (e.g., computer, visual, and data), as participants made statements such as "it's really useful to show it on maps because everybody kind of knows how to look for the place you are talking about" (R01) and "if you want you can get more in-depth information, but if you don't, you can just quickly see what you have" (R02). We understood from those comments that the map-based data visualization could be used by novice users to gain quick insights but also by intermediate or perhaps even advanced users for further analysis. This more in-depth analysis is usually triggered by interactions like one participant (G02) mentioned: " . . . because it's interactive. So you can play with it and get a better understanding of the information you're looking at." The preference for interactions in data visualizations was also addressed by a recent interview study conducted by Park et al. [57], which assessed the requirements for data visualizations among public health professionals. Interactions are important to enhance these analyses [74]. They have to be considered further in future research.

Considering the use and availability of interactions, no participant was overwhelmed by the datasets we used in our study, and four out of nine participants thought they could consume more datasets. Seven out of nine participants mentioned that the map-based visualization application contained datasets that the participants were not interested in. However, the participants understood that the datasets irrelevant to them were included in the application to consider the diverse aspects of vitality. We also learned that experts were looking for specific datasets related to their own projects, such as "the location and information of sports programs in a city" in addition to the vitality datasets we used in this study (e.g., Table 1).

In addition to its benefits, the map-based data visualization presented different challenges. The main challenge we found through this study was the specific contexts of domain experts' projects in the real world. Several participants provided insights into this issue through interviews. They stated that the map-based data visualization should have some themes, such as "vitality in public space", which one participant defined as a conceptual frame and others as the connection with certain policies. This could be realized by the design of the map-based data visualization, which supports users in finding vitality themes (likely presented by the combinations of several datasets) on which they would like to focus. One participant (B02) suggested a filter function that allows users to focus the interface on a neighborhood that users would like to analyze. In addition, one participant (R02) suggested grouping the overlay datasets by topics (e.g., bike paths, running routes, and roads as "traffic"). We think such functions may support creating or finding themes for each domain expert in order to slightly adjust to various experts' needs individually, similar to the concept of adaptive information visualization [75].

Throughout the study, we also recognized the domain experts' practice of collaborating with other partners and citizens. One participant discussed the difficulty of having in-person meetings with partners and citizens during the lockdown caused by the COVID-19 pandemic. Experiencing this challenge, there may be more demands on collaborative features on map-based data visualizations.

5. Limitations

This study also has some limitations that warrant discussion. First of all, this study is highly case-specific and limited to a specific city in the Netherlands, with a smaller number of participants who are all experts in the field of vitality. This limits the generalizability in some way. We had small samples due to experts' limited availabilities [41], for which reason we did not conduct a statistical analysis of the quantitative data. Furthermore, click events data likely limits the understanding of participants' behavior in depth. It may be necessary to consider collecting mouse movement data such as done by Krassanakis and Kesidis [76] and eye movement data as done in the study by Cybulski and Horbiński [77] in order to obtain richer quantitative data for the further analysis. The selection of the open-ended tasks for this study may have prevented generating specific insights among the interview participants, since we were not able to analyze the data systemically. For instance, we could not analyze which vitality-related datasets were useful as well as compare rigorously the differences in utilized datasets for specific tasks. Nevertheless, we could still obtain rich and interesting insights from this mixed-methods study, especially with the respect to the domain experts' practices on map-based data visualization in the real-word. This empirical evidence also provides insights into designing map-based data visualizations targeting domain experts in the information visualization and GIS research community.

6. Conclusions and Future Work

In this paper, we presented the results of a mixed-methods study to address how a map-based visualization containing various vitality data supports the visual analysis process among different domain experts. Our study confirmed the favoring of map-based data visualizations among those domain experts as well as several benefits, such as the efficiency of the data presentation and the ease of spatial analysis. However, we also found challenges when it was applied to domain experts' projects in the real world due to in-depth and specific requirements. Although the adaptability of map-based data visualization for diverse target audiences has already been considered, further considerations are necessary to support domain experts' work in practice. The provision of themes created by the combination of several datasets and shown together in map-based data visualizations might help cover each specific use case among various domain experts, which can be realized by interaction and feature designs that consider these adaptions.

Our future plan is to design a map-based data visualization that adapts to the various domain experts' projects based on the insights we obtained through this study. As we found collaboration was common practice in their projects, we also consider this an important factor for the adaption of our map-based data visualization.

As there has been growing interest and efforts to research the effective and efficient visualization of geospatial data for insight generation, information sharing, and decision-making in the cartographic and geographic information science community [78], more studies that investigate users' utilization in specific contexts in the real world are required. Our study contributes to the particular area of geovisualizations by providing new empirical evidence.

Supplementary Materials: The map-based data visualization application used for the study is available at: https://experiment1-tue.herokuapp.com.

Author Contributions: Conceptualization, K.W., G.W. and S.V.; methodology, K.W., G.W. and S.V.; software, K.W.; formal analysis, K.W.; investigation, K.W., G.W. and S.V.; data curation, K.W.; writing—original draft preparation, K.W.; writing—review and editing, K.W., G.W. and S.V.; visualization, K.W. All authors have read and agreed to the published version of the manuscript.

Funding: This research was funded by Vitality Living Lab, financed by Operational Program EFRO 2014–2020 South-Netherlands.

Data Availability Statement: The data are not publicly available due to the participants' privacy. Ethical approval applied only to the internal usage of the collected data.

Acknowledgments: We would like to thank all the participants who supported our research by participating in the study.

Conflicts of Interest: The authors declare no conflict of interest.

References

1. Few, S. Data Visualization for Human Perception. In *The Encyclopedia of Human-Computer Interaction*; Soegaard, M., Dam, R.F., Eds.; The Interaction Design Foundation: Aarhus, Denmark, 2013.
2. Tufte, E.R. *The Visual Display of Quantitative Information*, 2nd ed.; Graphics Press: Cheshire, CT, USA, 2001.
3. Tory, M.; Möller, T. Human Factors in Visualization Research. *IEEE Trans. Vis. Comput. Graph.* **2004**, *10*, 72–84. [CrossRef] [PubMed]
4. Zulkifli, H.; Kadir, R.A.; Nayan, N.M. Initial User Requirement Analysis for Waterbodies Data Visualization. In *Advances in Visual Informatics*; Zaman, H.B., Robinson, P., Smeaton, A.F., Shih, T.K., Velastin, S., Jaafar, A., Ali, N.M., Eds.; Springer: Cham, Switerland, 2015; Volume 9429, pp. 89–98. [CrossRef]
5. Gershon, N.; Eick, S.G. Information Visualization. *IEEE Comput. Graph. Appl.* **1997**, *17*, 29–31. [CrossRef]
6. Gilbert, E.W. Pioneer Maps of Health and Disease in England. *Geogr. J.* **1958**, *124*, 172–183. [CrossRef]
7. Fitterer, J.; Nelson, T.A.; Nathoo, F. Predictive Crime Mapping. *Police Pract. Res.* **2015**, *16*, 121–135. [CrossRef]
8. TransBASE. Available online: https://transbase.sfgov.org/dashboard/dashboard.php (accessed on 21 October 2021).
9. Plaisant, C. The Challenge of Information Visualization Evaluation. In Proceedings of the Workshop on Advanced Visual Interfaces AVI, Gallipoli, Italy, 25–28 May 2004.
10. MacEachren, A.M.; Kraak, M.-J. Research Challenges in Geovisualization. *Cartogr. Geogr. Inf. Sci.* **2001**, *28*, 3–12. [CrossRef]
11. Ruijer, E.; Grimmelikhuijsen, S.; Hogan, M.; Enzerink, S.; Ojo, A.; Meijer, A. Connecting Societal Issues, Users and Data. Scenario-Based Design of Open Data Platforms. *Gov. Inf. Q.* **2017**, *34*, 470–480. [CrossRef]
12. Osagie, E.; Waqar, M.; Adebayo, S.; Stasiewicz, A.; Porwol, L.; Ojo, A. Usability Evaluation of an Open Data Platform. In Proceedings of the 18th Annual International Conference on Digital Government Research (dg.o '17), Staten Island, NY, USA, 7–9 June 2017.
13. Smith, S.J.; Lloyd, R.J. Promoting Vitality in Health and Physical Education. *Qual. Health Res.* **2006**, *16*, 249–267. [CrossRef]
14. Ren, X.; Wang, Z.; Nast, C.; Ettema, D.; Brombacher, A. Integrating Industrial Design and Geoscience: A Survey on Data-Driven Research to Promote Public Health and Vitality. In Proceedings of the 9th International Conference on Digital Public Health (DPH2019), Marseille, France, 20–23 November 2019.
15. Sui, D.Z. Geographic Information Systems and Medical Geography: Toward a New Synergy. *Geogr. Compass* **2007**, *1*, 556–582. [CrossRef]
16. Wada, K.; Van Renswouw, L.; Wallner, G.; Lévy, P.; Vos, S. Studying Requirements for Designing a Vitality Data Sharing Platform from a Multi-Stakeholder Perspective. In Proceedings of the 8th International Conference on Kansei Engineering and Emotion Research, Tokyo, Japan, 7–9 September 2020.
17. Sieber, R. Public Participation Geographic Information Systems: A Literature Review and Framework. *Ann. Assoc. Am. Geogr.* **2006**, *96*, 491–507. [CrossRef]
18. Osborne, T. Vitalism as Pathos. *Biosemiotics* **2016**, *9*, 185–205. [CrossRef]
19. Van Steenbergen, E.; Van Dongen, J.M.; Wendel Vos, G.C.W.; Hildebrandt, V.H.; Strijk, J.E. Insights into the Concept of Vitality: Associations with Participation and Societal Costs. *Eur. J. Public Health* **2016**, *26*, 354–359. [CrossRef] [PubMed]
20. Guérin, E. Disentangling Vitality, Well-Being, and Quality of Life: A Conceptual Examination Emphasizing Their Similarities and Differences with Special Application in the Physical Activity Domain. *J. Phys. Act. Health* **2012**, *9*, 896–908. [CrossRef] [PubMed]
21. Ryan, R.M.; Frederick, C. On Energy, Personality, and Health: Subjective Vitality as a Dynamic Reflection of Well-Being. *J. Personal.* **1997**, *65*, 529–565. [CrossRef] [PubMed]
22. Hallal, P.C.; Andersen, L.B.; Bull, F.C.; Guthold, R.; Haskell, W.; Ekelund, U.; Alkandari, J.R.; Bauman, A.E.; Blair, S.N.; Brownson, R.C.; et al. Global Physical Activity Levels: Surveillance Progress, Pitfalls, and Prospects. *Lancet* **2012**, *380*, 247–257. [CrossRef]

23. I-Min, L.; Shiroma, E.; Lobelo, F.; Puska, P.; Blair, S.; Katzmarzyk, P. Impact of Physical Inactivity on the World's Major Non-Communicable Diseases. *Lancet* **2012**, *380*, 219–229. [CrossRef]
24. Kohl, H.W.; Craig, C.L.; Lambert, E.V.; Inoue, S.; Alkandari Ramadan, J.; Leetongin, G.; Kahlmeier, S. The Pandemic of Physical Inactivity: Global Action for Public Health. *Lancet* **2012**, *380*, 294–305. [CrossRef]
25. Janssen, M.; van den Heuvel, R.; Megens, C.; Levy, P.; Vos, S. Analysis of the Design and Engineering-Process towards a First Prototype in the Field of Sports and Vitality. In Proceedings of the 12th Conference of the International Sports Engineering Association, Brisbane, Australia, 26–28 March 2018.
26. Penninx, B.W.J.H.; Guralnik, J.M.; Bandeen-Roche, K.; Kasper, J.D.; Simonsick, E.M.; Ferrucci, L.; Fried, L.P. The Protective Effect of Emotional Vitality on Adverse Health Outcomes in Disabled Older Women. *J. Am. Geriatr. Soc.* **2000**, *48*, 1359–1366. [CrossRef]
27. Montgomery, J. Urban Vitality and the Culture of Cities. *Plan. Pract. Res.* **1995**, *10*, 101–110. [CrossRef]
28. Lopes, M.N.; Camanho, A.S. Public Green Space Use and Consequences on Urban Vitality: An Assessment of European Cities. *Soc. Indic. Res.* **2013**, *113*, 751–767. [CrossRef]
29. Marquet, O.; Miralles-Guasch, C. Neighbourhood Vitality and Physical Activity among the Elderly: THE Role of Walkable Environments on Active Ageing in Barcelona, Spain. *Soc. Sci. Med.* **2015**, *135*, 24–30. [CrossRef]
30. Lavrusheva, O. The Concept of Vitality. Review of the Vitality-Related Research Domain. *New Ideas Psychol.* **2020**, *56*, 100752. [CrossRef]
31. Friendly, M. A Brief History of Data Visualization. In *Handbook of Data Visualization*; Chen, C., Härdle, W.K., Unwin, A., Eds.; Springer: Berlin/Heidelberg, Germany, 2008; pp. 15–56.
32. Koç, H. Developing Valid and Reliable Map Literacy Scale. *Rev. Int. Geogr. Educ. Online* **2014**, *4*, 120–137.
33. Nöllenburg, M. Geographic Visualization. In *Human-Centered Visualization Environments. Lecture Notes in Computer Science*; Kerren, A., Ebert, A., Meyer, J., Eds.; Springer: Berlin/Heidelberg, Germany, 2007; Volume 4417, pp. 257–258.
34. Kahila-Tani, M.; Kytta, M.; Geertman, S. Does Mapping Improve Public Participation? Exploring the Pros and Cons of Using Public Participation GIS in Urban Planning Practices. *Landsc. Urban Plan.* **2019**, *186*, 45–55. [CrossRef]
35. Bugs, G. Assessment of Online PPGIS Study Cases in Urban Planning. *Lect. Notes Comput. Sci.* **2012**, *7333*, 477–490. [CrossRef]
36. Rinner, C.; Bird, M. Evaluating Community Engagement through Argumentation Maps—A Public Participation GIS Case Study. *Environ. Plan. B Plan. Des.* **2009**, *36*, 588–601. [CrossRef]
37. Gebre, E.H.; Morales, E. How "Accessible" Is Open Data?: Analysis of Context-Related Information and Users' Comments in Open Datasets. *Inf. Learn. Sci.* **2020**, *121*, 19–36. [CrossRef]
38. Kronenberg, C.; Woodward, L.; Dubose, B.; Weissman, D. Achieving Vision Zero: Data-Driven Investment Strategy to Eliminate Pedestrian Fatalities on a Citywide Level. *Transp. Res. Rec.* **2015**, *2519*, 146–156. [CrossRef]
39. Psyllidis, A.; Bozzon, A. A Platform for Urban Analytics and Semantic Data Integration in City Planning. In *Computer-Aided Architectural Design Futures. The Next City—New Technologies and the Future of the Built Environment. CAAD Futures 2015. Communications in Computer and Information Science*; Celani, G., Sperling, D.M., Franco, J.M.S., Eds.; Springer: Berlin/Heidelberg, Germany, 2015; Volume 527, pp. 21–36. [CrossRef]
40. Sui, D.Z.; Holt, J.B. Visualizing and Analysing Public-Health Data Using Value-by-Area Cartograms: Toward a New Synthetic Framework. *Cartographica* **2008**, *43*, 3–20. [CrossRef]
41. Elmqvist, N.; Yi, J.S. Patterns for Visualization Evaluation. *Inf. Vis.* **2015**, *14*, 250–269. [CrossRef]
42. Brewer, I.; MacEachren, A.M.; Abdo, H.; Gundrum, J.; Otto, G. Collaborative Geographic Visualization: Enabling Shared Understanding of Environmental Processes. In Proceedings of the IEEE Symposium on Information Visualization, Salt Lake City, UT, USA, 9–10 October 2000; pp. 137–141. [CrossRef]
43. Yang, Y.; Goodwin, S. What-Why Analysis of Expert Interviews: Analysing Geographically-Embedded Flow Data. In Proceedings of the IEEE Pacific Visualization Symposium, Bangkok, Thailand, 23–26 April 2019; pp. 122–126. [CrossRef]
44. Carpendale, S. *Evaluating Information Visualizations*; Kerren, A., Stasko, J.T., Fekete, J.-D., North, C., Eds.; Springer: Berlin/Heidelberg, Germany, 2008; Volume 4950. [CrossRef]
45. Lam, H.; Bertini, E.; Isenberg, P.; Plaisant, C.; Carpendale, S. Empirical Studies in Information Visualization: Seven Scenarios. *IEEE Trans. Vis. Comput. Graph.* **2012**, *18*, 1520–1536. [CrossRef]
46. Kandel, S.; Paepcke, A.; Hellerstein, J.M.; Heer, J. Enterprise Data Analysis and Visualization: An Interview Study. *IEEE Trans. Vis. Comput. Graph.* **2012**, *18*, 2917–2926. [CrossRef] [PubMed]
47. Roth, R.E. An Empirically-Derived Taxonomy of Interaction Primitives for Interactive Cartography and Geovisualization. *IEEE Trans. Vis. Comput. Graph.* **2013**, *19*, 2356–2365. [CrossRef] [PubMed]
48. Roth, R.E.; Çöltekin, A.; Delazari, L.; Filho, H.F.; Griffin, A.; Hall, A.; Korpi, J.; Lokka, I.; Mendonça, A.; Ooms, K.; et al. User Studies in Cartography: Opportunities for Empirical Research on Interactive Maps and Visualizations. *Int. J. Cartogr.* **2017**, *3*, 61–89. [CrossRef]
49. Haklay, M.; Tobón, C. Usability Evaluation and PPGIS: Towards a User-Centred Design Approach. *Int. J. Geogr. Inf. Sci.* **2003**, *17*, 577–592. [CrossRef]
50. Lloyd, D.; Dykes, J. Human-Centered Approaches in Geovisualization Design: Investigating Multiple Methods through a Long-Term Case Study. *IEEE Trans. Vis. Comput. Graph.* **2011**, *17*, 2489–2507. [CrossRef]
51. Mazza, R.; Berrè, A. Focus Group Methodology for Evaluating Information Visualization Techniques and Tools. In Proceedings of the International Conference on Information Visualisation (IV '07), Washington, DC, USA, 4–6 July 2007.

52. Suchan, T.A. Usability Studies of Geovisualization Software in the Workplace. In Proceedings of the 2002 annual national conference on Digital government research (dg.o '02), Los Angeles, CA, USA, 19–22 May 2022.
53. Bąkowska-Waldmann, E.; Kaczmarek, T. The Use of PPGIS: Towards Reaching a Meaningful Public Participation in Spatial Planning. *ISPRS Int. J. Geo-Inf.* **2021**, *10*, 581. [CrossRef]
54. Maguire, M. Methods to Support Human-Centred Design. *Int. J. Hum. Comput. Stud.* **2001**, *55*, 587–634. [CrossRef]
55. Angular. Available online: https://angular.io/ (accessed on 27 February 2022).
56. D3. Available online: https://d3js.org/ (accessed on 27 February 2022).
57. Park, S.; Bekemeier, B.; Flaxman, A.D. Understanding Data Use and Preference of Data Visualization for Public Health Professionals: A Qualitative Study. *Public Health Nurs.* **2021**, *38*, 531–541. [CrossRef]
58. Bolstad, P. *GIS Fundamentals: A First Text on Geographic Information Systems*, 4th ed.; Eider Press: White Bear Lake, MN, USA, 2012.
59. CBS StatLine. Available online: https://opendata.cbs.nl/ (accessed on 28 February 2022).
60. QGIS. Available online: https://qgis.org/ (accessed on 28 February 2022).
61. Eindhoven Open Data. Available online: https://data.eindhoven.nl/ (accessed on 30 March 2022).
62. GeoJSON. Available online: https://geojson.org/ (accessed on 28 February 2022).
63. Zacharopoulou, D.; Skopeliti, A.; Nakos, B. Assessment and Visualization of Osm Consistency for European Cities. *ISPRS Int. J. Geo-Inf.* **2021**, *10*, 361. [CrossRef]
64. Eindhoven in Cijfers. Available online: https://eindhoven.incijfers.nl/ (accessed on 30 March 2022).
65. Prieto, D.F.; Hagen, E.; Engel, D.; Bayer, R.; Hernandez, J.T.; Garth, C.; Scheler, I. Visual Exploration of Location-Based Social Networks Data in Urban Planning. In Proceedings of the IEEE Pacific Visualization Symposium, Hangzhou, China, 14–17 April 2015; pp. 123–127. [CrossRef]
66. Nesbitt, L.M.; Cliff, W.H. How the Story Unfolds: Exploring Ways Faculty Develop Open-Ended and Closed-Ended Case Designs. *Am. J. Physiol.-Adv. Physiol. Educ.* **2008**, *32*, 279–285. [CrossRef]
67. Wildemuth, B.M.; Freund, L. Assigning Search Tasks Designed to Elicit Exploratory Search Behaviors. In Proceedings of the Symposium on Human-Computer Interaction and Information Retrieval (HCIR '12), Cambridge, CA, USA, 4 October 2012.
68. Albers, M.J. Analysis for Complex Information: Focus on User Goals, Information Needs, and Information Relationships. In Proceedings of the First International Workshop on Coping with Complexity, Bath, UK, 16–17 September 2004.
69. Terry, M.; Mynatt, E.D. Side Views: Persistent, On-Demand Previews for Open-Ended Tasks. In Proceedings of the 15th Annual ACM symposium on User Interface Software and Technology, Paris, France, 27–30 October 2002.
70. Ahmed, A.; Hurwitz, D.; Gestson, S.; Brown, S. Differences between Professionals and Students in Their Visual Attention on Multiple Representation Types While Solving an Open-Ended Engineering Design Problem. *J. Civ. Eng. Educ.* **2021**, *147*, 04021005. [CrossRef]
71. Hasan, L.; Morris, A.; Probets, S. Using Google Analytics to Evaluate the Usability of E-Commerce Sites. In *Human Centered Design. HCD 2009. Lecture Notes in Computer Science*; Kurosu, M., Ed.; Springer: Berlin/Heidelberg, Germany, 2009; Volume 5619, pp. 697–706. [CrossRef]
72. Braun, V.; Clarke, V. Using Thematic Analysis in Psychology. *Qual. Res. Psychol.* **2006**, *3*, 77–101. [CrossRef]
73. Shneiderman, B. Eyes Have It: A Task by Data Type Taxonomy for Information Visualizations. In Proceedings of the 1996 IEEE Symposium on Visual Languages, Boulder, CO, USA, 3–6 September 1996.
74. Lu, M.; Liang, J.; Zhang, Y.; Li, G.; Chen, S.; Li, Z.; Yuan, X. Interaction+: Interaction Enhancement for Web-Based Visualizations. In Proceedings of the IEEE Pacific Visualization Symposium, Seoul, Korea, 18–21 April 2017; pp. 61–70. [CrossRef]
75. Carenini, G.; Conati, C.; Hoque, E.; Steichen, B.; Toker, D.; Enns, J. Highlighting Interventions and User Differences. In Proceedings of the CHI' 14: SIGCHI Conference on Human Factors in Computing Systems, Toronto, ON, Canada, 26 April–1 May 2014.
76. Krassanakis, V.; Kesidis, A.L. MatMouse: A Mouse Movements Tracking and Analysis Toolbox for Visual Search Experiments. *Multimodal Technol. Interact.* **2020**, *4*, 83. [CrossRef]
77. Cybulski, P.; Horbiński, T. User Experience in Using Graphical User Interfaces of Web Maps. *Int. J. Geo-Inf.* **2020**, *9*, 412. [CrossRef]
78. Jiang, B.; Li, Z. Geovisualization: Design, Enhanced Visual Tools and Applications. *Cartogr. J.* **2005**, *42*, 3–4. [CrossRef]

Article

A Constraint-Based Generalization Model Incorporating a Quality Control Mechanism

Natalia Blana [1], Ioannis Kavadas [2] and Lysandros Tsoulos [1,*]

[1] Cartography Laboratory, School of Rural, Surveying and Geoinformatics Engineering, National Technical University of Athens, 15780 Zografou, Greece
[2] Internal Quality Unit, Hellenic Cadastre, 15562 Holargos, Greece
* Correspondence: lysandro@central.ntua.gr

Abstract: Automation in map production has created the need for modeling the map composition process. Generalization is the most critical process in map composition, with considerable impact on the quality of features portrayed on the maps. Modeling of the generalization process has been an area of research for several years in the international cartographic community. Constraint-based generalization modeling prevailed, and it is evolving to an agent model or to other optimization models. The generalization model presented in this paper is based on constraint-based modeling. It introduces the standardization of the semantic and cartographic generalization process together with an evaluation mechanism for the assessment of the quality of the resulting cartographic data considering simultaneously the preservation of the shape of the portrayed linear and area features. For cartographers, quality management is a key factor in creating an evidence-based, reliable product. To achieve this objective, cartographers, drawing on international experience, should implement a quality policy and adopt a quality management system (QMS) as an integral part of the map production process, starting with the quality assessment of the input data and finishing with the evaluation of the final product.

Keywords: map quality; data quality model; semantic and cartographic generalization; generalization modeling; shape evaluation

1. Introduction

As a means of depicting the geography of an area, maps aim to store and display the geographic information of the area, considering the geographic features and their relationships. When considering the purpose of the map, scale restricts the display of geospatial entities (features' arrangement and their relationships), which is implemented through generalization (semantic and cartographic). The selection of the features to be depicted, along with their accuracy and clarity in portrayal together with the integrity of their relationships, are the goal of generalization.

Generalization is the most critical transformation in cartography, causing modification of features' shape and—occasionally—a partial to complete elimination of spatial information. Generalization modeling aims to control the process of generalization and has been a field of extensive research since the 1990s. A turning point in generalization modeling was the development of the constraint-based generalization model, which approaches generalization holistically through the integration of an evaluation mechanism for assessing the state of the data before, during and after generalization.

This article elaborates on the development of a constraint-based generalization model integrating a quality model with a shape evaluation mechanism, which was introduced partially in the previous work of the authors [1,2]. Considering generalization as the transition from a geospatial database (digital landscape model—DLM) to a cartographic one (digital cartographic model—DCM) as proposed by [3] and adopted by several European national mapping agencies [4], two complete topographic maps at scales 1:500,000 and 1:1,000,000 are composed. The maps produced are the result of the generalization process (semantic and cartographic) implemented on the EuroRegional Map geodatabase at scale 1:250,000 (area 15,143 km^2). The map feature classes include populated areas (points/polygons), coastline, road, railway and hydrographic network (linear features), and lakes and islands (polygons). Generalization is guided and evaluated in the framework of the constraint-based generalization model. A fundamental prerequisite for the accomplishment of the smooth and uninterrupted model function is the suitable quality of the input data. Therefore, the preliminary transition process from the geographic database to the initial spatial database is evaluated through the implementation of a separate quality model. This is also incorporated as a special issue in this article, together with a test case regarding the construction of the spatial database (at scale 1:25,000) derived from cadastral data. Attempting to extend the implementation of the introduced constraint-based generalization model to geodatabases at larger scales, containing cadastral data as proposed in [2], an additional test case is presented for the transition of the spatial database at scale 1:25,000 to a cartographic database at scale 1:50,000 and the production of the relevant map (with generalization applied on the road network feature class).

In the following sections, three processes are described for the successful construction of a cartographic database to be used for map composition, utilizing data of suitable quality and considering shape preservation of linear and polygonal features: (a) transition from a geographic database to the spatial database, (b) semantic generalization and (c) cartographic generalization. Each one of the three processes is based on a methodology for controlling data quality and securing an outcome of acceptable quality. Map specifications and ISO standards for spatial data quality are used, and new specifications and quality requirements, together with their corresponding measures and conformance levels, are composed. Test cases are demonstrated as a proof of concept for the validity of the proposed methodology.

1.1. Background and Recent Achievements on the Evaluation of Generalization

Generalization modeling has occupied the scientific community as a special research issue in automated map production since the 1990s. Three generalization models have been developed: (a) condition-action modeling or rule-based systems, (b) human interaction modeling and (c) constraint-based modeling, which prevailed among the three [5]. Constraint-based modeling introduced by [6] attempts to identify a state where a variety of constraints are satisfied [7]. Constraints are connected to measures and guide the generalization process through their satisfaction [5]. Constraint-based modeling constitutes the base for the development of optimization models (agent modeling, combinatorial optimization, continuous optimization) [5], as it integrates an evaluation mechanism to control the generalization process.

Quality evaluation and assessment in generalization has been identified as an inextricable part of the generalization models since the first attempts on the topic [8–12]. Current approaches regarding the integration of an evaluation process in generalization are based on the research conducted in the framework of: (a) the AGENT project (IGN, France), on the methodologies proposed by [13] and that of [14]; and (b) the EuroSDR project and the studies conducted by [15,16]. To encompass the scientific knowledge on generalization modeling and evaluation, three sub-processes are defined [17]:

i. evaluation for tuning before the commencement of generalization;
ii. evaluation for controlling during generalization;
iii. evaluation for assessing at the end of the generalization where the three processes are integrated, as proposed by [14].

In addition, considering the proposed conceptual framework by [17], the generalization model suggested by [9] and the methodologies proposed by [13,14] and [18] identify three basic components of the automated evaluation process:

i. definition and formation of map requirements as constraints;
ii. identification of measures for automated evaluation;

iii. execution of data matching between initial and resulting data.

In recent years, several national mapping agencies have implemented automated or semi-automated processes in map production (Ordnance Survey of Great Britain (OSGB); Institut Geographique National—IGN, France; The Netherlands Kadaster; Institut Cartografic de Catalunya—ICC, Spain; AdV—Germany; Swisstopo—Switzerland; KMS—Denmark; and USG-S—USA) [4,19–21] with multi-agent systems prevailing in generalization processes. Despite the evolution of automation in map production, there is a lack of a high-impact methodology concerning generalization modeling [22]. Emerging research on deep learning integration in generalization modeling has appeared, but it is still at an early stage [22–24].

1.2. Research Goals and Innovation

As it is pointed out in the introduction, the work presented in this article is the amalgamated outcome of the efforts presented in [1,2] concerning the design of a constraint-based generalization model, together with a quality model for each phase of generalization (semantic and cartographic) and its implementation for the construction of a complete topographic map. With the aim to contribute to the constraint-based modeling evolution, the work presented here covers special issues where scientific knowledge in generalization modeling needs to be enhanced with methods concerning the evaluation of shape preservation and legibility violation tolerances [18], as well as simplified techniques for the resolution of geometric conflicts which perform better—in some cases—than those used by the complex multi-agent systems [4]. It also incorporates the design of the semantic constraint-based generalization model applied to a geospatial database, which is considered a prerequisite for cartographic generalization in the current multi-agent systems but is not described formally in published scientific literature. In addition, a new shape measure is introduced along with a method for the selection of the appropriate generalized feature for display preserving shape [2].

In this article, a comprehensive methodology for the design of the proposed constraint-based generalization model is analyzed. The article is structured in three sections. In the first section, the proposed constraint-based generalization model is presented together with the special case of quality management in transitioning a geographic database to a geospatial one (Section 2.1). The semantic generalization process, first introduced in [1], is further analyzed to be the fundamental generalization process as it constitutes the reference for the creation of the cartographic database. A new technique for a network's density reduction is also developed, including legibility violation tolerances, based on the features' geometric characteristics. Cartographic generalization is also presented briefly (Section 2.3), based on [2], in order to prove the functionality of the proposed constraint-based generalization model as it results in the cartographic database used for display. Along with the synoptic approach to cartographic generalization, guidelines are provided for the configuration of the method introduced in [2] for the evaluation and assessment of shape preservation. In Section 2.4, a formulated example of the semantic and cartographic generalization of the road network at scale 1:500,000 is presented. In Section 3, the results of the test cases are presented with the corresponding maps. Finally, in Section 4, a discussion based on the results is included, followed by topics for future research.

Regarding the constraint-based model application environment, it is clarified that functions of the ESRI ArcGIS software (ESRI's file geodatabases, ESRI's point remove simplification algorithms, and ESRI's bend simplify algorithm) are used in combination with free-access library tools in the Python programming language (SciPy, https://scikit-learn.org/stable/, Scikit-learn, https://scipy.org/, Shapely, https://pypi.org/project/Shapely/, accessed on 20 January 2021). New functions have been developed in the Python programming language in the context of the research on similarity measures, shape representation techniques, measures of horizontal accuracy, topological consistency, conceptual consistency, relative position, legibility evaluation, network density reduction techniques and process automation. ESRI's ArcMap software is used to compose and display the maps.

2. A Constraint-Based Generalization Model Encompassing an Evaluation and Assessment Methodology for Cartographic Data

The proposed generalization model adopts the approach introduced by [3] that defines the generalization process as the transition from a spatial database originating from a geographic database to a cartographic one. Constraint-based modeling is used as the prototype for the design of the proposed generalization model, which integrates an evaluation routine designed according to [17] as a quality model for each phase of the generalization process (semantic and cartographic). The proposed quality model is composed of three elements and is constructed according to [18]. The three structural elements of the quality model are adequate for the implementation of each phase of the generalization process (introduced partially in [1]), and they are presented complete as follows:

i. Structural element 1: It includes a) the map specifications expressed as constraints along with their violation thresholds for guiding the generalization process, and b) the map quality specifications expressed as quality requirements along with their conformance levels for the evaluation and the quality assessment of the resulting cartographic data;

ii. Structural element 2: It includes the measures and techniques for the evaluation of the features' state, the assessment of their compliance with the constraints before and during generalization, and their compliance with the quality requirements after the generalization transformations;

iii. Structural element 3: It includes the constraint-based generalization process (semantic and cartographic) and the quality control stage configured as follows:

- The process for the selection of the appropriate generalization transformation with its corresponding algorithm through the evaluation and the assessment of the state of the features before generalization with respect to the set constraints;
- The execution of the transformation algorithms and the evaluation of the features' condition through the assessment of their compliance with the constraints during the generalization process. In case of non-compliance issues, a different calibration of the parameters of the algorithm used is performed, or a different algorithm suitable for the selected transformation is utilized;
- The quality checks evaluate the condition of the features at the end of each phase of the generalization process through the assessment of their compliance with the quality requirements. In the case of error detection, an extra generalization transformation is carried out, such as elimination or displacement.

The formulation of constraints is based on the EuroSDR project approach as described in [25] (legibility and appearance preservation constraints), enriched with new features concerning semantic generalization. Quality requirements are formed considering the three quality components: (a) geometric quality regarding the features' shape and position, (b) thematic quality regarding the features' categorization and their attributes' values, and (c) graphic/Gestalt quality regarding the map's legibility and its ability to represent geographic phenomena, namely the features' relationships (conceptual and topological).

As mentioned in the introduction, the knowledge of the quality of the input data is critical for the implementation of the proposed constraint-based generalization model. Therefore, a methodology for the assessment of the quality of the spatial data and the method for the transition of a geographic database to a spatial one are also incorporated in the next section as a special subject matter utilizing data from the Hellenic Cadastre (Section 2.1).

2.1. Quality Management in Transitioning Geographic Databases to Spatial Databases at Different Scales

In map composition, map producers use different types of geospatial data from a variety of sources collected for different purposes. They then integrate this data into software applications and process it using various procedures and methodologies, which are additional sources of error for the resulting product. It is important for cartographers that quality management is a key factor in the creation of an evidence-based, reliable product. To achieve this objective, the cartographer, drawing on international experience, should implement a quality policy and adopt a quality management system (QMS) as an integral part of the map production process. By applying QMS to the production of geospatial data, quality management is involved in all phases of its production, from the definition of user requirements to the delivery of the final product. The adoption of a QMS based on international standards will ensure the expected quality of the map to the satisfaction of its users.

In this context, and as far as quality management is concerned, cartographers are required to consider user requirements to define quality requirements and quality objectives at each implementation phase, to use monitoring indicators in order to determine whether or not the quality objectives are achieved, to adequately document the quality of the map produced, and to assess the degree of user satisfaction with a view to further improve the quality of the map. To optimize quality management within a QMS, it is indispensable—as best practice—to develop and implement a quality model that will form the core of the QMS.

Table 1 shows how quality management is involved in the main phases of the geospatial data production process.

Table 1. Interpretation of quality in different phases of production [26].

Phase of production	Quality Documentation	Goal for Quality	Quality Methods	Level
Before production	Specifications Quality model	Define quality requirements	Analysis of customer requirements	Entity/Feature type level
Production	Database Process history	Meet the specifications Record expected quality to database	Inspection	Entity/Feature instance
After production	Metadata Test reports	Measure conformance to quality requirements	Evaluation Reporting	Dataset level

Interpreting the contents of Table 1, the core of the quality system is the compilation and implementation of a quality model. In the following paragraphs, the methodology for developing and implementing the quality model applied to evaluate and document the quality of the spatial database created is elaborated.

2.1.1. Spatial Database Development—Data Model

A software application is developed to integrate the cadastral data held by the Hellenic Cadastre, at scale 1:1000 for urban areas and 1:5000 for other areas of Greece, into a spatial database. The aim of the application is to create the necessary spatial data to be used as reference data to produce a topographic map at scale 1:25,000 for the country.

The structure of the spatial database is implemented based on a predefined feature attributes coding system (FACS) that includes the following categories of entities:

- AdministrativeUnits;
- Topography;
- SpotElevation;
- Hydrography;
- TransportNetworks;
- PopulatedPlaces;
- LandUse;

- ProtectedSites;
- UtilityNetworks;
- NamedPlaces;
- GeneralFeatures.

For the coding of the entities, the selection of their attributes, and their field of definition, the technical specifications of the INSPIRE directive adapted to the data are used. This is because the geospatial database to be created will contain data fully compliant with the specifications of the INSPIRE Directive.

The design and implementation of the spatial database include the stages of conceptual, logical, and physical design. Following the building of the feature attribute coding system (FACS), the data's conceptual, logical, and physical model is compiled.

Figure 1 shows the implementation flow of the spatial database based on its conceptual and logical design.

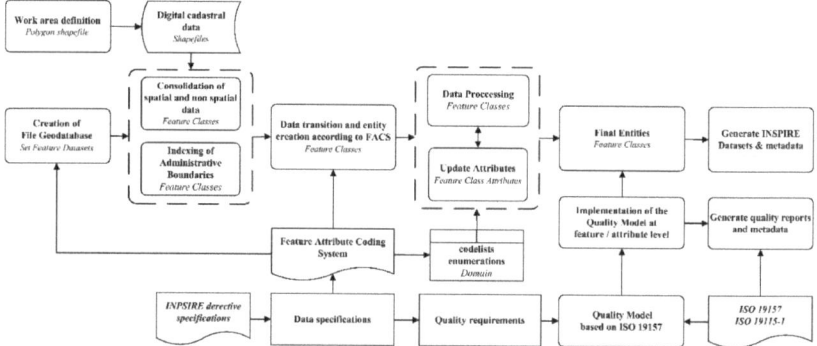

Figure 1. Workflow for the creation of the spatial database based on its conceptual and logical design.

A standalone software application for Microsoft Windows has been developed to create, feed, and update the spatial database and to assess the quality of the data. The application has been developed in the Microsoft Visual Studio environment, which is the main management platform of the application and is used in the implementation of its interface with the operator. The management of spatial information and the application of the quality model are executed in ArcMap. For data analysis, data integration and data processing code are developed in Python programming language using the ArcPy site package.

2.1.2. Compilation and Implementation of the Quality Model

According to [27], a quality model for geospatial data is defined as "a model describing the quality of a geospatial data set according to the technical specifications" (fit-for-purpose QM). According to [26], a quality model for geospatial data is defined as "a framework for the measurement and the representation of the quality of a dataset". The Quality Knowledge Exchange Network (Q-KEN) Committee of Eurogeographics, propose a more comprehensive definition, which defines the geospatial data quality model as "A framework for defining, evaluating, documenting, and presenting the quality of spatial data sets and geo-services according to their specifications" [28]. During its implementation, the differences between the dataset and the "Universe of Discourse" (UoD) are identified, detected and measured to assess their significance and to be documented in the quality reports and transcripts.

The "quality" of data is involved in all phases of the production process (see Table 1). The best methodology to ensure data quality and achieve quality objectives is the development and implementation of a spatial data quality model (SDQM) using international standards [26,29,30]. The goal of a successful implementation of an SDQM is to measure the extent to which the requirements of the specifications are met and to ensure that the needs of data users are met in a timely and efficient manner. When implemented, a SDQM provides (a) a common understanding of data quality issues across all stakeholders, (b) improved performance, (c) lower production costs, (d) confidence in the data, and (e) more effective management and monitoring of data quality.

Quality in geospatial data sets refers to the entity level, which is the basic building block. The SDQM identifies the quality requirements at the entity level, detects the sources of potential errors affecting data quality, and identifies the metrics required to quantify quality and to assess and ensure the quality of the data. The first and foremost step in the design and development of an effective quality model is the analysis and identification of quality requirements and objectives.

For each quality requirement, the quality parameters are selected consisting of a combination of a quality element and a quality measure. Based on the above, the quality model is developed using the ISO 19157:2013 [31] standard. For each combination of quality element and quality measure, a method of evaluation is used to assess the quality and quantify possible errors in the data set. Table 2 shows a part of the SDQM. It shows the quality parameters selected to assess the quality of the administrative unit's data set (polygon entities).

In addition, the cell color indicates the evaluation technique chosen to evaluate the quality and quantify the quality measure:

- Sampling inspection according to ISO 2859–1 [32] (yellow cells);
- Sampling inspection according to ISO 3951–1:2013 [33] to determine sample size and FGDC standard [34], [35] for the distribution of the checkpoints (green cells);
- Full inspection (orange cells).

Table 2. Quality model (part). It includes the set of quality elements proposed by the ISO 19157 Standard. The colored cells describe the combination of quality element and quality measure that is selected at the entity or entity attribute level of the data element. Each cell indicates the type of quality measure chosen with reference to the identification number compliant with ISO 19157 Annex D.

Entity Type & Attribute	Geospatial Database—Quality Model—ISO Quality Elements								
	Completeness		Logical Consistency				Positional Accuracy		
	Commission	Omission	Conceptual Consistency	Domain Consistency	Format Consistency	Topological Consistency	Absolute Accuracy	Relative Accuracy	Gridded Data Accuracy
AdministrativeUnit	Error count id 2	Error count id 6	Correctness indica-		Error indicator id 119				
	Error count id 2	Error count id 6							
inspireId				Error indicator id 14					
country				Error indicator id 14					
geometry	Error count id 4		Error count id 11			Error count id 23, id 24 id 25, id 26 id 27		id 28	
name									
nationalCode				Error indicator id 14					
HCCode				Error indicator id 14					
nationalLevel				Error indicator id 14					
nationalLevelName				Error indicator id 14					
surfaceArea									
beginLifespanVersion									
endLifespanVersion									

Table 2. *Cont.*

Entity Type & Attribute	Geospatial Database—Quality Model ISO Quality Elements					
	Temporal Accuracy			Thematic Accuracy		
	Accuracy of a Time Measurement	Temporal Consistency	Temporal Validity	Classification Correctness	Non-Quantitative Attribute Correctness	Quantitative Attribute Accuracy
AdministrativeUnit				Error count id 60		
inspireId						
country						
geometry						
name				Error count id 60	Error count id 65	
nationalCode					Error count id 65	
HCCode					Error count id 65	
nationalLevel					Error count id 65	
nationalLevelName					Error count id 65	
surfaceArea						LE99.8 id 73
beginLifespanVersion			Error indicator id 14			
endLifespanVersion						

2.1.3. Quality Results

The application of the quality model for each combination of quality element/quality measure results in a quality value. The software application developed provides specific functionality that helps the evaluator to implement the quality model and the chosen evaluation techniques. The results of the assessment are stored automatically or manually (depending on the evaluation technique used) in a specific table within the geodatabase (see Table 3). The evaluator then automatically derives the evaluation results in the form of a quality report and/or metadata file based on the requirements of ISO 19157 [31]. For the cartographer to decide whether and to what extent the geospatial data created are suitable for use to produce a map, they should assess the resulting quality outcome. The evaluation of the quality results is carried out in comparison with the quality objectives established in advance. If the results of data quality are appropriate, they can proceed to the next stage of simplification/generalization. If one or more of the quality objectives are not met, revision of the specifications, selection of new reference data sets, update of the quality model and/or revision of the levels of compliance set is required.

An example of the evaluation of the quality outcomes associated with the dataset for the administrative units in the work area is shown in Table 3. The cadastral data used as reference data have documented but unpublished quality.

For sampling inspection of completeness and thematic accuracy (yellow cells), recent data and the administrative division of Greece were used as references. As expected, the resulting qualitative results are zero, confirming the quality of the reference data. The logical consistency of the data is assessed automatically through full inspection. The quality results detected three topological errors referring to invalid sliver polygons. These errors are identified and quantified, and their location in the geodatabase is recorded. As their exact spatial location in the dataset is known, it is feasible to eliminate them in the next stage of the mapping process. The sliver polygons identified create very small gaps in the data in relation to the intended accuracy of the map, and their presence is not considered significant. The results of the positional accuracy checks, as expected, confirm the suitability of reference data. The inspection of temporal validity also gives zero results.

In conclusion, based on the evaluation of all quality results at the entity level of the spatial database, the predefined quality objectives are achieved, and the data are suitable for the production of smaller-scale maps. The data included in the spatial database are of acceptable quality and can be used as input data in the next stage of generalization.

Table 3. Implementation results of the QM of the spatial database (part).

FCID	FeatureType_Attribute	DQ ELEMENT	DQ Sub_ELEMENT	Name of Measure	Measure Identification	DQ_Quantitative Result	Result ValueType
AU01	Administrative Unit	Completeness	Commission	error count	2	0	Integer
AU02	Administrative Unit	Completeness	Omission	error count	6	0	Integer
AU03	Administrative Unit	Logical Consistency	Conceptual Consistency	correctness indicator	9	True	Boolean
AU04	Administrative Unit	Logical Consistency	Format Consistency	error indicator	119	True	Boolean
AU05	Administrative Unit	Thematic Accuracy	Classification Correctness	error count	60	0	Integer
AU06	inspireId	Logical Consistency	Domain Consistency	error indicator	14	True	Boolean
AU07	country	Logical Consistency	Domain Consistency	error indicator	14	True	Boolean
AU08	geometry	Completeness	Commission	error count	4	0	Integer
AU09	geometry	Logical Consistency	Conceptual Consistency	error count	11	0	Integer
AU10	geometry	Logical Consistency	Topological Consistency	error count	23	0	Integer
AU11	geometry	Logical Consistency	Topological Consistency	error count	24	0	Integer
AU12	geometry	Logical Consistency	Topological Consistency	error count	25	3	Integer
AU13	geometry	Logical Consistency	Topological Consistency	error count	26	0	Integer
AU14	geometry	Logical Consistency	Topological Consistency	error count	27	0	Integer
AU15	geometry	Positional Accuracy	Absolute Accuracy	Mean value of positional uncertainties	28	1.22	Meters
AU16	name	Thematic Accuracy	Non-quantitative Attribute Correctness	error count	60	0	Integer
AU17	name	Thematic Accuracy	Non-quantitative Attribute Correctness	error count	65	0	Integer
AU18	nationalCode	Thematic Accuracy	Non-quantitative Attribute Correctness	error count	65	0	Integer
AU19	nationalCode	Logical Consistency	Domain Consistency	error indicator	14	True	Boolean
AU20	HCCode	Thematic Accuracy	Non-quantitative Attribute Correctness	error count	65	0	Integer
AU21	HCCode	Logical Consistency	Domain Consistency	error indicator	14	True	Boolean
AU22	nationalLevel	Thematic Accuracy	Non-quantitative Attribute Correctness	error count	65	0	Integer
AU23	nationalLevel	Logical Consistency	Domain Consistency	error indicator	14	True	Boolean
AU24	nationalLevelName	Thematic Accuracy	Non-quantitative Attribute Correctness	error count	65	0	Integer
AU25	nationalLevelName	Logical Consistency	Domain Consistency	error indicator	14	True	Boolean
AU26	surfaceArea	Thematic Accuracy	Quantitative Attribute Correctness	LE99.8	73	True	Boolean
AU27	beginLifespanVersion	Temporal Accuracy	Temporal Validity	error indicator	14	True	Boolean

2.2. Semantic Generalization Process

In this section, the semantic generalization process is deployed in the framework of the proposed quality model based on constraint-based generalization modeling. The semantic generalization process may alter the features' categorization and attribution [36]. The presented generalization model adopted the semantic generalization transformations proposed by [36] on the schema level (class abstraction, class elimination, class composition, attribute elimination, attribute aggregation, modification of the feature class intension—namely the feature class joining rules) and the instance level (feature elimination, feature reclassification, features aggregation, feature merging, attribute values modification).

The semantic generalization constraints are formulated considering the process as a transition between the spatial and the cartographic databases [1]. It is implemented through the transfer of features from the spatial to the cartographic database and is based: (a) on the identification of the relation between the features classes of the initial database and those of the new one (one-to-one, many-to-one, one-to-none), and (b) to the determination of the semantic generalization transformations. Constraints include the legibility preservation requirement (features' separation, minimum area, and length), the preservation of appearance (features' arrangement/patterns and distribution), the compatibility between spatial and cartographic databases schemata (feature classes, feature attributes), the compatibility between spatial and cartographic databases physical structures (features' geometric types, attributes fields types, attributes domains, projections), and the features' compliance with their feature class rules (geometric and thematic). The quality requirements are formulated based on the quality components (thematic and graphic/Gestalt quality). The thematic quality checks include the examination of the information completeness of the features and their attributes, the features' classification correctness, the domain consistency, and the attribute values' correctness. The graphic/Gestalt quality checks include the examination of the legibility preservation (distance between features, density) and conceptual consistency. The constraints violation threshold and the quality requirements conformance levels are set to acceptable or unacceptable.

Quality measures provided by the ISO 19157 standard [31] for geospatial data quality are used for the evaluation of the features state and for the assessment of their compliance with the set thresholds and the quality requirements conformance levels. The ISO quality element "completeness" is used for the evaluation of feature classes and their attributes' presence in both databases—namely, the spatial and the cartographic databases schemata. The ISO quality element "logical consistency" is adopted for the evaluation of the features' conceptual consistency, the attribute values' compliance with their attribute domain, and the spatial and cartographic databases' physical structures compatibility. The ISO quality element "thematic accuracy" is adopted for the evaluation of the features categorization and their attribute values' correctness. The graphic/Gestalt quality regarding map legibility is evaluated with a simple technique based on buffer zones. A network's density reduction proved to be more complex; therefore, a special technique has been developed based on the features' geometric characteristics when semantic information is missing. Five cases are examined and resolved regarding a network's density reduction.

i. Junction of two lines (Figure 2a). A junction of two lines is detected when the endpoints of two lines coincide, and the lines are not closed (they do not have the same coordinates at the start and the endpoints). Two lists with the coordinates of the endpoints of the reference line are created, as well as the other two lists with the coordinates of the endpoints of the intersected lines. When the coordinates of the intersected lines lists belong to the lists of the reference line, then there is a junction of two lines. A line is eliminated when 20% of its length is included in the buffer zone (buffer zone width is set according to the separation distance limit of 0.25 mm at the generalization scale) of the reference line. Regarding railway and road networks, the line with the shortest length is the reference line because it is retained considering that the longest line is a siding line. The reverse case is applied on the hydrographic network considering that the longest line is the main river due to its shape sinuosity.

ii. Junction of three lines (Figure 2b). A junction of three lines is detected when two lines having a node coinciding with each endpoint of the reference line have also another coinciding node that does not belong to the reference line. The longest line is eliminated, considering it as a bend when 20% of its length is included in the buffer zone (buffer zone width is set according to the separation distance limit of 0.25 mm at the generalization scale) of the reference line.

iii. Junction of lines constitutes a polygon with an area less than the threshold. A polygon-to-area transformation is applied, and the longest line is eliminated in the case of the railway and road networks and the smallest in the case of the hydrographic network.

iv. Two non-connected lines distinction (Figure 2c). A buffer zone is created around a reference line (buffer zone width is set according to the separation distance threshold of 0.25 mm at the generalization scale) of the reference line. The examined line included in the buffer zone of the reference line is eliminated if it does not intersect the reference line. To retain road continuity and considering that a road consists of several segments, a list is created containing the intersecting lines with the eliminated line each time an action is implemented. Each time an elimination need occurs for two lines, the elimination of the line included in the list is preferred.

v. Elimination of lines with a dangling node that is not included in the buffer zone (buffer zone width is set according to the separation distance limit of 0.25 mm at the generalization scale) of a point or polygon is conceptually inconsistent considering that lines in a network should be connected to a location or to each other.

vi. "Orphan" lines. An "orphan" line is considered a line with dangling nodes at the endpoints. "Orphan" lines are eliminated as conceptually inconsistent.

The semantic generalization process is carried out per theme for each feature class following the order: polygons, lines, and points. Considering that: (a) the new cartographic database schema, and (b) the correspondence between feature classes and features attributes of the initial database schema with the new one is known; the progress of semantic generalization is carried out as follows:

i. Before generalization:
- Compatibility evaluation between the initial and the cartographic database schemata regarding features classes and features' attributes correspondence leading to the application of semantic transformations on features classes and features' attributes (transformations on the schema level);
- Compatibility of projections, feature classes' geometric types, features' attributes field types, and domains compatibility evaluation (transformations on the schema level).

ii. During generalization: Transferring data between databases (from the spatial database to the cartographic one), implementing transformations on the instance level, and assessing transformation results per feature class to resolve possible conflicts.
- Features' compatibility evaluation against each feature's class rules (geometric and thematic) leading to features reclassification/merging, elimination/aggregation, and their attributes' value modification (transformations on the instance level);
- Features' compatibility evaluation to legibility rules (features distinction, density) leading to the features' reclassification/merging, elimination/aggregation, and their attributes' value modification (transformations on the instance level;
- The three kinds of relationships between feature classes of the initial database and the new one (one-to-one, many-to-one, none-to-one) correspond to transformations on the schema level along with feature class attributes' transformation (attribute elimination, attribute aggregation). They signify the transformations to be applied on the instance level for the successful completion of the transferring process. Specifically, the class abstraction transformation applies feature reclassification or feature merging followed by attribute values modification. Class

elimination/class composition transformations apply feature elimination and feature aggregation;
- Quality controls per feature class regarding features compliance with quality requirements: features number completeness (compatibility to the feature class rules), features correct categorization when subcategories' attribute values are not null, attribute values completeness and correctness (no null values), attributes values compatibility to the attributes' domains (domain consistency), conceptual consistency regarding "holes" creation when features are eliminated or merged.

iii. At the end of the generalization process: Quality controls between feature classes.
- Conceptual consistency evaluation and assessment in feature relationships regarding invalid overlaps usually occur because of the polygons merging when the space between them is filled. Conflicts are resolved by altering the features participating in the merging process or by canceling the action;
- Legibility preservation evaluation regarding features distinction

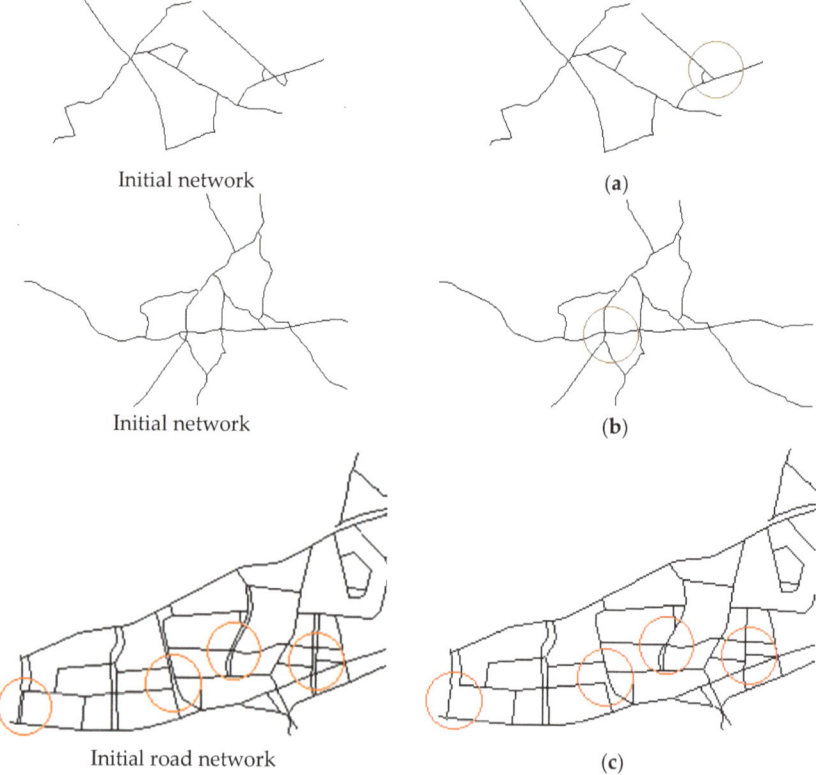

Figure 2. (a) refinement-junction of two lines, (b) refinement-junction of three lines, (c) refinement-two non-connected lines distinction. Reducing network density through lines elimination (red cycle).

With respect to map production at scales 1:500,000 and 1:1,000,000, legibility constraints are configured as follows: (a) the separation distance threshold is set at 0.25 mm at the generalization scale, (b) the polygons area threshold is set less than 1 km² at scale 1:500,000 and less than 3 km² at scale 1:1,000,000, (c) the lines length threshold is set shorter than 1 km at scale 1:500,000 and less than 2 km at scale 1:1,000,000 concerning lines in a network (railway, road, hydrographic) carrying one dangling node. Other constraints which lead to feature elimination or geometric transformation (e.g., polygon-to-point) are formulated based on thematic information like the built areas' population or the missing information like rivers without names which are considered of minor importance. Semantic generalization on the railway, road, and hydrographic network is implemented basically as network reduction by using the techniques mentioned earlier. Semantic generalization on polygonal features (building areas and lakes) is based on thematic information (same names) and legibility constraints, and it is implemented through merging along with the integration of a polygon-to-point geometric transformation regarding the building areas' feature class. The polygonal features at both scales (1:500,000 and 1:1,000,000) which are involved in a merging process, are derived directly from the initial spatial database at scale 1:250,000. The results of the quality controls at the end of the semantic generalization process are presented in Section 3.

2.3. Cartographic Generalization Process

In this section, the cartographic generalization process (following the semantic generalization phase) is deployed in the framework of the proposed quality model based on constraint-based generalization modeling. It aims to produce data suitable for display on the map. Cartographic generalization transformations have an impact on the features' geometry and alter their spatial rendering. Based on this approach, the constraints in cartographic generalization refer to features shape preservation: (a) position and orientation preservation and (b) shape preservation. Respectively, the quality requirements in cartographic generalization are related to the geometric and graphic/Gestalt quality. The geometric quality assumes features relative position correctness. The graphic/Gestalt quality assumes legibility preservation, topological consistency (connectivity), and conceptual consistency. The constraints violation threshold and the quality requirements conformance levels are set to acceptable or unacceptable except for the case of the shape preservation constraint. The ISO 19157 [31] standard on quality measures for spatial data quality is used to evaluate the features' condition and assess the features' compliance with the constraint's violation thresholds and the quality requirements conformance levels. The evaluation of the shape preservation constraint and the assessment of the features' compliance with it (elaborated in [2]) requires the comparison of the initial feature's shape with its new shape (after generalization). The shape-matching process is carried out through shape transformation (shape representation in another form, e.g., Fourier series, turning function, etc.) and measurement of its similarity using a similarity measure [37]. Considering the two approaches, guidelines are developed for the evaluation and assessment of the shape preservation degree during the generalization process. This includes:

- Parametric description of the feature's shape based on its geometric characteristics or its representation;
- Evaluation of the feature's shape condition through the application of a similarity measure for measuring the distance (dissimilarity) between the initial and the generalized feature, considering that a short distance corresponds to similarity and a long distance corresponds to dissimilarity [37];
- Evaluation of the feature's shape condition through the implementation of a legibility measure in the feature's geometric elements (vertices, part-lines) for the evaluation of its shape sharpness;
- Evaluation of the feature's shape state through the application of a horizontal accuracy measure;
- Evaluation of the feature's shape state through the application of a topological consistency measure regarding the feature's geometry for the evaluation of its shape integrity;
- Assessment of the feature's shape preservation degree based on the feature's compliance with legibility, horizontal accuracy, and topological consistency constraints;
- Assessment of the feature's shape through a technique for the determination of the suitable shape for portrayal.

Based on these guidelines, a new shape measure was introduced in [2] along with shape parameterization and a technique for the selection of the most suitable shape for portrayal (test case included the simplification algorithms examination: ESRI's point remove [38], and ESRI's bend simplify [39]). Specifically, the turning function weighted length difference was introduced as a new shape measure. It is configured as the difference between the weighted turning function length of the original feature to the weighted turning function length of the generalized feature considering weight as the ratio of the number of vertices of the generalized feature to the number of vertices of the original feature:

$$L_{tf}x\left(\frac{Ng}{No}\right), \text{weighted turning function length of the generalized feature}$$

$$L_{tf}x\left(\frac{No}{No}\right), \text{weighted turning function length of the initial feature}$$

- N_o, N_g = the number of vertices of the initial, generalized lines;
- L_{tf} = the turning function length considering the turning function as a step-function where on the x-axis, the normalized feature length [0,1] is set, and on the y-axis, the counterclockwise cumulative angle of the tangent at each feature vertex is set.

The proposed parameterization for shape description is based on the comparison between the shape measures and their suitability for the assessment of shape preservation in cartographic generalization. Hausdorff distance, modified Hausdorff distance, Fréchet distance, turning function distance as area, and distance between Fourier descriptors for different representation techniques were examined in [2]. Between them, the turning function weighted length and the modified Hausdorff distance proved to be the most appropriate for shape description as they are increasing along with spatial information reduction. The modified Hausdorff distance [40] between lines A and B is defined as follows:

$$f(d(A,B), d(B,A)) = \max(d(A,B), d(B,A))$$

- $d(A,B) = \frac{1}{Na}\sum_{a\in A} d(a,B)$,
  the distance between the set of points on line A and the set of points on line B;
- $d(B,A) = \frac{1}{N\beta}\sum_{b\in B} d(b,A)$,
  the distance between the set of points on line B and the set of points on line A;
- $Na, N\beta$ = the number of points in each set of points on lines A and B;
- $d(a,B) = \min||a-b||$;
  the minimum Euclidean distance between point a on line A and the set of points on line B;
- $d(b,A) = \min||b-a||$,
  the minimum Euclidean distance between point b on line B and the set of points on line A.

The legibility constraints are related to the distinction between the features' geometric elements (minimum accepted resolution of 0.25 mm at generalization scale). They are evaluated on the basis of measures estimating the "bottleneck phenomenon" and very sharp corners. The horizontal accuracy constraint is evaluated through the measurement of the percentage of the length of the generalized line located outside the buffer zone of the original line [41]. Aiming to avoid visual conflicts between features, the horizontal accuracy acceptable conformance level is set according to the minimum accepted resolution (0.25 mm) at the generalization scale. Topological accuracy constraints are evaluated based on measures provided by the ISO 19157 standard [31] regarding self-intersections and self-overlaps. Techniques for the implementation of the legibility measures, the horizontal accuracy and the topological consistency constraints are also provided in [2]. The selection of the suitable feature for portrayal is made from the group of features complying with legibility, horizontal accuracy, and topological consistency constraints. The hierarchical clustering process is applied to the feature's shape description parameters estimated per the tolerance value of the simplification algorithm. For each cluster, a representative having the highest silhouette correlation coefficient is identified, and among them, the representative corresponding to the maximum tolerance value is considered the most appropriate for portrayal. In Figure 3, a test case of the proposed method for the selection of a suitable generalized line for portrayal is presented.

The cartographic generalization process is carried out in two stages. In the first stage, the generalization algorithm (simplification) is applied, and the selection method of the suitable feature for portrayal is carried out. In the second stage, quality controls are implemented for the evaluation and assessment of the resulting features in the first stage, including (a) topological consistency (overshoots, undershoots, sliver polygons); (b) conceptual consistency (invalid overlaps); (c) relative position preservation; and (d) legibility preservation (features distinction). Techniques for the application of the measures of the quality requirements concerning topological consistency, conceptual consistency, relative position accuracy, and legibility preservation are also provided in [2].

The simplification algorithm of ESRI's point remove [38] is applied on the road and railway network, and ESRI's bend simplify [39] is applied on polygonal features and hydrographic network to produce the maps at scales 1:500,000 and 1:1,000,000. Regarding the simplification of the road network at scale 1:50,000, the ESRI's point remove [38] algorithm is utilized.

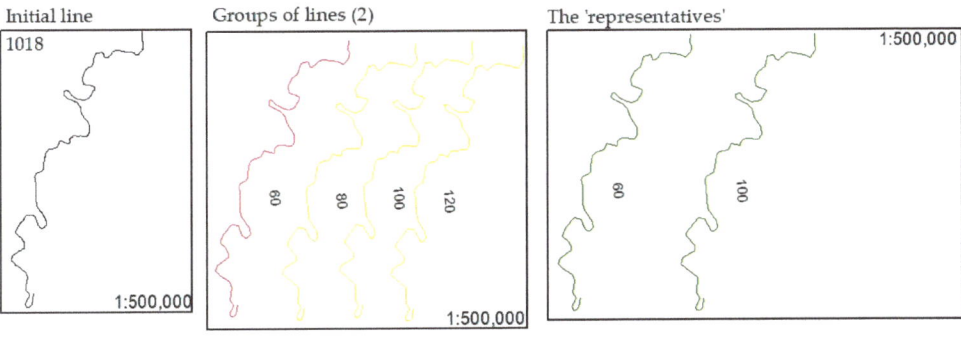

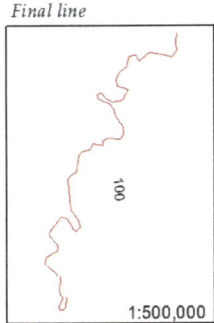

Figure 3. Test case for the selection of the suitable generalized line for portrayal according to the proposed proceedure.

2.4. Road Network Generalization Example

Specifications: Horizontal accuracy is set to 500 m at scale 1:500,000 and 1000 m at scale 1:1,000,000. The minimum separation distance is set to 125 m at scale 1:500,000 and 250 m at scale 1:1,000,000.

2.4.1. Semantic Generalization of the Road Network (scale 1:500,000)

Constraints: Compatibility between the initial and the new schema must exist regarding features geometric types, attributes fields types, attributes domains, and projections to ensure the successful features transfer from the initial to the final geodatabase. Legibility must also be retained. The constraints' conformance levels are set to acceptable or unacceptable.

Quality requirements: Domain consistency attribute values' correctness, and legibility preservation (minimum separation distance) must be retained. The quality requirements conformance levels are set to acceptable or unacceptable.

The process:

i. Geodatabases compatibility controls (initial vs. final). Geometric types, attributes' field types, and their domains and projections are compatible. All features are transferred from the geodatabase at scale 1:250,000 to the geodatabase at scale 1:500,000.
ii. Three out of the four categories of the road network are retained. The "national", "primary" and "secondary" roads are retained. The "local" roads are eliminated.
iii. Junction cases (i), (ii), and (iii) described in Section 2.2 are simplified to achieve the network's density reduction. The minimum separation distance is set to 125 m and the threshold of the polygon area considered as a junction (case iii) is set to 1 km^2.
iv. The road hierarchy (national, primary, and secondary roads) is retained in case there is a need for feature elimination.
v. Elimination of lines with a dangling node that does not fall in the buffer zone of 500 m (map specification) of a built-up area.
vi. "Orphan" lines elimination.
vii. Quality controls are carried out on the feature class level regarding attribute fields with "null"/"none" values and attributes fields values compatibility to their domains. No extra quality control regarding the network's density is required.
viii. Quality controls are carried out between feature classes with respect to conceptual consistency (overlays) and legibility (features belonging to different classes) when the semantic generalization process is completed for each feature class. The road network's conceptual consistency is checked against features of aggregated lakes (roads are not allowed to pass through lakes unless their initial condition implies that). The road network's feature separation is checked against the railway and hydrographic network. In the case of conflicts, only the conflicts where elimination is applied are resolved. Displacement as a solution to resolve visual conflicts is implemented in cartographic generalization.
ix. Results are shown in Section 3.

2.4.2. Cartographic Generalization of the Road Network (scale 1:500,000)

Constraints: Shape preservation and horizontal accuracy. The horizontal accuracy threshold is set to 125 m based on the minimum separation distance to avoid visual conflicts.

Quality requirements: Features legibility, relative position consistency, topological consistency (overshoots, undershoots), and conceptual consistency (overlays). The quality requirements conformance levels are set to acceptable or not acceptable.

The process:

i. Point remove simplification algorithm [38] is applied. Tolerance is set in the range 20 m to 1000 m with 20 m intervals resulting in 50 generalized lines corresponding to each line of the initial road network;
ii. Legibility between features geometric elements ('bottleneck phenomenon' and very sharp corners), horizontal accuracy, and features topological consistency (self-intersections, self-overlaps) is checked for each generalized line. A group of generalized features complying with conformance levels is created, which corresponds to each initial line of the road network. Each feature of the group is bound to a tolerance value;

iii. Modified Hausdorff distance between the initial and the generalized line and the difference between the turning function weighted lengths of the initial and the generalized line are computed for each line in each group formed in the previous step (ii). These two parameters describe the shape of each line in each group;
iv. Hierarchical clustering is carried out on each group. Shape parameters computed in the previous step (iii) are used in clustering. The process is applied for the different number of clusters and different linkage criteria (Ward's, average, complete, single). The best number of clusters of each group is chosen, the one which: a) retains the highest mean silhouette correlation coefficient, and b) clusters with members that present a positive value for the silhouette correlation coefficient. For each cluster of each group, the member with the highest silhouette correlation coefficient is selected as the "representative" one. Among the representative members, the one corresponding to the maximum tolerance value is selected as suitable for display on the map;
v. Quality control at the feature class level is not necessary. Topological inconsistencies (overshoots, undershoots) are not expected as the applied point remove algorithm retains the endpoints of the lines. Quality control is carried out between feature classes. Legibility errors, such as features separation, are expected in cases where features displacement is required. Results are shown in Section 3.

3. Results and Conclusions

Sections 2.2 and 2.3 elaborate on the design of the proposed constraint-based model along with its implementation on (a) the EuroRegional Map geodatabase at scale 1:250,000 for the creation of two maps at scales 1:500,000 and 1:1,000,000, and (b) on a geodatabase at scale 25,000 with cadastral data for the creation of a map at scale 1:50,000 (the generalization model was applied only on the road network). In Figures 4 and 5, maps at scales 1:500,000 and 1:1,000,000 are shown. In addition, in Figure 6, the road network at scale 1:50,000 is displayed in comparison to its initial form at scale 1:25,000.

Semantic generalization results concerning spatial information reduction are presented in Table 4, and quality controls at the end of the process are as follows:

- Twelve (12) legibility conflicts were identified concerning roads and rivers (4364 lines were examined), fourteen (14) legibility conflicts were identified concerning roads and railways (3792 lines were examined) at scale 1:500,000;
- Twenty-seven (27) legibility conflicts were identified concerning roads and rivers (3974 lines were examined), twenty (20) legibility conflicts were identified concerning roads and railways (3699 lines were examined) at scale 1:1000,000.

Cartographic generalization results regarding quality controls at the end of the process are presented below:

- Four (4) legibility conflicts were identified concerning roads and rivers (4364 lines were examined), 2 legibility conflicts were identified concerning road and railway networks (3792 lines were examined) at scale 1:500,000;
- Twenty-eight (28) legibility conflicts were identified concerning roads and rivers (3974 lines were examined), twenty (20) legibility conflicts were identified concerning road and railway networks (3699 lines were examined), one (1) legibility conflict was identified involving rail and rivers (479 lines were examined) at scale 1:1,000,000. Semantic and cartographic generalization quality control on the geodatabase at scale 1:50,000 with cadastral data resulted in no errors (as expected).

Analyzing the quality results, the satisfactory functionality of the proposed constraint-based generalization model is documented. As shown, a small number of errors occur, which allows the visual inspection of each case and the manual handling of errors, where needed.

Figure 4. Topographic map at scale 1:500,000.

Figure 5. Topographic map at scale 1:1,000,000.

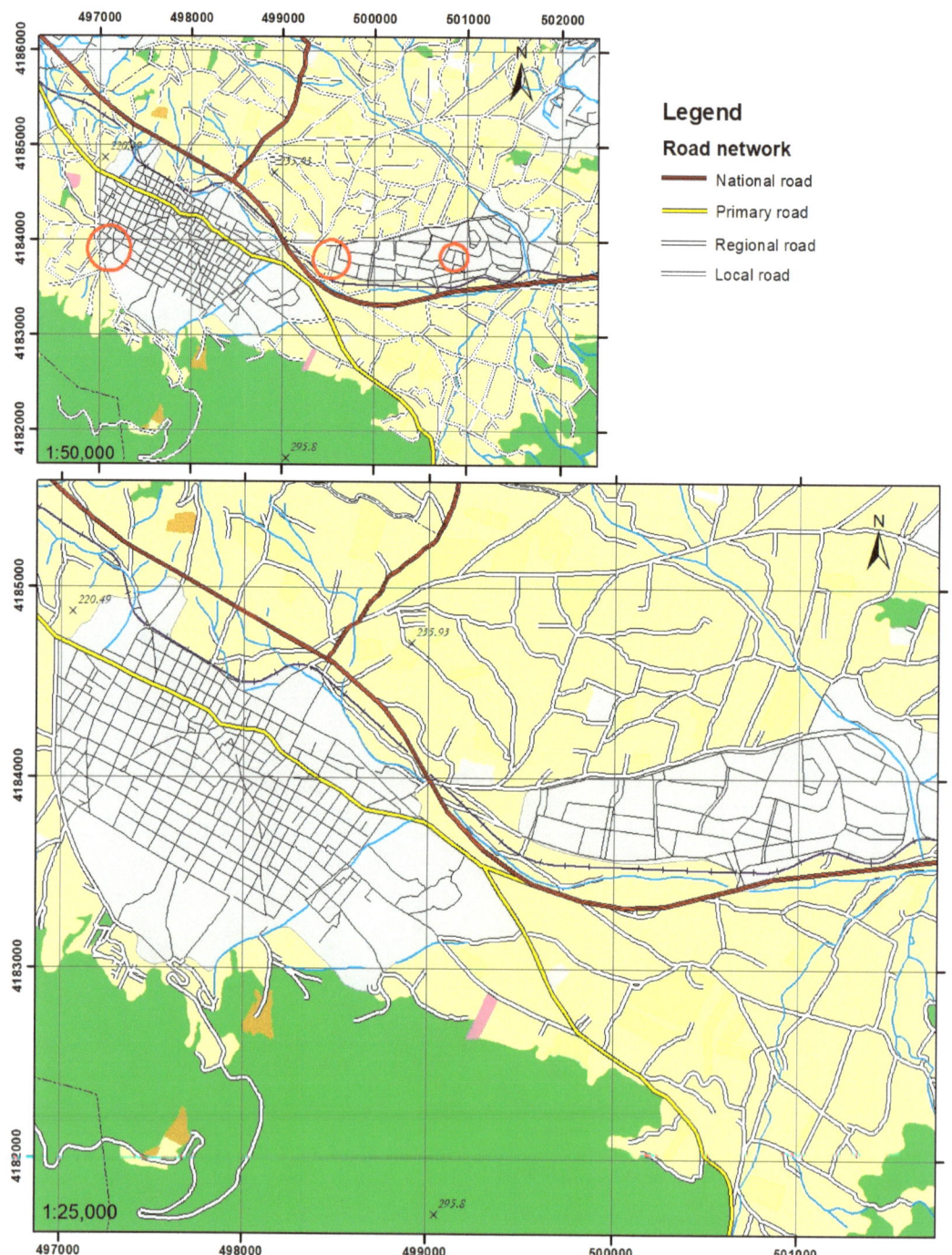

Figure 6. Road network map at scales 1:25,000 (initial geodatabase) and 1:50,000. Red circles displayed on the map at scale 1:50,000, indicate the impact of semantic generalization.

Table 4. Features reduction per feature class caused due to semantic generalization.

	1:250,000	1:500,000	1:1,000,000
Built area (polygon)	210	113	63
Built area (point)	1829	552	317
Road network	14,522 km	9014 km	8831 km
Railway network	1680 km	987 km	957 km
Lake	1329	49	17
Watercourse (polygon)	184	1	1
Watercourse (line)	5968 km	4294 km	2551 km
Island	85	20	8
Coastline (None of its parts are deleted)	1356 km	1356 km	1356 km

4. Discussion and Future Work

In this article, a constraint-based generalization model with a quality evaluation mechanism, as introduced originally by the authors in [1,2], is presented together with its implementation to produce topographic maps. The proposed model provides a concise organizational framework and a comprehensive generalization methodology for linear and area features. The proposed techniques are simple with straightforward parameterization compared to more sophisticated generalization systems such as multi-agent systems. The new shape measure and the new parameterization method of the features' shape introduced are more sensitive in capturing any change of shape caused due to generalization in comparison to the existing measures in the literature. Finally, quantitative legibility violation thresholds are configured for the selection of the suitable feature's shape for portrayal. The methodology developed incorporates the fundamental constraints, the quality requirements, the quality measures, and the implementation techniques for the evaluation and assessment of the cartographic data resulting from generalization together with a new method for the selection of the suitable feature for portrayal on the map with respect to the preservation of its shape. As it is derived from the examination of the maps produced (Figures 4–6), the implementation of the proposed model results in the composition of high-quality maps at any scale. The novelty of the work presented is based on: a) the analysis and standardization of the semantic generalization process, which is not demonstrated sufficiently in published work; b) the integration of the quality model with the aforementioned new shape evaluation mechanism; c) the location and resolution of legibility violations according to quantitative conformance levels; d) the network's density reduction techniques for the resolution of geometric conflicts in a simplified way using quantitative legibility violation thresholds; e) the application of the ISO 19157 Standard on quality and the associated map specifications. An additional advantage of the proposed constraint-based generalization model is its applicability in any geographic information system environment.

Future work will be related to the expansion of the proposed model. Methods for the evaluation of the information density and legibility regarding symbolization could be integrated. In addition, optimization techniques that will trigger automated displacement of the features for the resolution of geometric conflicts could also be incorporated.

Author Contributions: Conceptualization, N.B., I.K. and L.T.; methodology, N.B., I.K. and L.T.; software, N.B. and I.K.; validation, N.B., I.K. and L.T.; investigation, N.B., I.K.; resources, N.B., I.K. and L.T.; data curation, N.B., I.K.; writing—original draft preparation, N.B., I.K.; writing—review and editing, L.T.; visualization, N.B. and I.K; supervision, L.T. All authors have read and agreed to the published version of the manuscript.

Funding: This research received no external funding.

Data Availability Statement: Data made available by the NTUA Cartography Laboratory.

Conflicts of Interest: The authors declare no conflict of interest.

References

1. Blana, N.; Tsoulos, L. Constraint-Based Spatial Data Management for Cartographic Representation at Different Scales. *Geographies* **2022**, *2*, 258–273. [CrossRef]
2. Blana, N.; Tsoulos, L. Generalization of Linear and Area Features Incorporating a Shape Measure. *ISPRS Int. J. Geo-Inf.* **2022**, *11*, 489. [CrossRef]
3. Grünreich, D. *Computer-Assisted Generalization*; Papers CERCO Cartography Course; Institut für Angewandte Geodäsie: Frankfurt, Germany, 1985.
4. Duchêne, C.; Touya, G.; Taillandier, P.; Gaffuri, J.; Ruas, A.; Renard, J. *Multi-Agents Systems for Cartographic Generalization: Feedback from Past and On-Going Research*; Research Report; IGN (Institut National de l'Information Géographique et Forestière); LaSTIG, équipe COGIT: Saint Mandé, France, 2018; Available online: https://hal.archives-ouvertes.fr/hal-01682131/document (accessed on 28 February 2022).
5. Harrie, L.; Weibel, R. Modelling the overall process of generalisation. In *Generalisation of Geographic Information: Cartographic Modelling and Applications*; Mackaness, W., Ruas, A., Sarjakoski, T., Eds.; Series of International Cartographic Association; Elsevier Science: Amsterdam, The Netherlands, 2007; pp. 67–88.
6. Beard, K. Constraints on rule formation. In *Map Generalisation: Making Rules for Knowledge Representation*; Buttenfield, B.P., McMaster, R.B., Eds.; Longman Group: Harlow, UK, 1991; pp. 121–135.
7. Sarjakoski, L.T. Conceptual models of generalization and multiple representation. In *Generalisation of Geographic Information: Cartographic Modelling and Applications*; Mackaness, W., Ruas, A., Sarjakoski, T., Eds.; Series of International Cartographic Association; Elsevier Science: Amsterdam, The Netherlands, 2007; pp. 11–37.
8. McMaster, R.B.; Shea, K.S. *Generalization in Digital Cartography*; Association of American Geographers: Washington, DC, USA, 1992.
9. Weibel, R. Three essential building blocks for automated generalization. In *GIS and Generalization: Methodology and Practice*; Mueller, J., Lagrange, J.P., Weibel, R., Eds.; Taylor & Francis: London, UK, 1995; pp. 56–70.
10. Ehrliholzer, R. Quality assessment in generalization: Integrating quantitative and qualitative methods. In Proceedings of the 17th International Cartographic Conference, Barcelona, Spain, 3–9 September 1995.
11. João, E.M. *Causes and Consequences of Map Generalization*; Taylor and Francis: London, UK, 1998.
12. Brazile, F. Semantic Infrastructure and Methods to Support Quality Evaluation in Cartographic Generalisation. Ph.D. Thesis, Department of Geography, University of Zurich, Zurich, Switzerland, 2000.
13. Bard, S. Quality Assessment of Cartographic Generalisation. *Trans. GIS* **2004**, *8*, 63–81. [CrossRef]
14. Bard, S.; Ruas, A. Why and How Evaluating Generalised Data? In *Developments in Spatial Data Handling, Proceedings of the 11th International Symposium on Spatial Data Handling*; Springer: Berlin/Heidelberg, Germany, 2004; pp. 327–342.
15. Burghardt, D.; Schmid, S.; Duchêne, C.; Stoter, J.; Baella, B.; Regnauld, N.; Touya, G. Methodologies for the evaluation of generalised data derived with commercially available generalisation systems. In Proceedings of the 11th ICA Workshop of the ICA Commission on Generalisation and Multiple Representation, Montpellier, France, 20–21 June 2008.
16. Stoter, J.; Baella, B.; Blok, C.; Burghardt, D.; Duchêne, C.; Pla, M.; Regnauld, N.; Guillaume, T. *State-of-the-Art of Automated Generalization in Commercial Software*; EuroSDR Publication: Frankfurt, Germany, 2010.
17. Mackaness, W.; Ruas, A. Evaluation in the map generalisation process. In *Generalisation of Geographic Information: Cartographic Modelling and Applications*; Mackaness, W., Ruas, A., Sarjakoski, T., Eds.; Series of International Cartographic Association; Elsevier Science: Amsterdam, The Netherlands, 2007; pp. 89–111.
18. Stoter, J.; Zhang, X.; Hanna, S.; Harrie, L. Evaluation in Generalisation. In *Abstracting Geographic Information in a Data Rich World. Methodologies and Applications of Map Generalisation Lecture Notes in Geoinformation and Cartography*; Burghardt, D., Duchêne, C., Mackaness, W., Eds.; Springer: Cham, Switzerland, 2014; pp. 259–297.
19. Stoter, J.; Post, M.; Van Altena, V.; Nijhuis, R.; Bruns, B. Fully automated generalization of a 1:50k map from 1:10k data. *Cartogr. Geogr. Inf. Sci.* **2014**, *41*, 1–13. [CrossRef]
20. Regnauld, N.; Touya, G.; Gould, N.; Foerster, T. Process Modelling, Web Services and Geoprocessing. In *Abstracting Geographic Information in a Data Rich World. Methodologies and Applications of Map Generalisation Lecture Notes in Geoinformation and Cartography*; Burghardt, D., Duchêne, C., Mackaness, W., Eds.; Springer: Cham, Switzerland, 2014; pp. 197–225.
21. Duchêne, C.; Baella, B.; Brewer, C.; Burghardt, D.; Buttenfield, B.; Gaffuri, J.; Käuferle, D.; Lecordix, F.; Maugeais, E.; Nijhuis, R.; et al. Generalisation in Practice Within National Mapping Agencies. In *Abstracting Geographic Information in a Data Rich World. Methodologies and Applications of Map Generalisation Lecture Notes in Geoinformation and Cartography*; Burghardt, D., Duchêne, C., Mackaness, W., Eds.; Springer: Cham, Switzerland, 2014; pp. 329–391.
22. Touya, G.; Zhang, X.; Lokhat, I. Is deep learning the new agent for map generalization? *Int. J. Cartogr.* **2019**, *5*, 142–157. [CrossRef]
23. Kronenfeld, B.J.; Buttenfield, B.P.; Stanislawski, L.V. Map Generalization for the Future: Editorial Comments on the Special Issue. *ISPRS Int. J. Geo-Inf.* **2020**, *9*, 468. [CrossRef]
24. Sester, M. Cartographic generalization. *J. Spat. Inf. Sci.* **2020**, *21*, 5–11. [CrossRef]
25. Burghardt, D.; Schmid, S.; Stoter, J. Investigations on cartographic constraint formalisation. In Proceedings of the Workshop of the ICA Commission on Generalization and Multiple Representation at the 23nd International Cartographic Conference ICC, Moscow, Russia, 4–10 August 2007.
26. Jakobsson, A.; Holmes, J. (Eds.) *Update Guideline for Implementing the ISO 19100 Geographic Information Quality Standards in National Mapping and Cadastral Agencies*; EuroGeographics Quality Knowledge Exchange Network (Q-KEN): Brussels, Belgium, 2018.

27. Rocha, L.A.; Montoya, J. *Spatial Data Quality Model for "Fit-For-Purpose" Methodology in Colombia*; FIG Working Week 2020: Amsterdam, The Netherlands, 2020.
28. Eurogeographics Quality-Knowledge Experts Network (Q-KEN). Creating a Data Quality Model. In Proceedings of the 3rd International Workshop on Spatial Data Quality, Valetta, Malta, 28–29 January 2020; Eurogeographics Q-KEN: Brussels, Belgium, 2020.
29. Kavadas, I. ISO Standards in the Development of a Spatial Information Quality Model. Postgraduate Thesis, Geoinformatics Postgraduate Programme, School of Rural and Surveying Engineering, National Technical University of Athens, Athens, Greece, 2007. (In Greek)
30. Kavadas, I. Assessment of Spatial Information Quality using the ISO International Standards. In Proceedings of the 11th National Cartography Conference, Nafplio, Greece, 8–10 November 2010; Hellenic Cartographic Society: Thessaloniki, Greece, 2010; pp. 467–483. (In Greek)
31. *ISO 19157*; Geographic Information—Data Quality. International Organization for Standardization: Geneva, Switzerland, 2013.
32. *ISO 2859-1*; Sampling Procedures for Inspection by Attributes—Part 1: Sampling Schemes Indexed by Acceptance Quality Limit (AQL) for Lot-By-Lot Inspection. International Organization for Standardization: Geneva, Switzerland, 2006.
33. *ISO 3951-1*; Sampling Procedures for Inspection by Variables—Part 1: Specification for Single Sampling Plans Indexed by Acceptance Quality Limit (AQL) for Lot-By-Lot Inspection for a Single Quality Characteristic and a Single AQL. International Organization for Standardization: Geneva, Switzerland, 2013.
34. *No FGDC-STD-007.3-1998*; Geospatial Positioning Accuracy Standards—Part 3: National Standard for Spatial Data Accuracy. FGDC: Washington, DC, USA, 1998.
35. *No FGDC-STD-002-1999*; Spatial Data Transfer Standard (SDTS). FGDC: Washington, DC, USA, 1999.
36. Regnauld, N.; McMaster, R.B. A synoptic View of Generalisation Operators. In *Generalisation of Geographic Information: Cartographic Modelling and Applications*; Mackaness, W., Ruas, A., Sarjakoski, T., Eds.; Series of International Cartographic Association; Elsevier Science: Amsterdam, The Netherlands, 2007; pp. 37–66.
37. Veltkamp, R. Shape matching: Similarity measures and algorithms. In Proceedings of the International Conference on Shape Modeling and Applications, Genova, Italy, 7–11 May 2001; pp. 188–197.
38. Douglas, D.; Peucker, T. Algorithms for the Reduction of the Number of Points Required to Represent a Digitized Line or its Caricature. *Can. Cartogr.* **1973**, *10*, 112–122. [CrossRef]
39. Wang, Z.; Muller, J.C. Line generalization based on analysis of shape characteristics. *Cartogr. Geogr. Inf. Sci.* **1998**, *25*, 3–15. [CrossRef]
40. Dubuisson, M.P.; Jain, A. A Modified Hausdorff distance for object matching. In Proceedings of the 12th International Conference on Pattern Recognition, Jerusalem, Israel, 9–13 October 1994; Volume 1, pp. 566–568.
41. Goodchild, M.; Hunter, G. A Simple Positional Accuracy Measure for Linear Features. *Int. J. Geogr. Inf. Sci.* **1997**, *11*, 299–306. [CrossRef]

Disclaimer/Publisher's Note: The statements, opinions and data contained in all publications are solely those of the individual author(s) and contributor(s) and not of MDPI and/or the editor(s). MDPI and/or the editor(s) disclaim responsibility for any injury to people or property resulting from any ideas, methods, instructions or products referred to in the content.

Article

Geovisualization of Historical Geospatial Data: A Web Mapping Application for the 19th-Century Kaupert's Maps of Attica

Georgios Lampropoulos [1,*], George Panagiotopoulos [2], Christina Giannakoula [1] and Alexandros Kokkalas [1]

[1] Dipylon Society, 6 Omirou Str., 10564 Athens, Greece; christing136@hotmail.com (C.G.); akokkalas@gmail.com (A.K.)
[2] Metsovio Interdisciplinary Research Center, National Technical University of Athens, 9 Iroon Polytechniou Str., 15780 Athens, Greece; g.panag@metal.ntua.gr
* Correspondence: giorglmbr@gmail.com; Tel.: +30-6942687697

Abstract: This paper presents the development procedure and significance of a web mapping application designed for disseminating, exploring, and analyzing Kaupert's 19th-century Maps of Attica, Greece. The application facilitates historical and geographical study by providing access to high-resolution map images and overlaying multiple vector layers of geospatial data. The paper outlines the methods used to create the application, which includes the process of interpreting, digitizing, and organizing the original mapped data, georeferencing the historical cartographic sheets, and developing the web-based mapping application. The results of this work include a comprehensive and interactive digital reference tool for studying the ancient topography of Attica, as well as a framework for future research. Overall, this work highlights the potential of digital technologies to transform the way we approach and study historical maps and other cultural artifacts.

Keywords: archaeological cartography; historical maps; geospatial data; webGIS; cultural heritage; digital humanities; geovisualization; web mapping application; Johann A. Kaupert

1. Introduction

1.1. The 19th-Century Topographic-Archaeological Mapping of Attica

Historical maps are essential records that provide valuable insights into the past [1–4], often being the only available source for reconstructing historical events. However, the reliability of such maps can vary depending on factors such as the period they were created in, the techniques employed, and the skill level of the cartographer [5,6]. Therefore, researchers need to be mindful of the uncertainties present in historical maps, as they can pose challenges for analyzing data over specific time frames and require careful consideration in developing methodologies. In addition, the limited accuracy of early cartographic maps adds further complexity to this issue [7].

Nevertheless, the Maps of Attica, created by Kaupert and his team, is a remarkable example of a comprehensive topographic study of a complex region. Immediately after the establishment of the German Archaeological Institute in Athens in 1874, the institute's mastermind, the archaeologist Ernst Curtius, expressed the necessity of mapping the Attic land on single topographic-archaeological maps, as the area has been a cradle of civilization since ancient times and was full of archaeological monuments and remains. The German Empire supported this venture, intending to gain access to the East and gain primacy in the study of the classical world. However, to complete the archaeological mapping of the region, geographical background maps were required. As the newly established Greek nation still needed to have ready-constructed ones, the decision was taken to create them from scratch [8]. Thus, the Maps of Attica, a two-decade project (1875–1894), focus not only on specific topographic elements, such as the road network, settlements, or place names but also constitute a comprehensive topographic study of the area. Moreover, the fact that a region of complex topography with remote areas and rugged terrain was mapped, resulting in a series of maps of such detail using the equipment of the time, indicates the professional work of Kaupert and his team. Furthermore, these results are in accordance with prior research examining the surveys conducted by German topographers in the Attica region [9–11].

1.2. Web Mapping Applications in Spatial Humanities and Cultural Heritage

Web mapping applications provide a powerful tool for scholars in the field of spatial humanities to explore, visualize, and analyze various forms of geographical data and maps [12]. They play a crucial role in spatial humanities research as they facilitate the processing and analysis of vast amounts of spatial data. These systems allow researchers to create interactive maps, query and analyze data, and share their findings with other scholars in a way that is easy to access and interpret.

In spatial humanities research, web mapping can be used to study various phenomena that have spatial components, such as migration patterns, cultural landscapes, and urban development [13]. Such tools can also be utilized to map and analyze historical events, such as the movements of armies, trade routes, and the spread of disease [14,15].

Web mapping tools can also help scholars explore and understand complex spatial relationships. For example, the visualization of historical data on a map can help researchers identify patterns and relationships that might not be immediately apparent in text-based sources. This can be particularly useful in fields such as archaeology, where researchers can use digital mapping to analyze the distribution of artifacts across a landscape [16].

The interactivity offered by digital mapping allows users to filter the data at the desired scale and can include a plethora of additional information that allows interdisciplinary analysis [17]. The addition of the web element offers more possibilities for the dissemination and exchange of data among researchers.

Web mapping applications are widely used in cultural and archaeological heritage to visualize and share information about historical sites, monuments, artifacts, and landscapes [18]. Such applications offer users the opportunity to explore the cultural heritage of an area in a visual and interactive way, allowing them to experience the heritage site from a virtual perspective [19]. Additionally, web mapping applications can be used to create digital archives of cultural heritage data, providing a more accessible and sustainable way to preserve cultural heritage [20].

There are a few examples of cultural heritage web mapping applications, such as the "Mapping Ancient Athens" project (https://mappingancientathens.org, accessed on 30 March 2023) and the "Kitchener's survey of Cyprus 1878–1883" project (https://kitchener.hua.gr, accessed on 30 March 2023). Both aim to provide a better understanding of historical locations and their significance. For instance, the "Mapping Ancient Athens" project unveils an unknown side of Athens by mapping rescue excavations and highlighting connections between archaeological sites and the present-day urban landscape. It makes vast amounts of archaeological data more accessible to a broader audience, including researchers, professionals, citizens, and visitors [21]. Similarly, the "Kitchener's survey of Cyprus 1878–1883" project documents and arranges information from Kitchener's historical map of Cyprus, making it easily accessible to users via a dedicated web application. The online application encourages the sharing and utilizing of this data by individuals interested in historical cartography and geography [22]. Both projects allow for basic and advanced searches, and the data are presented in a user-friendly format to appeal to a broad audience.

The effective utilization of web mapping applications in cultural heritage preservation and presentation relies on the development of accurate spatial databases to support detailed digital maps. In this case, the "Karten von Attika in the Era of Digital Humanities" project is achieved through the use of powerful tools and methodologies as the project team was able to effectively manage large quantities of spatial data, which included various types of geographical features and historical maps.

Relevant literature, such as "PostGIS in Action" by Obe and Hsu [23] and "Historical GIS: Technologies, Methodologies, and Scholarship" by Gregory and Ell [24], provides valuable guidance and insight for spatial database development in humanitarian studies. The development of this database is in line with emerging trends in historical GIS and the spatial humanities, which emphasize the importance of GIS and related technologies for humanities scholarship [24,25]. Other related works that address the implementation and use of GIS-based systems for heritage protection, management [26,27], and tourism [28,29] further demonstrate the versatility and significance of GIS for various fields. Moreover, cultural databases are gaining attention; thus, standards for data collection, organization, and analysis must be improved and widely adopted to address the unique challenges posed by cultural data [30]. The creation of a spatial database, as demonstrated in this project, is therefore essential for managing and analyzing spatial data in a comprehensive and efficient manner.

1.3. Research Aim

The objective of this article is to present the development of an online cartographic platform as a tool to disseminate and analyze Kaupert's Maps of Attica. Previous studies have demonstrated the usefulness of online mapping applications for this purpose [21,22,31,32]. In this research, state-of-the-art technologies are employed to accomplish the goal, aiming to present Kaupert's work with utmost precision and dependability, while ensuring easy accessibility for both the scientific community and the general public.

2. Materials and Methods

In this chapter, the materials and methodology employed for the project are presented in detail. A schematic representation of this work can be seen in Figure 1. Firstly, the 24 sheets of 19th-century Kaupert's Maps of Attica were merged and georeferenced to create a seamless image mosaic. Then, the database was designed to store and link descriptive and geospatial data, facilitating their management and retrieval. Next, the historical-geographical content of the map was interpreted, categorized, and digitized using a GIS environment. The final step of the methodology involves the design and creation of the interactive web mapping application that incorporates all the information gathered and processed in the earlier phases and makes them publicly available.

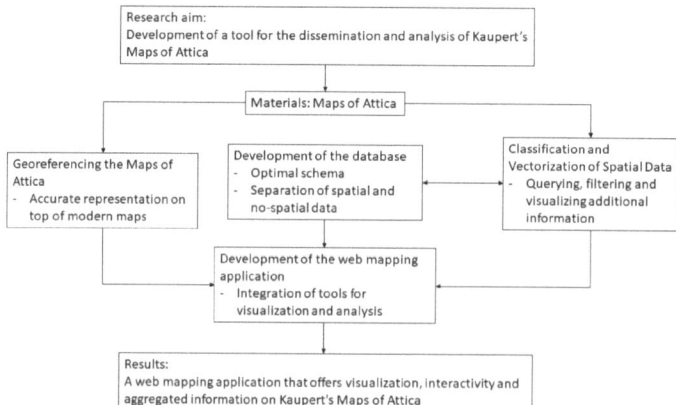

Figure 1. Representation of the steps of the methodology to achieve the research aim of this work.

2.1. Cartographic Material

Twenty-four adjacent cartographic sheets from the extensive 19th-century Karten von Attika project [33] were selected for visualization on the cartographic platform, namely those numbered 3–26 (III–XXVI) (Figure 2). On a scale of 1:25,000, these sheets depict the

19th-century attic land to its entire extent. In addition, cartographic sheets 1 and 2 (I and II), which are not among those analyzed, show in greater detail the areas of Athens and Piraeus, respectively, at a scale of 1:12,500. All the above cartographic sheets were acquired from the rich collection of maps of the Melissa publishing house, specifically from the translated in Greek and edited by Manolis Korres publication of Karten von Attika [34]. Moreover, freely accessible cartographic backgrounds were used to identify the ground control points (GCPs) for georeferencing the unified Maps of Attica.

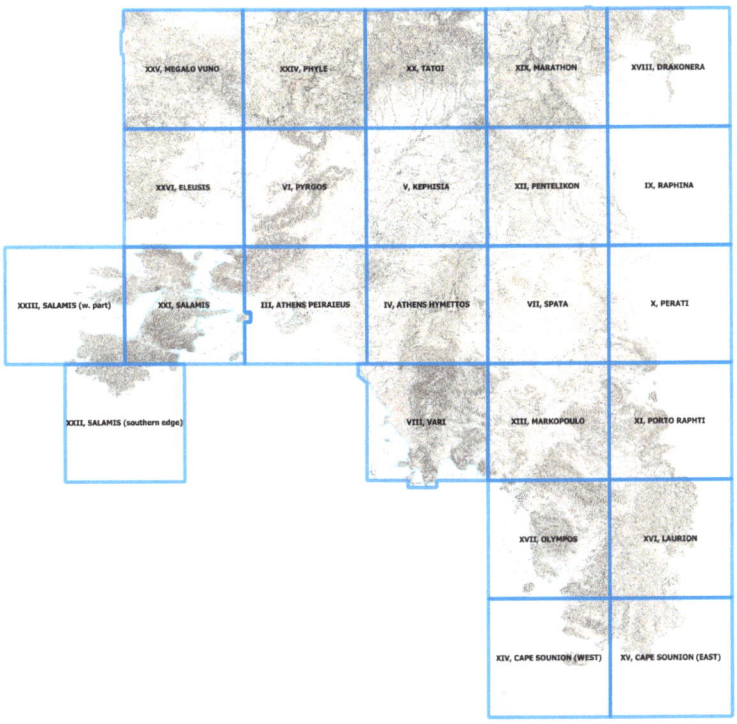

Figure 2. The twenty-four stitched adjacent cartographic sheets of Kaupert's Maps of Attica.

2.2. Methods

2.2.1. Classification and Vectorization of Spatial Data

In order to systematize the cartographic data depicted on the Maps of Attica, a separation of the data into cartographic signs and cartographic labels was initially carried out. Symbols are identified as signs, while the words that appear on the maps are identified as labels. Recognizing symbols and words is often a demanding process as, despite the excellent resolution of the digitized cartographic sheets, the distinction of the letters in words can be a difficult task (Figure 3).

For the identification of the cartographic signs, information was drawn from symbols of multiple legends provided by the original 19th-century work. The critical legend was the general legend of the cartographic sheet I, "Athens and surroundings", which contains the most crucial information about the road network, hydrographic network, architectural remains, natural features, buildings, and other human-made constructions. As annotated in the rest of the cartographic sheets, the explanations of the symbols are those given on the first cartographic sheet [33]. Furthermore, the additional legends of sheets XIV, XV, "Cape Sounion", and XVI, "Laurion", have been used to identify the red signs depicted on the Maps of Attica. According to the annotated cartographic information, the red signs are recognized as ancient remains [33]. Moreover, to further verify the explanation of the symbols, we examined the legend of another cartographic product of the same map series, the "Overview Map of Attica", a map of the region's full extent, in scale 1:100,000 produced by the merging of partial cartographic sheets. A considerable part of cartographic signs regarding the human-made environment was recorded in the database, as well as the total number of cartographic labels.

Figure 3. Difficulty identifying the word. Tränke (DE)/Brücke (DE).

The cartographic data are classified into 16 thematic categories and, at a second hierarchical level, into 56 sub-categories, as shown in Table 1. The categories contain cartographic signs and labels with related concepts, e.g., the terms 'cistern', 'basin', and 'reservoir' are classified under the term 'cistern', which in turn is classified under the broader category of 'water supply'. A quantitative analysis of the categorized cartographic signs and labels is presented in Table 2.

Table 1. The classification of cartographic data depicted on the Maps of Attica.

Domestic Space	farm/metochi	house	settlement/village			
Defense	fortifications	military facilities	naval base			
Transport	coastal navigation	railroad	road network			
Water Supply	cistern	fountain	hydraulic structure	water conduit	well	
Cult	church	monastery	sanctuary			
Funerary Space	cemetery	grave	tumulus			
Port Infrastructures	ferry	lighthouse	port	shipshed		
Economy	agriculture	animal husbandry	coastal activities	industry	mines/quarries	services
Recreation	hippodrome	observation tower	stadium	theater	wildlife park	
Health	bath	hospital	quarantine			
Civil	parliament					
Education	educational institution	museum	observatory			
Sites						
Scattered Material	architectural	burial	sculptures	various		
Other Remains	architectural	excavation	inscriptions	various		
Natural Features	fluvial features	human intervention	landform features	marine features		

Table 2. Signs and labels data entries.

	Signs Data Entries	Labels Data Entries
domestic space	163	475
defense	124	137
transport	343	103
water supply	677	704
cult	587	491
funerary space	471	300
port infrastructures	13	22
economy	636	693
recreation	6	7
health	5	6
civil	1	1
education	4	5
sites	0	107
scattered material	45	65
other remains	824	551
natural features	145	673

The cartographic signs have been digitized into spatial vector data using all possible geometries (point, line, polygon). For example, map signs for towers are registered as points (Figure 4), water conduits as lines (Figure 5), settlements as polygons (Figure 6), etc. Regarding the digitization of the cartographic labels, they were digitized as lines. The vector lines match the length of the words or phrases depicted on the map (Figure 7). The translation of the cartographic labels, except those concerning toponyms, into Greek and English was based on the translation of Manolis Korres in Creation, Content and Value of Kaupert's Maps of Attica [8].

Figure 4. The towers were digitized using point instead of line geometry, avoiding reflecting their floor plan that sometimes appears on the map. In this case, the aim was to preserve the position of the archaeological remains rather than their geometry.

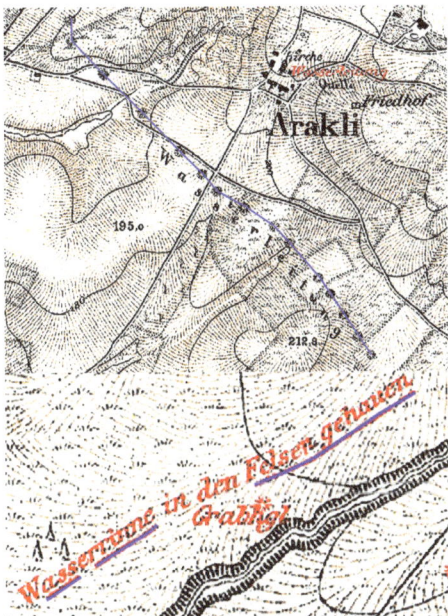

Figure 5. The water conduits were digitized using line geometry. In two different cases, by joining the individual point symbols as they indicate the original/surviving length of the aqueduct or by digitizing the line symbol. The aim was to demonstrate the continuity and the length of the aqueducts.

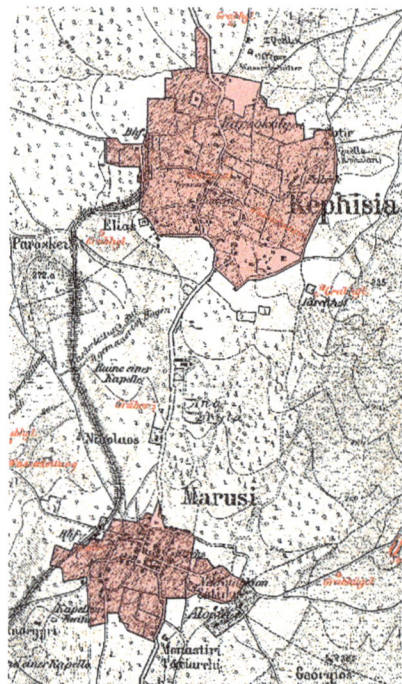

Figure 6. The settlements were digitized using polygon geometry. The polygon was implemented to enclose all the black signs, which are identified as houses, trying in this way to reflect the extent of each settlement.

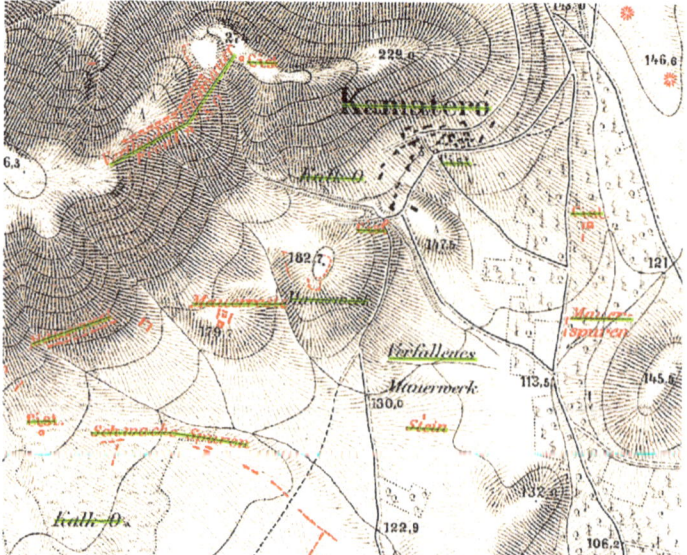

Figure 7. The labels were digitized using line geometry, following the shape of the word. If the label is written in two lines, then the digitization line is placed between them. The location of the digitization line reflects the position of the label in the web mapping application.

2.2.2. Georeferencing the Maps of Attica

Georeferencing is essential for aligning historical maps with modern ones to extract valuable information about the landscape over time [35]. After obtaining the high-resolution scanned map sheets, the first process was to crop them at the edges and stitch them together, creating a seamless image mosaic. The whole process was implemented in ArcGIS software. Then, the georeferencing procedure was carried out in two stages.

In the first stage, a rough georeference was generated based on the study of the cartographic directions followed for the overall 19th-century Karten von Attika project. According to Korres [8], the shape of the earth's surface was taken as the ellipsoidal shape proposed already in 1842 by Friedrich Bessel, while the meridian of Ferro Island, the westernmost of the Canary Islands, was used as the First Meridian. Accordingly, the coordinates given at the four edges of each map sheet were transformed and registered in the World Geodetic System (WGS) 84, EPSG 4326. In this way, a new grid was created (Figure 8), according to which the georeferencing of the single image mosaic was performed.

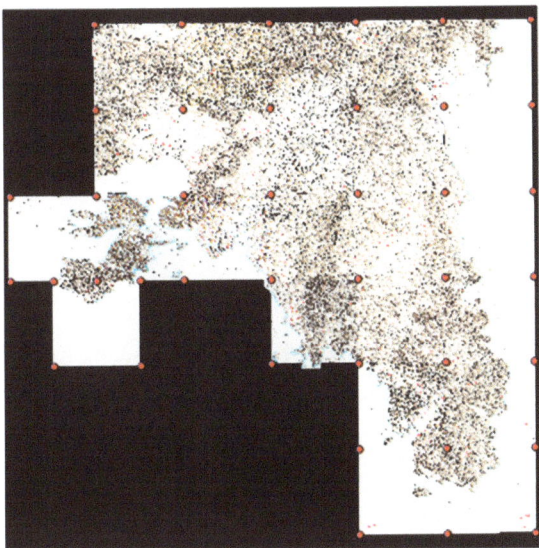

Figure 8. An artificial grid constructed on Kaupert's Maps of Attica by transforming the coordinates at the edges of each map sheet.

According to Livieratos et al. [36] in their study on the geometric infrastructure of the Maps of Attica, an error is found in the coordinates of the Athens Observatory (which is given in the 19th-century work, as the Observatory is one of the vertices of the triangulation network of the maps). Therefore, after georeferencing the image mosaic, a geometric correction was made so that the coordinates of the Observatory are identical to those obtained from the modern background. As a result, a temporary alignment of the maps is available.

In the second stage, a transformation based on ground control points (GCPs) for greater accuracy was chosen. The task of identifying and gathering GCPs from historical maps is a challenging one that requires significant effort and attention to detail. It is due to the need for in-depth examination and thorough evaluation of supplementary materials such as narratives of people who have traveled to these particular locations, other old maps, and historical literature to ensure that the geographical features from the historical map correspond to locations on modern maps accurately [22]. In addition, a considerable amount of GCPs is necessary to enhance the overall accuracy. Therefore, our study concentrates on identifying control points, specifically on landmarks, such as churches and monasteries, which have remained in the exact same location without any significant changes. We also analyzed and identified archaeological remains, road intersections, remarkable buildings, and coastline features. This process aims to determine the locations of GCPs with high accuracy initially. Next, the GCPs were validated using supplementary material, such as different modern maps, various websites with historical information about churches and monasteries of Attic land, and Milchoefer's explanatory text. The text is an integral part of the overall project, as it accompanies the Maps of Attica and often contains information that clarifies or revises what is displayed on them. Eventually, 470 GCPs were collected, and a 1st-degree polynomial (affine transformation) was performed on this set of points. On completion of this procedure, a mean error of 62.4 m was calculated.

The transformed image mosaic was then examined to detect and remove GCPs, resulting in significant distortions, and to identify and add new ones. Most of the GCPs with large residuals were discarded. However, others with significant residuals, most often collected in remote areas, were retained. In cases such as these, with limited reference information and a lack of identifiable locations in historical and modern background, these GCPs were considered to serve as rough anchor points contributing to local scale georeference. Additionally, it was considered essential to maintaining consistency and continuity by including most of the available data due to spatial considerations regarding the analyses of a considerably large area that Kaupert's Maps of Attica covers. After this procedure, a set of 514 GCPs that were aligned with the reference map, distributed as shown in Figure 9, were generated. For further inspection of the validation of the GCPs, we observed the continuity of linear elements across the map sheets, such as the road and the water supply network.

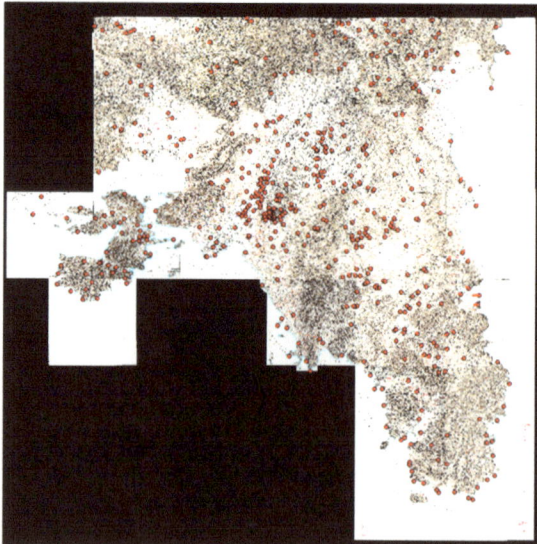

Figure 9. The distribution of the 514 GCPs.

The selected software for the georeferencing process is QGIS. The transformation function used was a 1st-degree polynomial (affine transformation), which included translation, rotation, and scale change, and the registration was made in the Greek Geodetic Reference System (GGRS) 87, EPSG 2100. The mean error of the procedure was calculated at 59.5 m, which corresponded to 2.38 mm in the historical map's scale. The mean error represents the difference between the actual and desired link positions, and it is dependent on the accuracy of the historical map and the satellite imaginary [37]. In Schaffer and Levin's "Reconstructing nineteenth century landscapes from historical maps–the Survey of Western Palestine as a case study" [38], the georeferencing of merged sheets of a historical map for the area of Palestine (surface area of approximately 14 square kilometers) was carried out using 123 GCPs, an affine transformation and an error of 74.4 m. While in Chalkias et al. [22], where a slightly different approach to the georeferencing procedure was used for the merged sheets of the 19th-century map of Cyprus (surface area of approximately 9 square kilometers), 340 GCPs were identified both on the historical map and a modern background with an error of 68.76 m. For the generated image mosaic of the Maps of Attica, a surface area of approximately 3.5 square kilometers, according to Conolly and Lake [39], the error of 59.5 m is considered significant. However, it is acceptable for the framework of this project, considering comparative literature and specificities of the map itself, such as the age of the maps, the multiple sheets produced by different cartographers, and the large area they covered.

Regarding a further deepening of the spatial distribution of the GCPs with the most significant residuals, Figure 10 shows the distribution of GCPs on the map, with the size of the arrow proportionally reflecting the size of the residual of each GCP. Excluding the Athens city region (sheets III, IV, VI) from our analysis, as in this region denser control points were taken for the georeferencing procedure, we observe that the most significant residuals were found in specific map sheets. These are the sheets V, VII, X, XI, XIII, XX, XXI, and XXV, most of which include coastline or mountainous areas, concluding that the accuracy is higher in relatively smooth surface areas.

Figure 10. The distribution of GCPs on the map with the size of the arrow proportionally reflects the size of the residual of each GCP.

2.2.3. Development of the Web Mapping Application

There are two fundamental types of architectures for webGIS and web mapping applications: thin-client and thick-client. In the former, the majority of data processing and analysis is conducted on the server side, with the client being responsible primarily for visualization. In the latter, these operations are largely performed on the client side [40]. Our application utilizes a hybrid system that combines aspects of both architectures;

however, given that most of the processing is executed on the client side, it could be classified primarily as a thick-client application.

The web mapping application for this project must be capable of displaying both raster and vector geospatial data to achieve the project's goal. The raster data, which are Kaupert's Maps of Attica, and the vector data include the digitization of all elements of the map, accompanied by their relevant information, as well as auxiliary spatial data such as archaeological sites and modern municipalities of the area. Given the diverse types of data, we adopted both thin-client and thick-client architecture approaches to develop the application, ensuring optimal visualization concerning load speed, interactivity, functionality, and response times.

The general architecture of the web application is given in Figure 11. The components of the application can be separated into two basic categories, those on the server side and those on the client side. On the server side, there are four components. The first is the database, which manages all the data in tables and their relationships. The two main types of data are the spatial references of the raster image tiles and the digitized features, along with their non-spatial information. Additionally, disk storage is used to store the created tiles (PNG image files) derived from the raster image of the Maps of Attica.

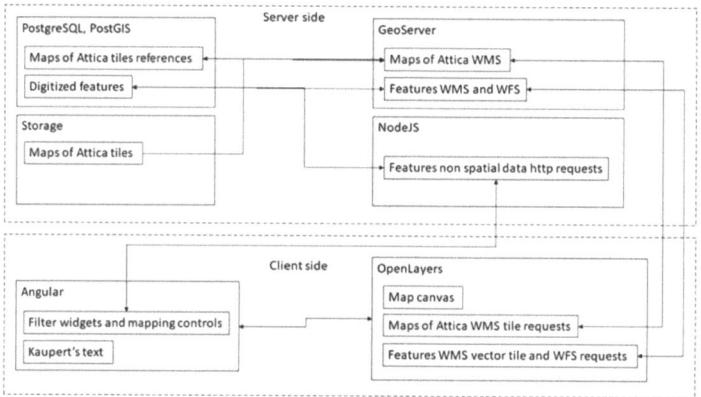

Figure 11. The general architecture of the web mapping application.

The PostgreSQL database (https://www.postgresql.org/, accessed on 30 March 2023) with the PostGIS extension (https://postgis.net/, accessed on 30 March 2023) was used to store and manage the digitized features of the Maps of Attica. To achieve efficient storage and retrieval, the spatial and non-spatial data are divided into separate tables within the database. The spatial data is stored in dedicated tables optimized for computational efficiency. Non-spatial data is stored in separate tables, linked by foreign key constraints that enforce referential integrity. This separation allows for streamlined processing and quick retrieval of spatial information when generating the web map. To minimize redundancy and enhance space utilization, lookup tables (also known as LUT tables) are employed to store frequently referenced values. These tables mitigate duplication of data, leading to improved storage efficiency. Furthermore, the web application can independently access these lookup tables, thereby facilitating enhanced loading times. Additionally, indexes were created on columns that are frequently queried, and spatial indexes were created on the geometry columns of tables that contain spatial data. These indexes enhance data retrieval performance, particularly for spatial queries.

The next two server components, GeoServer and NodeJS, are responsible for retrieving and delivering data from the server to the client side. The non-spatial information is retrieved through HTTP requests, which, through NodeJS, lead to appropriate queries in the database and then return the information to the client side. Spatial data, before it can be visualized on a map on the client side, must be converted to Web Map Services (WMS) or Web Feature Services (WFS) [41]. GeoServer is used for this purpose. In the case of the vector features, the process is to retrieve the spatial data through queries in the database from the GeoServer and create the corresponding WFS or WMS. For raster data, the process is different. There are two ways that GeoServer can convert a raster file into a WMS. The first is by simply importing a raster file. In this way, GeoServer reads the file, and all the required conversions to WMS are performed on the fly, following the request from the client side. GeoServer can read most file formats such as ASCII, TIFF, Geopackage, etc. The second way is by converting the raster file into an image mosaic, i.e., the pre-production of the tiles for the various zoom levels and viewing area of the map on the client side. This process requires specifying the basic elements of the raster file (size in pixels and reference system) and the generated tile size in pixels (e.g., 256 × 256). Moreover, it is necessary to define the pyramids (zoom levels), which can be estimated from the size of the image based on the formula:

$$\text{number of pyramids} = \log(\text{pixel size of image})/\log(2) - \log(\text{pixel size of tile})/\log(2) \quad (1)$$

(https://docs.geoserver.org/2.19.x/en/user/tutorials/imagemosaic-jdbc/imagemosaic-jdbc_tutorial.html, accessed on 30 March 2023).

Both methods can be used by various client-side libraries to visualize raster data with the WMS or web map tile service (WMTS) protocols. The main reason for the choice of method has to do with the size of the raster file. GeoServer has the ability (it also depends on the capabilities of the server it is running on) to perform optimally up to a file size of 2 GB. For larger files, it is preferred to be converted to image mosaics first and then served to GeoServer via a PostgreSQL with the PostGIS extension database (https://docs.geoserver.org/latest/en/user/tutorials/imagepyramid/imagepyramid.html#:~:text=GeoServer%20can%20efficiently%20deal%20with,below%20the%202GB%20size%20limit, accessed on 30 March 2023). Maps of Attica are large raster files as they cover a large spatial area and are of high resolution so that all the elements of the map, which are drawn by hand, can be rendered correctly. Large-size raster images can be converted from RGB 24-bit to pseudo-color table (PCT) 8-bit images. However, with this conversion, the sharpness of the image is significantly reduced, and depending on its use, the result may not be desirable. In this work, both methods were considered. The original raster image of the Maps of Attica is almost 7 GB. The size converted to PCT is almost 1 GB, which is sufficient to import as a TIFF image to GeoServer.

On the client side, there are two main components. The Angular framework was used to develop all the elements of the user interface except for the map. This includes the various filters for the spatial features, the layers tools, the map tools, and the accompanying Milchoefer's Explanatory Text. Apart from the text, all other information is dynamically retrieved from the database through NodeJS. Since Milchoefer's Explanatory Text is a historical artifact that will not change over time, it was provided as simple text with the required spatial references and was not stored in the database to improve loading speed.

The open-source library OpenLayers is used to render the spatial data in the map element of the application. Raster data is retrieved as a WMS tile layer via the appropriate OpenLayer's method, (https://openlayers.org/en/latest/apidoc/module-ol_source_TileWMS-TileWMS.html, accessed on 30 March 2023). Two more OpenLayers tools were used on the raster data for better map exploration, the 'Layer Spy' (https://openlayers.org/en/latest/examples/layer-spy.html, accessed on 30 March 2023) and the 'Layer Swipe' (https://openlayers.org/en/latest/examples/layer-swipe.html, accessed on 30 March 2023). With these tools, the user has the ability to overlay the raster data on a base map (e.g., OpenStreetMap), as shown in Figure 12.

Figure 12. Screenshots of the web mapping application displaying the two key tools used in the raster image (the historical Maps of Attica) to facilitate map exploration based on a modern map.

Most of the vector features are rendered on the map with the vector tile method of OpenLayers (https://openlayers.org/en/latest/apidoc/module-ol_layer_VectorTile-VectorTileLayer.html, accessed on 30 March 2023). With this method, it is possible to retrieve vector data with the WMS, significantly reducing the loading time and the responsiveness of the map, while rendering numerous features. Given the large data volume of the two main layers of the application (the cartographic labels and the cartographic signs, which account for more than 9000), a specific method was chosen for these layers.

3. Results

The present study introduces a web application that is unique worldwide in offering visualization, interactivity, and aggregated information on Kaupert's Maps of Attica, a work of significant historical and archaeological value for the study area and beyond. This platform provides a valuable tool for spatial humanities research and education as it offers deep mapping features that allow users to create spatial narratives in multiple ways. The web mapping application can be accessed at the following address: https://dipylon-kartenvonattika.org/ (accessed on 30 March 2023).

The digitization of the map features, combined with their classification and additional information, provides a comprehensive visualization for users when browsing and analyzing the Maps of Attica. This information can stimulate more in-depth analysis of the data in GIS software or serve as a simple assessment of the characteristics of the area at that time. The features can be overlaid on both the Maps of Attica and modern cartographic backgrounds (Figure 13, offering more flexibility and utility in the analysis and composition of spatial narratives.

The platform offers the possibility of overlaying the Maps of Attica on modern cartographic backgrounds, thereby integrating the maps into today's reality (Figure 13). The georeferencing of the Maps of Attica carried out in this project provides a great advantage, as users can easily compare the natural and built environment of that time with today's. The average error obtained in this study is relatively large compared to current standards (59.5 m). Nonetheless, considering the nature of the study material and comparing it with similar works, the result is satisfactory. Furthermore, it provides the opportunity, for the first time, to overlay the Maps of Attica on modern cartographic backgrounds.

A significant addition to the application is Milchoefer's Explanatory Text of the Maps of Attica, which offers a huge amount of additional information to the map. Users can view the explanatory text in conjunction with the map and navigate the map via links in the text for all the words associated with a spatial entity (Figure 14). The two-way interaction between the map and the text allows users to connect from one media to the other, making it easy to access additional information about a spatial entity or locate a spatial entity on the map.

Figure 13. Screenshot of the final version of the web mapping application, showing the capabilities of overlaying the Maps of Attica and the digitized features on top of a modern cartographic map.

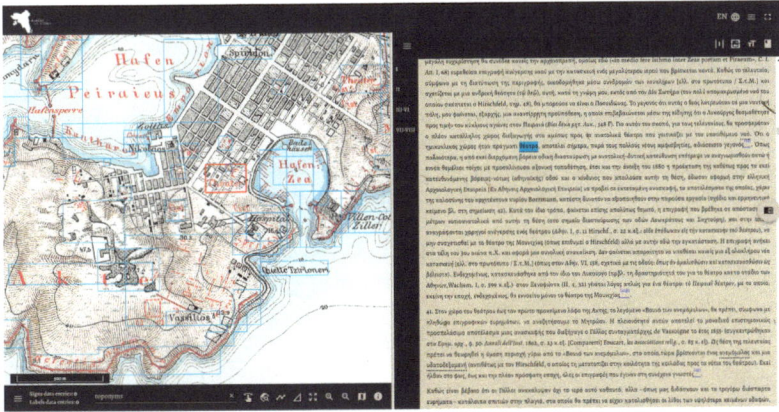

Figure 14. Screenshot of the final version of the web mapping application, showing the feature of linking Milchoefer's Explanatory Text with the Maps of Attica and vice versa.

The creation of a database containing map elements provides the opportunity for quantitative analysis of Kaupert's Maps of Attica. Users can observe quantitative aspects of each data category in conjunction with specific spatial filters. For example, Figure 15 demonstrates the utilization of a spatial filter to isolate cartographic signs and labels belonging to the 'domestic space' category for the island of Salamina. The user receives quantitative data pertaining to the selected area's relevant digitizations. In addition to querying and filtering, various other tools are available to assist users in navigating and analyzing the data. These tools include measurement functionalities for distances and areas, a map-based search feature, legends, and more.

Figure 15. Screenshot of the final version of the web mapping application, demonstrating the filtering functionality.

Additionally, the data will soon be available for download through the platform, enabling researchers to further study the data and their accompanying information in more detail.

Despite the abundance of spatial and non-spatial information, the application performs flawlessly on most modern browsers. Additionally, the application can operate normally on mobile devices with some minor limitations, particularly in displaying the explanatory text simultaneously with the map. These features make the application accessible to both academics and the public.

Overall, the web application developed provides valuable tools for the dissemination and study of Kaupert's Maps of Attica. The interactivity and the aggregated and detailed information offered by the application make it an educational and scientific tool that can be used by anyone interested in studying this important work.

4. Discussion

In this study, we employed historical Maps of Attica within a webGIS framework to collect and visualize geographical data. To our knowledge, this represents one of the first comprehensive web mapping applications for the Attica region. The use of GIS technology enables the construction of a historical-geographical framework, facilitating the exploration of significant heritage, such as Kaupert's Maps of Attica. Enhancing the value of historical data is achievable by identifying their geographical locations within modern cartographic backgrounds.

A critical step in this process was georeferencing the historical map using carefully selected GCPs. The overall mean error was found to be 59.5 m. While the global mean error is a widely recognized metric that provides an approximate estimate of georeferencing accuracy, it fails to convey the actual spatial distribution of inaccuracies across the map. Data collection using 19th-century equipment by multiple survey teams over a two-decade period (1875–1894), covering an area of approximately 3.5 square kilometers, and producing 24 different cartographic sheets, resulted in notable disparities in the precision of Kaupert's Maps of Attica across different regions. Consequently, the digital data generated from the georeferencing process had to account for variations in accuracy across different map areas. The most significant discrepancies in accuracy were identified in the map's periphery (e.g., Porto Rafti, Daskaleio) and over hilly terrain (e.g., Parnitha mountain). Large deviations along the coastline were expected due to changes that occurred over the last century and a half (e.g., Piraeus and Faliro regions). In contrast, mapping and defining the trigonometric network required special effort in mountainous or generally inaccessible areas, as mentioned before. Identifying trustworthy GCPs, primarily churches, proved to be a demanding and time-intensive task, requiring researchers to rely on supplementary historical and contemporary information to verify the precise locations of these GCPs.

The developed web application utilizes the latest web mapping technologies, and the employed architecture allows for flexible data visualization using a variety of tools without impacting data loading or map responsiveness. The application's map symbols are used to depict various features or phenomena, and these symbols are associated with specific concepts that differentiate one type of map element from another. However, a lack of information on the map's legend may cause readers to rely on their familiarity and ability to anticipate appropriate symbols for interpretation [42]. To mitigate personal bias in the interpretation process and reduce subjective perspective when interpreting symbols that are not explicitly defined in the legend, we refer to a subsequent map of the same series, the Overview Map of Attica. This map, which depicts the region's full extent at a scale of 1:100,000, includes a separate legend rich in information. To aid recognition of the map symbols, a general legend is provided for the recognition of black-colored signs and labels, and two additional legends are provided for the recognition of red-colored signs and labels. Nonetheless, it is not certain that the symbols will be interpreted as intended, which introduces an additional factor of personal bias in the interpretation process. Thus, the choice to refer to the Overview Map of Attica is crucial for the accurate classification of cartographic data.

The results of this study can deepen our understanding of the geography, topography, and archaeology of the Attica region in the late 19th century and stimulate further inquiry into Kaupert's Maps of Attica. Despite the limitations and assumptions mentioned earlier, this work offers valuable insights into the historical landscape of Attica during this period and can make a significant contribution to the field of digital humanities through interdisciplinary research.

Author Contributions: Conceptualization, G.L., G.P. and C.G.; Data curation, G.L., G.P., C.G. and A.K.; Formal analysis, G.P.; Investigation, G.L., G.P. and A.K.; Methodology, G.L., G.P., C.G. and A.K.; Project administration, C.G.; Resources, G.L.; Software, G.P. and A.K.; Supervision, G.L. and C.G.; Validation, G.P.; Visualization, G.P.; Writing—original draft, G.L., G.P. and A.K.; Writing—review & editing, G.L. and G.P. All authors have read and agreed to the published version of the manuscript.

Funding: The project was funded by the John S. Latsis Public Benefit Foundation (https://www.latsis-foundation.org/eng, accessed on 27 March 2023), the George Vergottis Memorial Fund (https://vergottisfoundation.org/?lang=ENG, accessed on 27 March 2023), the J. F. Costopoulos Foundation (https://costopoulosfoundation.org/en/, accessed on 27 March 2023) and the Loeb Classical Library Foundation (https://lclf.harvard.edu/, accessed on 27 March 2023).

Data Availability Statement: The data presented in this study are available on request from the corresponding author.

Acknowledgments: We would like to express our gratitude to Dipylon Society's (https://dipylon.org/en/, accessed on 30 March 2023)ounding members, research team, and external collaborators for their contribution to the project, Manolis Korres, John Mckesson Camp II, Sylvian Fachard and Dylan K. Rogers for their scientific remarks, the Archaeological Society at Athens for the authorization to use archaeological plans, Athina Ragia and Melissa Publishing House for kindly providing digital copies of Kaupert's Maps of Attica. Finally, we would like to express our gratitude to the two anonymous reviewers for their invaluable feedback and insightful comments that greatly improved this manuscript.

Conflicts of Interest: The authors declare no conflict of interest.

References

1. Kienast, F. Analysis of Historic Landscape Patterns with a Geographical Information System—A Methodological Outline. *Landsc. Ecol.* **1993**, *8*, 103–118. [CrossRef]
2. Grossinger, R.M.; Striplen, C.J.; Askevold, R.A.; Brewster, E.; Beller, E.E. Historical Landscape Ecology of an Urbanized California Valley: Wetlands and Woodlands in the Santa Clara Valley. *Landsc. Ecol.* **2007**, *22*, 103–120. [CrossRef]
3. Levin, N.; Elron, E.; Gasith, A. Decline of Wetland Ecosystems in the Coastal Plain of Israel during the 20th Century: Implications for Wetland Conservation and Management. *Landsc. Urban. Plan.* **2009**, *92*, 220–232. [CrossRef]
4. Hopkins, D.; Morgan, P.; Roberts, J. The Application of GIS to the Reconstruction of the Slave-Plantation Economy of St. Croix, Danish West Indies. *Hist. Geogr.* **2011**, *39*, 85–104.
5. Plewe, B. The Nature of Uncertainty in Historical Geographic Information. *Trans. GIS* **2002**, *6*, 431–456. [CrossRef]
6. Leyk, S.; Zimmermann, N.E. A Predictive Uncertainty Model for Field-Based Survey Maps Using Generalized Linear Models. In *Proceedings of the Geographic Information Science*; Egenhofer, M.J., Freksa, C., Miller, H.J., Eds.; Springer: Berlin/Heidelberg, Germany, 2004; pp. 191–205.
7. Lukas, M.C. Cartographic Reconstruction of Historical Environmental Change. *Cartogr. Perspect.* **2014**, *78*, 5–24. [CrossRef]
8. Korres, M. *Creation Content and Value of Kaupert's Maps of Attica*; Melissa Publishing House: Athens, Greece, 2008; ISBN 960-204-292-3.
9. Livieratos, E. *Germans Map Greece–from the 16th till the 19th Century*; National Map Center for Maps and Cartographic Heritage-National Map Library: Thessaloniki, Greece, 2001.
10. Dasaklis, S.; Sigalos, G.; Loucaidou, B.; Oikonomou, K.; Mavrakis, A.; Fotopoulos, N. Kaupert Maps as an Environmental Information Source for Attica. In Proceedings of the 7th National Conference HellasGIS, Athens, Greece, 17–18 May 2012; Volume 9.
11. Witmore, C. The World on a Flat Surface: Maps from The Archaeology of Greece and Beyond. In *Re-presenting the Past: Archaeology through Text and Image*; Brown University: Providence, RI, USA, 2013; pp. 125–150, ISBN 978-1-78297-231-0.
12. Blundell, D.; Lin, C.; Morris, J. Spatial Humanities: An Integrated Approach to Spatiotemporal Research. In *Big Data in Computational Social Science and Humanities*; Springer: Cham, Switzerland, 2018; pp. 263–288, ISBN 978-3-319-95464-6.
13. Jessop, M. The Inhibition of Geographical Information in Digital Humanities Scholarship. *Lit. Linguist. Comput.* **2008**, *23*, 39–50. [CrossRef]
14. Jack Gieseking, J. Where Are We? The Method of Mapping with GIS in Digital Humanities. *Am. Q.* **2018**, *70*, 641–648. [CrossRef]
15. Hamraie, A. Mapping Access: Digital Humanities, Disability Justice, and Sociospatial Practice. *Am. Q.* **2018**, *70*, 455–482. [CrossRef]
16. Lin, N.; Chen, S.; Wang, S.; Yeh, C. Displaying Spatial Epistemologies on Web GIS: Using Visual Materials from the Chinese Local Gazetteers as an Example. *IJHAC* **2020**, *14*, 81–97. [CrossRef]
17. Meccarelli, M.; Sastre, M.J.S. *Spatial and Temporal Dimensions for Legal History: Research Experiences and Itineraries*; Duve, T., Vogenauer, S., Eds.; Max Planck Institute for Legal History and Legal Theory: Frankfurt am Main, Germany, 2016; Volume 6, ISBN 978-3-944773-05-6.
18. Vacca, G.; Fiorino, D.R.; Pili, D. A Spatial Information System (SIS) for the Architectural and Cultural Heritage of Sardinia (Italy). *ISPRS Int. J. Geo-Inf.* **2018**, *7*, 49. [CrossRef]
19. Luppichini, M.; Noti, V.; Pavone, D.; Bonato, M.; Ghizzani Marcìa, F.; Genovesi, S.; Lemmi, F.; Rosselli, L.; Chiarenza, N.; Colombo, M.; et al. Web Mapping and Real–Virtual Itineraries to Promote Feasible Archaeological and Environmental Tourism in Versilia (Italy). *ISPRS Int. J. Geo-Inf.* **2022**, *11*, 460. [CrossRef]
20. Sánchez-Aparicio, L.J.; Masciotta, M.-G.; García-Alvarez, J.; Ramos, L.F.; Oliveira, D.V.; Martín-Jiménez, J.A.; González-Aguilera, D.; Monteiro, P. Web-GIS Approach to Preventive Conservation of Heritage Buildings. *Autom. Constr.* **2020**, *118*, 103304. [CrossRef]
21. Theocharaki, A.M.; Costaki, L.; Papaefthimiou, W.; Pigaki, M.; Panagiotopoulos, G. Mapping Ancient Athens: A Digital Map to Rescue Excavations. In *Proceedings of the Trandisciplinary Multispectral Modelling and Cooperation for the Preservation of Cultural Heritage*; Moropoulou, A., Georgopoulos, A., Doulamis, A., Ioannides, M., Ronchi, A., Eds.; Springer International Publishing: Cham, Switzerland, 2022; pp. 55–65.
22. Chalkias, C.; Papadias, E.; Vradis, C.; Polykretis, C.; Kalogeropoulos, K.; Psarogiannis, A.; Chalkias, G. Developing and Disseminating a New Historical Geospatial Database from Kitchener's 19th Century Map of Cyprus. *ISPRS Int. J. Geo-Inf.* **2023**, *12*, 74. [CrossRef]
23. Obe, R.O.; Hsu, L. *PostGIS in Action*; Manning: Shelter Island, NY, USA, 2011; ISBN 978-1-935182-26-9.
24. Gregory, I.N.; Ell, P.S. *Historical GIS Technologies, Methodologies, and Scholarship*; Cambridge University Press: Cambridge, UK, 2007; ISBN 978-0-521-85563-1.
25. Bodenhamer, D.J.; Corrigan, J.; Harris, T.M. *The Spatial Humanities GIS and the Future of Humanities Scholarship*; Indiana University Press: Bloomington, UK, 2010; ISBN 978-0-253-22217-6.
26. Marian, C.V.; Iacob, M. The ArchTerr Project—A GIS-Based Integrated System for Cultural and Archaeological Heritage Protection (Pilot Phase Tested in Romania). *Appl. Sci.* **2022**, *12*, 8123. [CrossRef]
27. Costantino, D.; Angelini, M.G.; Alfio, V.S.; Claveri, M.; Settembrini, F. Implementation of a System WebGIS Open-Source for the Protection and Sustainable Management of Rural Heritage. *Appl. Geomat.* **2020**, *12*, 41–54. [CrossRef]

28. Kokkalas, A.; Patenidis, A.T.; Stathopoulos, E.A.; Mitsopoulou, E.E.; Diplaris, S.; Papadopoulos, K.; Vrochidis, S.; Votis, K.; Tzovaras, D.; Kompatsiaris, I. E-Tracer: A Smart, Personalized and Immersive Digital Tourist Software System. In *Proceedings of the Information Integration and Web Intelligence*; Pardede, E., Delir Haghighi, P., Khalil, I., Kotsis, G., Eds.; Springer Nature Switzerland: Cham, Switzerland, 2022; pp. 581–587.
29. Paliokas, I.; Patenidis, A.T.; Mitsopoulou, E.E.; Tsita, C.; Pehlivanides, G.; Karyati, E.; Tsafaras, S.; Stathopoulos, E.A.; Kokkalas, A.; Diplaris, S.; et al. A Gamified Augmented Reality Application for Digital Heritage and Tourism. *Appl. Sci.* **2020**, *10*, 7868. [CrossRef]
30. Slingerland, E.; Atkinson, Q.; Ember, C.; Sheehan, O.; Muthukrishna, M.; Bulbulia, J.; Gray, R. Coding Culture: Challenges and Recommendations for Comparative Cultural Databases. *Evol. Hum. Sci.* **2020**, *2*, E29. [CrossRef]
31. Kuna, J.; Jeremicz, J.; Kociuba, D.; Niedźwiadek, R.; Janus, K.; Chachaj, J. Interactive HGIS Platform Union of Lublin (1569): A Geomatic Solution for Discovering the Jagiellonian Heritage of the City. *J. Cult. Herit.* **2022**, *53*, 47–71. [CrossRef]
32. Tice, J. The GIS Forma Urbis Romae Project: Creating a Layered History of Rome. *Humanist Stud. Digit. Age* **2013**, *3*, 70–85. [CrossRef]
33. Curtius, E.; Kaupert, J.A. Karten von Attika 1895. Available online: https://digi.ub.uni-heidelberg.de/diglit/curtius1895a/0001/image,info (accessed on 27 March 2023).
34. Korres, M. *Maps of Attica*; Curtius, E., Kaupert, J.A., Attiki Odos, S.A., Eds.; Melissa Publishing House: Athens, Greece, 2008; ISBN 978-960-204-292-2.
35. Cajthaml, J. Methods of Georeferencing Old Maps on the Example of Czech Early Maps. In *Proceedings of the 25th International Cartographic Conference*; ICA: Paris, France, 2011.
36. Livieratos, E.; Boutoura, C.; Koussoulakou, A.; Ploutoglou, N.; Tsorlini, A. Karten von Attika: A Major German Contribution to Greek Cartographic Heritage and Its Digital Approach. In *Proceedings of the 26th International Cartographic Conference*; ICA: Dresden, Germany, 2013; pp. 25–30.
37. Pethen, H. Errors, Inaccuracies, Resolution and RMSE: Georeferencing a Difficult Map of Abu Rawash's Pyramid and Cemeteries. *Scribe in the House of Life: Hannah Pethen Ph.D.* 2021. Available online: https://hannahpethen.com/2021/04/28/errors-inaccuracies-resolution-and-rmse-georeferencing-a-difficult-map-of-abu-rawashs-pyramid-and-cemeteries/ (accessed on 27 March 2023).
38. Schaffer, G.; Levin, N. Reconstructing Nineteenth Century Landscapes from Historical Maps—The Survey of Western Palestine as a Case Study. *Landsc. Res.* **2015**, *41*, 360–379. [CrossRef]
39. Conolly, J.; Lake, M. *Geographical Information Systems in Archaeology*; Cambridge University Press: Cambridge, UK, 2006; ISBN 978-0-511-80745-9.
40. Kulawiak, M.; Dawidowicz, A.; Pacholczyk, M.E. Analysis of Server-Side and Client-Side Web-GIS Data Processing Methods on the Example of JTS and JSTS Using Open Data from OSM and Geoportal. *Comput. Geosci.* **2019**, *129*, 26–37. [CrossRef]
41. Bećirspahić, L.; Karabegović, A. Web Portals for Visualizing and Searching Spatial Data. In Proceedings of the 2015 38th International Convention on Information and Communication Technology, Electronics and Microelectronics (MIPRO), Opatija, Croatia, 25–29 May 2015; pp. 305–311.
42. Keates, J.S. *Understanding Maps*, 2nd ed.; Routledge: Abingdon-on-Thames, UK, 1996; ISBN 978-0-582-23927-2.

Disclaimer/Publisher's Note: The statements, opinions and data contained in all publications are solely those of the individual author(s) and contributor(s) and not of MDPI and/or the editor(s). MDPI and/or the editor(s) disclaim responsibility for any injury to people or property resulting from any ideas, methods, instructions or products referred to in the content.

MDPI AG
Grosspeteranlage 5
4052 Basel
Switzerland
Tel.: +41 61 683 77 34

Geographies Editorial Office
E-mail: geographies@mdpi.com
www.mdpi.com/journal/geographies

Disclaimer/Publisher's Note: The title and front matter of this reprint are at the discretion of the Guest Editors. The publisher is not responsible for their content or any associated concerns. The statements, opinions and data contained in all individual articles are solely those of the individual Editors and contributors and not of MDPI. MDPI disclaims responsibility for any injury to people or property resulting from any ideas, methods, instructions or products referred to in the content.

www.ingramcontent.com/pod-product-compliance
Lightning Source LLC
LaVergne TN
LVHW072357090526
838202LV00019B/2567